A MAP TO
GOD

AWAKENING SPIRITUAL
INTEGRITY

Winchester, UK
Washington, USA

First published by O Books, 2007
O Books is an imprint of John Hunt Publishing Ltd.,
The Bothy, Deershot Lodge, Park Lane, Ropley, Hants, SO24 0BE, UK
office1@o-books.net
www.o-books.net

Distribution in:

UK and Europe
Orca Book Services
orders@orcabookservices.co.uk
Tel: 01202 665432 Fax: 01202 666219 Int. code (44)

USA and Canada
NBN
custserv@nbnbooks.com
Tel: 1 800 462 6420 Fax: 1 800 338 4550

Australia and New Zealand
Brumby Books
sales@brumbybooks.com.au
Tel: 61 3 9761 5535 Fax: 61 3 9761 7095

Far East (offices in Singapore, Thailand, Hong Kong, Taiwan)
Pansing Distribution Pte Ltd
kemal@pansing.com
Tel: 65 6319 9939 Fax: 65 6462 5761

South Africa
Alternative Books
altbook@peterhyde.co.za
Tel: 021 447 5300 Fax: 021 447 1430

Text copyright Susie Anthony 2007

Design: Stuart Davies

ISBN: 978 1 84694 044 6

A CIP catalogue record for this book is available from the British Library.

Printed in the UK by Ashford Colour Press

A MAP TO
GOD

AWAKENING SPIRITUAL
INTEGRITY

SUSAN ANTHONY

BOOKS

Winchester, UK
Washington, USA

Dr Susie Anthony bears her beautiful soul and displays her accomplished writing style to convey her personal story, witty, painful, amusing it lurches the reader along a roller coaster of universal deja-vu scenarios until it arrives at the station of moral integrity and peace by way of a map from God.
Heather Bird-Tchenguiz BA Hons, MBA. Chairperson UK Anti-Ageing Society, Owner of HB Health.

"A Map to God" is a way-shower of the spiritual terrain we all traverse as we journey home to the awareness and wholeness of who we really are. Susie has walked every step of this path herself. The profound challenges she encountered and overcame, makes her eminently qualified to share the perennial wisdom embodied in this book. Susie is inspirational wise and loving being. Her book expertly unfolds a practical map to the divine within everyone of us.
Dr Jude Currivan, author of *The Wave*, MD in Physics Quantum Theory and PhD in Archaelogy.

Written by a true visionary, Susan Anthony's "A Map to God" is an engaging road map to spiritual awakening. Merging powerful spiritual and psychological concepts, this book provides a creative, fresh and inspiring approach to personal growth and empowerment. For anyone interested in spiritual development, this is a must read.
Dr Lana Israel

If you truly want to understand, awaken and work with the infinite, potential capabilities that the universe offers us all as our birthright, then this powerful and informative book takes you on the most important spiritual journey of all – the ultimate journey within.
Hazel Courteney, award winning alternative health and spiritual journalist, former *Sunday Times* columnist and best selling author.

Dr. Susan Anthony writes from the heart, yet also weaves ancient wisdom into a stimulating text that awakens us on all levels. Her book does not simply describe spiritual wisdom, it teaches us how to apply these profound principles into our daily lives. I am most moved by authors who have lived through life situations where they personally have learned of the wisdom they teach. Susan Anthony is such an author, and brings us a wonderful book which teaches authentic spirituality.

Dr. Lee Jampolsky is the author of seven books, in over ten languages, his work has been featured in *The Wall St Journal, Business Week, The Los Angeles Times* and *Womens World.*

This book is dedicated to my Mom, Grace and to my brother JA.

I'd like to give a special heartfelt thanks to some dear friends who have supported and inspired me so much:

Hazel Courteney, Heather Bird Tchenguiz, Venessa Cowham, Raul & Gerdi Alvarado, Richard & Lana Israel, Thea Soroyan, Peter Gabriel, Dr Jude Currivan, Carey Ravden, Octavia Kenny, Cheryl van Blerk, Robert Frost, Ian Patrick, and the PSA team – Savannah Alalia, Judy Mazsa, Reinier File, Harry Foster-Holt, Zoisa Holder, Jackie Fowler, Chantal Hudson, Marie Moxey, Liam Roper, Kayla Wentworth, Lucy Wills, Simon Hinton, Simon Ledson and Psalm. And to Adam and Martine Fellows at Goodfellows – thanks for all the awesome cakes and bless everyone for your loving kindness and encouragement.

PS Make sure you read as much as you can of anything written by my dear friends Hazel Courteney and Dr Jude Currivan.

CONTENTS

FOREWORD

Many of us have moments when we feel the need – the necessity – to dig deeper and to (re)connect with that aspect of self that we know exists but have forgotten how to find. It's like a tip-of-the-tongue experience: you know the answer is there. You know you know it. You just need to access it. But sometimes the answer never seems to come, or finding it is a difficult and frustrating process. At critical moments like this, true blessing is having someone with a pure and powerful heart, mind and soul to guide you. Dr Susan Anthony has become that guide for me.

After a ten-day retreat with Susie and her amazing team at The Well House, I feel like a flower blossoming in fast motion. The most amazing part of this process is the realization that, like a flower, we have the power to absorb light, love, energy and the positivity and guidance that the universe offers in order to live truly extraordinary lives. Susie's depth of heart, knowledge, goodness and commitment inspire transformation. She walks her talk. And, with pure intention, authenticity and humour, she clears, attunes and calibrates for each person so that when they leave the retreat they are able to live their truth. That has been my experience.

I had many lessons and realizations during the retreat. It was amazing. However, since the retreat, I've experienced a shift in my outlook, orientation and focus that has empowered and realigned me. I know that some of this is due to my own revitalized will, intention and practise of the energy work that Susie teaches. I also know that some of this is due to the 'invisible' behind-the-scenes work that Susie initiated lovingly and wisely during the retreat. Susie is dedicated to assisting others in leading true, authentic lives. She is dedicated to seeing others succeed. I now approach every day knowing that I have the tools and the power within me to create and live my dreams. We all do.

Sure there are challenging moments. And Susie's work provides tools for taking challenges in your stride, learning from them, and continuing to grow and create. What can be more wonderful and important than learning about and becoming the magnificent beings that we are? And who better to guide us on this journey than Susie via this new and exciting book?

Dr Lana Israel

Dr Israel travels the world lecturing to students, parents, educators and business people about learning techniques. In recent years she has won the Glenn T. Seaborg Nobel Prize Visit Award, been named 'The Brain of the Year' (joint recipient) by the British Brain Trust, elected a Rhodes Scholar, and received her doctorate in Experimental Psychology from the University of Oxford and her bachelor's degree in Psychology from Harvard University.

INTRODUCTION

'You can have anything you want, but you will have to work for it.'
Richard Bach

The most enlightening experiences in my life have come from mistakes, heartbreak and pain. The gift of all that suffering, I have discovered, is that we don't have to throw away a whole life just because we get messed up a little. Losers deserve a second chance so that they can become winners and that's what this book is all about. The fairy tale of my life began as a nightmare. This book describes how this led to my awakening. As a result of a series of near death experiences, I was blessed to receive through 'direct knowing' vital spiritual knowledge (gnosis). I was given to understand that all kinds of gifts and tools for transformation are being made available to us at this crucial crossroads in human evolution. I was then guided through a chain of synchronistic and unusual events to various spiritual and psychological teachings. I met powerful spiritual people who recognized my awakening state. Each teacher was expert in his or her own field and was able to assist me to heal a different part of myself. I accessed powerful tools to begin to open up and re-connect to my inner world of invisible helpers. I began to heal others in turn, but realized there is no magical instant healing fix – it's about taking responsibility for our lives, changing everything within us to live in harmony with spirit, about being whole.

This book, the first of two, is the result of all that. It has been formulated from recondite Gnostic and other ancient wisdoms, as revealed over many thousands of years. Relatively few yet know about such traditions. Established religions, at least in their practice if not their origins, ignore them. It has been our loss, and this volume attempts to redress the balance. It makes it possible at last for every kind of spiritual seeker to rediscover their bliss and achieve a constant, upward spiral of spiritual growth, while contending with the demands and challenges of everyday modern living in a substantially toxic world. Incidentally, recent statistics show that nowadays, in just one day, we are subjected to more toxins than our grandparents encountered in an entire lifetime. Something has to give... We truly need to learn how to live higher spiritual principles in order to transform ourselves and heal our world. As we all learn to live these simple principles, our world will transform!

The book's premise is that all of contemporary society's problems stem from a loss of connection to spirit. Our technology-based, must-have consumer lifestyles cause many distractions so that we forget 'best self' (spirit), and thus our lives lack any real purpose, passion or bliss. Loss of connection to spirit ultimately disconnects us from the rest of our world. When we live out of harmony with spirit, we are more liable to cause harm to ourselves, to others and to our environment. Typically, best self then calls us to awaken, most often through a series of 'spiritual emergencies'. These 'breakdown to breakthrough' experiences can sometimes be mysterious and exciting, yet most often they are dramatic, traumatic and frightening. Without the ancient maps and a teacher, the quest to restore our spiritual integrity may take an entire lifetime, or worse still, due to unconscious psychological blocks and denials, may never happen at all. This is a tragedy because, ultimately, when we fail to deal with our own personal shadow defects, planetary shadow issues escalate and we tend to get the corrupt governments, corporations and fundamental religions we deserve.

'All you need is a Map and a Teacher.'

JOSEPH CAMPBELL

Campbell's notion that dreams are private myths and myths are public dreams had a big impact on me and inspired this book. Joseph Campbell did not restrict the term 'hero' to warrior or life-saver; he used it to describe anyone who had the courage to follow his or her calling, obtain the necessary knowledge and skills, and then use that wisdom and experience for the benefit of his or her people. For him, slaying the dragon or other monsters – a regular feature of these stories – was symbolic of overcoming the self-centred demands of the ego.

Like many famous playwrights and directors, television journalist Bill Moyers found himself entranced by Mr Campbell's ideas and, beginning in 1986, he sat down with the mythologist for 24 hours of interviews, most of which were recorded at George Lucas' Skywalker Ranch in Northern California. Their final talk took place at the American Museum of Natural History in New York, where Mr Campbell saw his first American Indian artefacts as a boy.

Mr Campbell died on October 30th, 1987, at age 83. Mr Moyers' interviews, edited down to six one-hour broadcasts, premiered on PBS a little over a month later. They quickly became one of the most-watched shows in the network's history, and Mr Campbell's books began to sell at a rate they had never reached while he was alive. While Mr Campbell would no doubt be pleased with this response, he never ached for greater recognition during his lifetime. He never sought money or fame, and he never made much money. He and his wife (dancer and choreographer Jean Erdman, a former student of his at Sarah Lawrence) lived in a tiny one-bedroom apartment – and the bedroom was his study. They slept on the couch. He didn't have much, but he had everything. Today I know what this means: I have made the sacrifices required to find my bliss, I am teaching others *how* and I have a '*map*', the map of the ancients – the 7 Alchemical Levels.

With a map and a teacher the journey is made simple and becomes radically fast-tracked. This book contains the map of that unfolding and describes the quest of the true initiate.

Of all the ancient traditions, one stands out above all others that I have come to know as a tremendously powerful way to transform the self and break through the bondage of depression, self-doubt and despair. This is the ancient mystical way of alchemy. It's the word used by the ancients, going back to at least Egyptian times, to describe one substance being changed, or refined, to another. It was also used to describe the spiritual process (whether this came first, and physical alchemy followed later, or vice versa, is uncertain). Both interpretations have been key to our modern understanding of alchemy. Indeed, the tradition gave birth to chemistry through the work of such men as Roger Bacon. In the 20th century, with the emergence of Depth Psychology, particularly under the influence of Jung, the tradition re-emerged as a source of knowledge that informs the practice of psychotherapy. Basically, as each of us commits to rediscovering our best selves, mind-body-spirit awareness and inner emotions are awakened. Thus begins the challenge of turning the lead of personality into spiritual gold. Overcoming the chaos of transformation and living a best potential destiny daily, in moment-to-moment awareness, is the journey of the spiritual hero. Once we are made aware that something is imbalanced in our lives, we can learn how to transform it. Inspired choices lead to positive changes. As each one of us truly becomes our best self, our world also becomes better.

The process of change is rarely a sudden one. Alchemy has been described as having anywhere from 6 to 75 stages. Here I use the traditional 7, with this volume covering the first four stages. It is a model for you to use for yourself rather than a prescriptive tool or creed. I also bring in a host of guides and helpers who have assisted me, and I trust can help you. Along the way we work not only with the light, but also the dark shadow aspects of our personalities. It is by thoroughly reviewing our lives, and especially by examining our anti-social, compulsive, destructive thoughts and behaviours that we discover how and why we have deviated from the path to wholeness. Resolving these issues is absolutely necessary for success in spiritual alchemy. Those who avoid clearing these often unpleasant but very important issues leave obstacles that will block their progress. Trying to be good is not enough. As Jung said, 'It is better to be whole than to be good.' Resolving and transmuting the shadow gives character strength and genuine power to achieve. This book differs from most spiritual books in that it goes deeply into resolving the issues of the shadow – work essential to awakening spiritual integrity. It contains a synthesis of all the purest and most powerful teachings that I have gathered. These enable us to purify on all the levels – physical, mental, emotional, spiritual – and to align these noble principles in our daily lives.

Use this map well. I offer it to you humbly. It represents all that I understand so far. There is always more and that's where my passion and my bliss thrive, in discovering more ways that can serve others so that they too can find their passion and be in their bliss. As more of us progress upon the path and create powerful inner peace, the great dreams of world peace will manifest as well.

Finally, spiritual alchemy may begin with knowledge, but knowledge not lived and mastered is just so much mental baggage. This book does more than inform. It provides the vision, the lived examples, the attunements and the practical work necessary to guide the reader effectively step-by-step through the progressive stages of spiritual awakening, all the way to enlightenment.

The work of awakening spiritual integrity fulfils Socrates' injunction to 'know thyself'. When we know who we are, we will discover the true purpose of our lives. Then our actions will reflect our higher purpose and make this world a better place.

A FAIRY TALE

Traditional fairly tales reveal the deepest darkest fears and most fervent desires of the collective. These fairy tales reflect our own personal dramas and stories of lost hopes and dreams of a better way, a higher path. Yet how do we find this potential best self and higher destiny?

Once upon a time there lived a little girl who was a princess, but this noble birthright had been hidden from her. Nevertheless, she dreamed of growing up to be kind, generous and very beautiful, finding a prince and living happily ever after with 2.4 children and a white picket fence...

Just like the ugly duckling, she was raised by a family who had fallen asleep and were unable to recognize her beauty. They all demonstrated negative behaviour, typical of the wicked kingdom they lived in. The girl tried to show her family how to be loving and good, and to feel their inner riches. But they ignored her, because they were so caught up in their own fears of poverty, shame and victim-consciousness. At the same time, they denied their inner despair by smoking too much and watching tell-a-vision, falling asleep in the spell of all the do-have-consume messages. The girl's father was lost in lust and had delusions of grandeur. Her mother was lost in fear; she felt stupid and not good enough. Both parents were competing, judging, attacking and denying everything, so great was their stupor and the depth to which they had fallen from Grace. Unable to express their real feelings to each other, they directed their anger, frustration and fear towards their children.

The girl was still small when her brother ran away to a place where the streets were paved with gold. He came back one day, rich, famous and powerful, but she could tell he wasn't happy. He was taking a secret potion to try to disguise his pain, but she could see and feel it all. It was terrible. Then her father left and never came back – she was devastated. She decided that life had betrayed her and she was very angry. Without realizing it she began to close her heart to protect herself from so much pain and the chaotic feelings and thoughts of others. She started to watch tell-a-vision, ate chocolate, drank coffee, got lost in all the lies of the matrix (the material world). It was less painful to be like them than trying to nurture her own spiritual well-being.

Eventually, the ugly duckling bloomed into a beautiful swan, although deep inside she still felt she was an ugly duckling and a misfit. She had suffered much due to poverty and lack, just like the parents who had raised her, so she worked very hard, determined to have as much money as possible. Tell-a-vision had convinced her that the more money she had, the safer she would be. Without help, she did achieve all that she had been 'programmed' to desire. She seemed to have the Midas touch, and created a life of luxury for herself. Surely she had it all? People said that she was truly the fairest of them all, yet her magic mirror never confirmed this. There was always someone to compete with and feel 'worse than'. This created another nasty trait; she began to belittle others in her mind so she would feel 'better than'. Her ego ran riot and became very powerful, judgemental, critical and harsh. For a while possessions and power, sex and money, all the glamorous people, places and things made her think she was feeling good. 'Tell me who I am with and I will show you who I am' became her credo.

Secretly she began to experience a terrible fear. Even though she had all these external symbols of power, she never felt safe because she feared she might lose them all or that people didn't love her for herself, they were only attracted to the false symbols of external power. So she withdrew from people totally. She worked harder and harder, longer and longer, amassing more and still more. People envied her and were jealous of her good fortune.

Like Peter Pan, she didn't wish to grow up. She avoided spiritual maturity, preferring to lust after pleasure in sick co-dependent relationships that somehow never worked out. She avoided pain, pursued pleasure and, with so many distractions, resisted the challenge of change and growing up. She became self-indulgent and would only help others if they gave her something in exchange. She never forgot who was indebted to her.

She searched endlessly for a prince, kissing many frogs, but she only found big bad wolves and evil warlocks. Her status and looks never brought her the happiness and peace she so craved. Her disappointment and pain compelled her to work even harder and to over-achieve. She was caught in the trap of perfectionism without realizing that 'perfect' was so limiting. If it was already perfect, it could never get better... One day, finally, in an all-consuming crisis, she broke down and cried her heart out. She was finally becoming conscious of the lie that she was living and how much energy it was taking from her to perpetuate the lie. The ultimate realization was that the gold that she had found at the end of her rainbow was only fool's gold and all the Chanel, Gucci and Prada were the Emperor's

New Clothes.

Afraid and in bondage to the system and all its false values, just like the tin man without a heart and the cowardly lion, she couldn't find the strength, or access the courage to change her ways. She didn't want to let go of the fool's gold, renounce or give up anything. She was so asleep in the matrix, she couldn't hear the voice of her Fairy Godmother who told her to take a blind, empty-handed leap of faith into the void with an expectation of nothing. This would have been her salvation. Ego said, 'Do more, consume more and have more – then you'll be happy!' And she did, but she was never happy.

Her shallow, meaningless, superficial life of the lie continued. She wouldn't admit defeat. Her search for happiness redoubled and became all-consuming. Inner chaos increased as she tried valiantly to deny the pain that continuing to live the lie caused. The veils of illusion were thinning… the inner conflict and disharmony were like a time bomb waiting to explode inside her – tick, tick, tick. She felt anxious, confused and depressed most of the time now. She had accumulated more and more things, yet nothing fixed her any more. Yet still she used all her energy to deny the emptiness and the pain, trying in vain to fit in and find some solace in all her 'possessions'.

So many meaningless lives she observed. Eventually, she gave up all hope of ever meeting anyone wise and kind. Could anyone really love, co-operate, share and live with integrity? Could she? Lost in a shadow world, in darkness and afraid, she told herself that everyone was truly lost to lust, vanity, shame, greed, fear, envy, jealousy, anger, hatred and guilt. She couldn't see any love or light. She had forgotten completely her magic inner universe and all the powerful secrets it contained. She expected hell on earth and somehow she always managed to create that. She was unaware of the universal law of attraction and the great secret that life tends to give us what we expect. She couldn't see that where we focus our attention, energy is magnified. Thus it was that she created her own long dark night of the soul and hell on earth. Yet she was soon to discover that out of chaos comes order and where there is greatest darkness there is greatest light and love.

Occasionally she had glimpses of a foggy memory of how this all began. She vaguely remembered how when she saw no hope of happiness and goodness around her as a young girl, she had closed herself down and had begun to lose her way in darkness. She had denied her heart and lost herself in the matrix ego-programming of doing, having and consuming. The busy-ness of doing, having and consuming kept her distracted so she didn't have to feel. She had lost her innocence and with that her connection to the magical inner world. Even seeing all the signs of bondage in her life, she was powerless to wake up. The magic inner universe put out a clarion call to her in the form of terrible loss and tragedy hoping this would help her to awaken.

All her life she had wished for love and received, at best, only temporary lust, but more often painful betrayals and disappointment. Finally, overwhelmed by sadness, she began to take a deadly potion to relieve her of the pain of unrequited love and broken promises. She fell further into darkness, emotionally bankrupt, mentally toxic, unreachable, numb and empty. The angels watched her destroy her life-spark – it was always part of the great plan. They truly hoped she'd ask for help so, without interfering with her free will, they could assist her to become the beautiful swan, her best self, as she was always destined to be.

She was filled with the poisonous potion and mental and emotional poison from all the toxic feelings suppressed, yet the angel of death embraced her. As her spirit left her body, she entered the magic universe calling out for help in terror and in shame. Finally her prayer was answered and her wish came true. A deep blue guiding light revealed the presence of her guardian angel. This powerful being helped her understand the true meaning of life.

Her best self and magical destiny were revealed to her. She had reconnected to her universal family. In the magic of this higher love and light, she was guided to forgive everyone. She forgave herself and let go of the past. She was healed. She was shown a new blueprint for her life and told that once back in the physical body she'd be permanently reconnected to this divine love, wisdom and power from the magic universe. Filled with Grace, reborn and regenerated, she now knew what ailed this world most. In the matrix world people had lost their connection to divine magic. They had forgotten all the powerful secrets of creation and love. Reconnected to all that love and power she began to remember the secrets. She especially recalled that wherever we focus our attention, energy is magnified. She remembered the secret of the law of attraction. She was shown that if we are asleep in the matrix world, we unconsciously attract and create what we fear in ignorance.

She remembered that creativity is a fundamental part of being human. To many philosophers, this is one of the most important reasons for being here on planet earth: to create! Some will argue that we are always creating every minute of every day... However, she came to understand that there is a big difference between creating unconsciously and creating consciously. At the unconscious (un-awakened) level of creating we are unknowingly using our creative powers to re-enforce a reality and lifestyle that is less than satisfying and has few rewards. It can be said with great certainty that the majority of people everywhere are creating unconsciously through the filters of unawareness and unrecognized, self-defeating thinking and behaviour. In other words, most people spend the vast amount of their creative energy repeating patterns of thought, behaviour and actions, even though the outside form may look different in each situation. An example of unconscious creation is the person who repeatedly gets involved with abusive people. Such a person – through their inability to recognize their patterns and through their inability to change their thinking and habits – continually 'creates' and unknowingly attracts the reality that their unconscious mind is most familiar with. Simply put, if we don't respect ourselves, we will attract those who don't respect us. Or we will be afraid to stand up for ourselves and ask for respect. Or we will be afraid to simply walk away if respect isn't coming.

The awakened person, she learned, has come to recognize that what they believe about themselves has drawn in the matching experience. The truly awakened then put forth the effort to change their thinking and behaviour, which automatically begins to change their life experiences. Little by little – or sometimes in great leaps and bounds – the person who once attracted abuse or disrespect is now attracting a different reality and creating a different way of dealing with these situations: either by taking a stand for him/herself in a more self-respecting way, or by finally being able to walk away and end the unhealthy interactions more rapidly than before.

She realized that if we are able to practise mindfulness, we can combat lack of consciousness. Then from such loving higher consciousness, lived in moment-to-moment awareness, we can consciously choose whatever it is we wish to experience! Mindfulness is appreciating that the only gift we have is 'now'. The past is gone and we can do nothing about it. The future is not yet here, so there's no need to worry. The only gift of life we have is now. That's why we call this gift of life our 'present'. She learned how to always remain mindful in the present – stop future fear projections and let go of the regrets of the past.

Previously, she'd believed in hell and attracted it. Perhaps her favourite author, Ernest Hemmingway, had programmed her to expect pain when he said, ' The best people possess a feeling for beauty, the courage to take risks, the discipline to tell the truth, the capacity for sacrifice. Ironically, their virtues make them vulnerable; they are often wounded, sometimes destroyed.' (*A Farewell to Arms*)

Now she believed in something different: love didn't have to equal pain. Pain she learned comes from attachment and co-dependency. She believed in true love – the love coming from her loving universal family of light, who even when she stopped believing in them, had never given up on her. Because she believed and learned to focus her attention on what she chose to experience, she was guided to all the right teachers, people, places and things. She learned how to travel into hidden invisible worlds containing magical guides, angels, ancestors, animal power totems, nature spirit guides, teachers and wise ones from ancient times. Now she was able to look back at the old web of destruction she had created and to realize that all the she'd experienced was always destined to become her greatest resource to teach others about how to wake up and live in harmony with spirit. Knowing the secret and believing in it with all her heart, practising mindfulness, she began to weave another web, where the dreams of the innocent child within her could be realized.

Her heart had opened and she was learning to listen with the ears of the heart, see with the eyes of the heart. Tree people communicated with her. Animals gave their sacred healing energies to her and protected her. Crystals energized her. Sensing her new-found beauty, innocence and purity, a powerful dragon emerged from the mountains of a faraway land, endowing her with limitless magical energies. Unicorns befriended her, re-establishing peace within. All of nature, all kinds of animal, mineral, insect and spider brothers and sisters reconnected to her, guiding her, empowering her. She was protected, cherished and loved. She was beginning to dance her dreams alive. She was awakened – the sceptic says, 'I'll believe it when I see it,' but the mystic says, 'I'll see it when I believe it.'

She moved to a place with magic wells, where she was endowed with all of nature's treasures and precious secrets from the heavens. Knowing how to work with the law of attraction, having no limits, she magnetized pure powers from so many sources. Finally in unity consciousness with Mother Earth and Father Sky, she found the gold of truth, divine love, power and wisdom to use for the greatest good of the whole.

Today she is living happily ever after near the magic wells, teaching her apprentices about all the great alchemical secrets of this magic universe. Her incredible journey to wholeness has bestowed in her a light we can all trust. If we listen carefully, we may hear her wise voice calling out into the darkness and if we look carefully we may see a golden white light... the light of miracles, healing and transformation.

CHAPTER 1

IN BONDAGE

'Every saint has a past and every sinner has a future.'
OSCAR WILDE

OVERVIEW

Both my parents came from extremely impoverished, humble, working-class backgrounds in the North of England. My mother worked hard to keep the family together, to provide a roof over our heads and a meal on the table. My father was a gambler and had delusions of grandeur. He was also into pornography, which angered and alienated my mother, and also shocked, titillated and confused my older brother and me. Pornography and my father's behaviour influenced all the family to misguidedly dishonour the feminine, confuse lust with love, seek thrills and avoid true intimacy. Many times my father squandered everything on gambling and pornography and we went without food. When he left, my mother and I were destitute. I was so afraid, I remember declaring to myself that I would get as much money as possible as soon as I could so I would never feel this frightened or insecure ever again. In my fear and desperation to achieve this, I forgot about all my noble intentions of helping people. I became self-obsessed, self-absorbed and self-indulgent.

I studied and worked very hard. Hollywood films became my teachers and Cosmopolitan magazine was my Bible… On my own merits I worked my way up, job by job, until I worked directly for some of the richest men in the world: Robin Stubbs, South African sidekick to Tiny Rowland, once referred to in the UK press as the 'unacceptable face of capitalism', and Harunori Takahashi and Bungo Ishizaki in Japan – Takahashi was once featured on the cover of Asia Magazine, and described as 'The busiest man on earth'. Ishizaki was the inventor of Big Mac economics.

And I made it – I had amassed all the things Cosmopolitan said would make me happy. I was rich, beautiful, wore designer labels and had more diamonds than Cartier. I had large homes, vintage luxury cars, famous friends and lovers. I had power, influence and all the trappings of success. In terms of what society, the system – the matrix – taught me to value, I had it all. However, after a time, I realized I was still insecure. I always wanted 'more' and I never felt as though more was enough. I still didn't feel as if I fitted in, either with the rich and famous or the poor.

The business world I moved in was about hostile mergers and acquisitions; dog-eat-dog exploitation, maverick behaviour that was often unscrupulous and at times totally corrupt. When I discovered all this, I wanted out. But I didn't want to give up my grand lifestyle, lose anything or let anything go. I had a high maintenance lifestyle, big bills, big mortgages, big credit card repayments, and with so many financial demands and being unwilling to simplify my life, I needed to continue earning vast amounts of money to service it all. I felt that if I gave it all up, people would judge me as a failure, a weak person just like my father. Accordingly, I continued to do what I increasingly hated. I loathed myself for doing so. I was stuck in bondage to a system with values I had never chosen, but blindly believed in. These false beliefs truly controlled me and I could see no way out.

Perpetuating the lie, I eventually became listless, empty, drained. Friends directed me to Harley Street doctors who catered to the rich and famous. They supplied me with diet pills that both gave me extra energy and helped me become super-model thin. I was working 18-hour days, six days a week. With the exhaustion and stress, like many of my high-flying contemporaries, when diet pills ceased to give me the lift I wanted, I moved on to drugs. In two years cocaine was costing me $1000 a day. At that time in my life, I didn't believe in angels or God. I was fond of saying that I worshipped at the altar of Gucci, Prada and Chanel. Yet, insecure and fickle to the very last, I was covering all bets by asking for divine help. No human could have reached me, incidentally, because I had so isolated myself from everyone – friends, family – because of a huge dose of false pride and really due to ever-increasing self-loathing and shame about what I had become. No amount of Chanel could hide the fact that I was in hell.

In retrospect now, this was my saving grace. The archetype of the destroyer in the form of the addict systematically dismantled and destroyed my big lifestyle and all the false beliefs that helped create it. In terms of cash resources, what friends failed to steal or embezzle from me, I spent on drugs. My house of cards gradually fell in on me. Today I thank God for this and can laugh. At the time it was the end of my world.

Eventually, on Good Friday 1992, during a cocaine binge alone in an apartment in Johannesburg, I passed out. When I woke up I was looking down on my body, which was convulsing on the floor in the last throes of death.

As I became aware of my life-force leaving my body, I was surrounded by a field of incredible sapphire-indigo blue light. I was aware that this energy was alive and conscious and communicating with me. I knew I was dead and so I thought the blue light must be God. It certainly felt like God – I had never experienced such love, such power and such compassion. I knew at last I was safe and where I belonged, integrated back into Source… oneness and holy love.

I found myself before some kind of angelic Life Review Board. An angel-like figure spoke to me telepathically, telling me that he was called Michael and was my guardian angel. Michael said I was dying, but it was not yet my time. Just before I was about to be returned to my body, I was given a telephone number.

When I regained consciousness, I was on my bed. I felt incredibly euphoric, as though I had been reborn. On the table next to me was a huge pile of drugs, but they no longer held any appeal. Then the number the angel had given me popped into my head. I felt my hand was being guided when I dialled the number.

It turned out to be a film producer friend I had last seen in Los Angeles three years before. We had lost touch and she had just moved back to South Africa. At the time, she was just the person I needed to see. She had been through similar experiences and was very spiritual; she really helped me to understand and integrate what had just happened to me. So it was that I began the hero's quest to overcome ego, shadow and persona and become reconnected to spirit.

People will say I was hallucinating – but hallucinations don't give you ex-directory numbers. From that day on, I felt protected by spirit and the angels day and night. They always guided me to people who could help me transform my consciousness.

Thus I called for divine intervention, and to my absolute shock, wonder and awe I did receive it – in the form of this formless electro-magnetic energy field. It was a few days later when I learned the identity of this divine messenger. It was the Archangel Michael, who is the Archangel of Mercy.

During this out-of-body experience, I was guided through a complete life review rather like the Life Inventory we have to complete in a 12-step programme to overcome addiction. The reward for completing this successfully was that I was given a glimpse of several potential futures for our planet. I was allowed to choose which one I wished to co-create. Ultimately, I was somehow energetically rewired, fast-tracked to embody higher aspects of my best self in order to achieve my best potential destiny and to help others.

It was a major choice point for me. I chose to come back and serve by helping to elevate consciousness on this planet. I was literally reborn, miraculously healed from the ravages of drug addiction. Embodying a much higher consciousness than was at first comfortable, I was guided to the right teachers, people, places and things to help me to learn how to integrate this experience and these divine gifts. They taught me how best to interpret this supernatural experience and then how best to teach others about the power of unconditional love, and wisdom.

To be honest, it was all incredibly simple, BUT it wasn't easy. At first I lacked discipline, faith and commitment and it was very difficult to conquer old ego-based patterns, false beliefs, attachments and desires. I felt alone and afraid. People thought I had gone mad. I thought I had gone mad. It was a time of great tests, trials, challenges and tribulations. When I listened to ego, I fell back into iniquity – I confess that I did this several times in those early years. Yet each time I stumbled and died again and again and again, I then found more powerful tools and was further blessed by spirit. I learned from spirit that each mistake contained an important teaching and was therefore valuable. It took quite a series of mistakes, as well as mystical and magical events, for me to finally get the message and understand the bigger picture.

Now, nothing in the material world I call 'the matrix' holds any temptation for me. I've already had an excess of everything money can purchase and some things it cannot. Time and again, as a zealous hedonist, I overdosed on all the 'glamours' of the matrix. Finally, today, instead, thanks to mindfulness and learning to let go of the past, I have found my passion and rediscovered the courage it takes to follow my passion. The result is bliss.

Living a lie

This book sets out the levels of awakening. It is set out in levels because the path is not easy, and short cuts rarely work. There are many in the West who regard themselves as 'saved', but though they might talk the talk, they do not walk the walk. They have not spent the time exploring and marrying the unconscious, conscious and super-conscious minds. As a result most of us live in a state of unconscious incompetence – not knowing that we do not know. The first step is to move to conscious incompetence – knowing that we don't know; then conscious competence – knowing that we know; and finally unconscious competence – a state of being so competent that we no longer have to think about it.

About Alchemical Level 1

We are alerted to Level 1 of the alchemical map when we consciously develop an awareness that something is missing; something is lacking in our lives. Activities that we always enjoyed before now seem meaningless. We feel empty and we cannot see the point of anything any more. We realize that all our possessions, our status, power, prestige and our achievements mean nothing. We may 'have it all' but still feel miserable. It all seems so worthless, so empty. But what is missing? Typically, at this level most people struggle to keep things as they were. This is not a good idea! Resistance to the call of spiritual integrity is futile and the only reward is pain. The structures of our lives lived in ego are beginning to break down. Certainly this is rather frightening to the ego-personality self. However, this is extremely good for the spirit.

Deepak Chopra has some great advice on ego: 'You want to reach a state of bliss, then go beyond your ego and the internal dialogue. Make a decision to relinquish the need to control, the need to be approved, and the need to judge. Those are the three things the ego is doing all the time. It's very important to be aware of them every time they come up.'

This first level of alchemy is called Calcination, or burning. Physically, it's when a substance is pulverised and then heated over an open flame or in a crucible to eliminate water and other volatile compounds until it is reduced to ashes. Spiritually, it's similar. It's where we get to know our ego. We identify our illusions and so destroy our attachment to material possessions. We learn how to recognize all the diverse examples of bondage in our lives. Such awareness is usually precipitated by all the challenges of our lives finally wearing us down. Perhaps we have experienced a personal loss, illness or disaster. Everything begins to fall apart. We begin to feel that life is empty and utterly meaningless. We may feel like giving up and that there is no point in continuing on in the old way. We begin to realize that we are living a lie in a matrix-type system where we have been taught to avoid intimacy and pain, pursue pleasure and resist change.

We have been influenced to avoid conscious awareness of the lie by being pressured to do, have and consume, fit in and conform. We have been trained to perpetuate the lie as a result of programming, conditioning and socialization in the matrix – a state of disconnected consciousness where, in the illusion of separation from Source, we have forgotten to live in harmony with spirit.

So here we evaluate who and what we really are, and what's important. It is generally a truly challenging experience to undergo because the ego fights back to protect the status quo, even if the status quo doesn't necessarily work. However, dismantling of the ego is essential to the success of the higher stages – this is the inner ground which must be prepared by the ego's deflation before the higher levels of being may be experienced.

The world as a lie

It's not just us as individuals living a lie, being fooled by the matrix. We're all part of it. We've collectively put humanity on a collision course with environmental disaster, industrial collapse and social chaos. You and I were put on the planet as caretakers. All we have done is taken and not cared.

Per person, the US consumes the most energy and pollutes the most of any country in the world. Thus they have the greatest responsibility to clean up their act. However, again and again the US has blocked international action to reduce carbon dioxide emissions, claiming that it would interfere with industrial productivity. It seems that the US government is still following the path of comfort, profit and greed. Organizations like Greenpeace work continually to bring these issues into the news and thereby into public awareness.

Whether the governments of the industrialized nations will realize the danger and act soon enough to avoid environmental collapse and the consequent collapse of civilization as we know it is still unknown. We may well be heading for a new kind of Dark Ages with mass starvation, collapse of industry, plagues, looting and collapse of governments. If the dark predictions become reality, survival will depend upon doing what the Hopis recommend: 'Where is your water? Know your garden. Create your community. Be good to each other.' Will we allow ourselves to enter ever more deeply into bondage or will we awaken and preserve life on earth? If we choose to create peace on earth, then it must start in our own hearts with reconnection to spirit. It's vital that we understand that all of life is an initiation to reconnect to spirit. Initiation, I have been taught by many great teachers, is the chosen method to elevate consciousness on this planet.

How did we get this way?

Our parents or other caretakers conditioned us. They domesticated and trained us to conform to the social norms of our time. Their intention was to influence us to believe and behave only in ways that they and society found acceptable. And, for the most part, they were successful. Briefly, during our teens and early twenties we may have rebelled against the system and truly tried to be different. But for the most part, we became a product of the times and eventually learned to behave just like everybody else we met. Sometimes an outrageous 'Shirley Valentine-type' impulse might have surfaced. But generally, our conditioning taught us to ignore any such liberating inclinations.

We have learned to desire that which we were trained to desire. It began with our parents and continues unabated in the media today, especially through advertising. Advertising teaches us what to long for, desire and strive for. Accordingly, we have become obsessive and compulsive about our image, our appearance, our social position, our job, our status and especially our possessions – our holidays, our clothes, our car, our home, our garden.

As we built up experiences, some of them brought us fear, pain, and of course fear of more pain. As we tried to make sense of these experiences, we made false interpretations through our ego lens misperceptions. We then generalized these misperceptions into beliefs – false beliefs. For example, if we experienced unrequited love, if we were rejected and repeatedly hurt, we most likely came to believe that love = pain. This false expectation became a self-fulfilling prophecy. Life tends to bring us that which we most fear, deny, judge or expect. The reality of how creative energies work is that wherever we focus our attention, energy is magnified. We generate our experiences largely from our expectations. We make our poor or otherwise limited expectations come true. When they do come true, we believe that this confirms our false belief, which becomes more rigid than ever before. This is one way that people close themselves off from so many new possibilities, and of course from spirit. They come to have very limited beliefs as to what is possible for them. They become victims and hostages to their own limited or false expectations. This is hell and precipitates either disappointment or grandiosity, both of which are negative ego states.

Like everyone else in our culture, we were taught to give away power to others. The powers that be (governments, fundamental religious organizations, etc.) find it easier to rule if people are weak-willed and cannot think for themselves. And so it suits their purpose if people have little self-worth and little will or power of their own. Consider the meaning of sayings such as: 'Man is conceived in sin', 'Man's righteousness is as dirty rags before God.' If we believe these popular religious teachings, our self-worth is reduced to near nothing before we ever leave Sunday school.

Can it be true that we really consciously choose to give our power away to others? Do we truly consciously choose to be manipulated by others? Or would we rather have high self-worth and be in control of our lives by making our own choices? Are people like Oprah Winfrey or Sir Richard Branson easy to rule? Of course not – they lead themselves. Consider this well. If we have any aspirations for healing the environment or creating peace in this world, we will be required to heal ourselves first, to develop high self-worth – otherwise we will fail.

Perhaps we don't yet realize how much of a mess our lives have become or how far off track we have gone. Our reasoning mind tries to find logical solutions to our problems. However, our habitual programming is so strong still that we rationalize and deny truth – we tell ourselves rational lies. We fabricate reasons why it seems right to go on doing what we want to do in the way we have always done, never mind that it doesn't work and we are unhappy.

At this level, old habits die hard. We are well and truly stuck in a rut.

ll this can be changed. We start to understand that we are responsible for all our experiences in life. As we surrender to the Level 1 process and allow our old ego and false personality life to be destroyed, all the energies we channelled into perpetuating the lie are returned. We begin to feel incredible. And in enjoying the resultant higher energy this creates, we begin to notice fascinating coincidences that appear to be guiding us towards something better.

Distraction

When the going gets tough, our first defence is to redouble our efforts, to distract ourselves with our preferred excesses (TV, food, excess alcohol, sex, work, and any compulsive behaviour). For a short while, if drastic and excessive enough, such activities keep us from feeling the pain, loneliness and uselessness of our lives devoid of any higher purpose. Sometimes we may become so sick and tired of life that we perhaps secretly consider ending it all. But something inside prevents this. Actually, this 'something inside' is spirit beginning to communicate with us. Thoughts of the uselessness and lack of meaning in our lives prevail. Sometimes, these blend with our fears about death and what that really means. All the joy is gone from living and yet we also fear dying in ignorance. Life seems to be falling apart. Is this a breakdown? No, on the path of spiritual integrity, it can be a breakthrough!

Depression and fears

Most people don't even realize spiritual emergencies exist, let alone that they are experiencing one or what it means. But these emergencies don't have to be dramatic. Perhaps the most common is simply depression. It can range from the severe and suicidal down to the mild 'are you unhappy with your life?' The most terrible thing about serious depression is the stigma around it; how strongly society judges us and worse still, how fiercely we judge and condemn ourselves for being depressed. Today, the anti-depressant drug is the most over-prescribed drug in the world, surely indicating the level of depression and imbalance being experienced in our lives. However, drugs don't fix depression – at best they offer merely a temporary escape.

At Alchemical Level 1, depression is one of the most challenging states of imbalance to overcome. The negative energies associated with depression, combined with self-criticism about being depressed, ensure a truly overwhelming and devastating experience, which seems to the uninitiated almost insurmountable. How does it serve us to adopt a harsh, critical and judgemental attitude towards ourselves for feeling depressed? It does not serve us and yet this is what we do. Self-judgement only feeds and perpetuates the depression or imbalanced state. Judging ourselves deepens the fear and feeds the negativity. We feel weak, lost and defeated when we criticize ourselves and accept others criticism about feeling depressed. Then we become more depressed... and so we spiral down into hell and remain in bondage to depression for years, or even a lifetime.

Other people fear looking into the mirror of our depression. They choose to deny and avoid what this negative state in us reflects back about themselves. They tell us to pull ourselves together, snap out of it, buy a new dress, go on holiday, find a new partner or new job, buy a new house, decorate the old house, and so on. Their lack of understanding and compassion fuels the power of depression. We begin to feel isolated and we become more depressed. Welcome to Alchemical Level 1 and the concepts of bondage and powerlessness.

What Alchemical Level 1 is teaching us is that depression is about a breaking down of the old that no longer works. Breaking through occurs when we are able to recognize that the loss of what was known or believed no longer serves us or works. We can then let go of the old and transform to embrace the new. This is, in fact, opportunity disguised as loss. If we will only listen to and learn from the message of depression, we can discover new beliefs and new attitudes about life that do work, serving our best selves and creating our best destinies. We must begin by understanding that usually anything we wish to avoid tends to have great meaning or power, and is serving our growth and the greatest good.

The meaning of depression we discover is that it's a wake-up call telling us that somewhere we have been living our lives out of harmony with spirit. The resultant lack of meaning in our lives causes fear, pain and anger. When we deny these negative feelings, we feel depressed. Ultimately, we are also depressed because we have forgotten our best selves and our best destinies. In Alchemical Level 1, we are ignorant or in denial of best self and best destiny, but what we have learned is that no amount of distraction – do/have/consume or avoidance – works anymore or can help us.

Self-criticism about being depressed is just such an avoidance. It forces our focus away from the true purpose of why we are being held hostage by some dark shadow aspect of ourselves. How can I explain this? Well, in nature as winter approaches, certain creatures go into hibernation. Depression is one way that our best selves call us to go within to recognize ourselves more completely. If we listen to this call to retreat and do the work, this is how we are awakened to the bigger picture and higher meaning of life, beyond the do/have/consume. If we are already beginning to wake up and are somewhat self-aware and accepting of all aspects of ourselves – the good, the bad and the ugly – then this cyclic immersion into unexplored regions of darker and best self will be an adventure, undertaken bravely even though it could be unpleasant. The big question is whether we are going to be able to say a hearty 'yes' to our adventure. We must be willing to get rid of the life we've planned, in order to have the life that is waiting for us. What inspires us to continue is the knowing that we will be transformed and always into something better. Unfortunately, in Alchemical Level 1, we are usually trapped in unconscious self-deprecating patterns of lack of self love and esteem, so we will perceive such a descent into darkness as proof positive of our unworthiness and/or terrible confirmation of all those dark shadow aspects of ourselves that we fear.

My own personal experience of breaking down to break through comes from almost twenty years of feeling a lack of any real purpose or true meaning in my life. I felt depressed most of the time and this precipitated suicidal episodes. I had tried all the do/have/consume tactics to distract myself from my depressing feelings and to avoid how I felt, but nothing worked. I then explored many different approaches to heal the depression, including taking anti-depressants – of the legal and illegal variety – and trying out various holistic therapies. Nothing worked until I was ready to listen to the message of my depression. My life was unmanageable and I was powerless to change anything. I feared change. I believed I was a victim of and powerless over depression, until one day something changed for me. Instead of denying or fighting the depression, I allowed myself to embrace the darkness and entered into it. Inside the darkness, I learned I was not a victim. I discovered that depression had been calling to me for years and that it held a gift, a powerful message of transformation. My depression contained many valuable messages for me and I had ignored them all because of fear. I feared that if I went deeper into the black hole of my depression, I'd never be able to climb out. I feared what I might find inside this black hole and I feared what other people would think, that I was insane or weak, just like my father... I feared most of all, unconsciously, that I would find my best self, the hero within, and that I would have to change my life. I feared this so strongly because the matrix had taught me very carefully to resist change, pursue pleasure and avoid pain.

All of those fears at Alchemical Level 1 fuelled and fed my unbalanced ego structure, which refused to permit me to expand and evolve my perceptions of reality. As I became willing to explore what depression had been trying to tell me all along, I came to know that I actually had more courage than I had believed. This was when I began to discover best self and reconnect to my best destiny. It was ironic when I realized that my true terror was the fear of truly being my best self – all the changes and sacrifices this would mean and how much effort it would take to realign to my best destiny. I feared being the only person in the room, the marriage, the family and the community. At work, I feared others who were aware of the bigger picture and were willing and powerful enough to do something about it. Yet when I gave in, broke down and allowed myself to break through, I began to know that anything was possible.

Self-destructive thoughts and self-limiting beliefs hold us back until the right time comes to break down, break through, rediscover our best selves and shine. That was definitely the case for me and has proved true for many of my students. The trials and tribulations of breakdown and depression, loss, defeat and disillusionment are in actual fact the necessary ingredients of the rich compost of fulfilment. Thich Nhat Hanh teaches that the rose needs the unpleasantness of the manure in order to become itself, and, in turn, it must eventually become the compost to guarantee life's balance. There are spiritual teachers, angel workshop teachers that I know personally, who promote rejection of the 'compost'. These 'teachers' are dangerous because they are actually teaching imbalance. It is only the person who can accept themselves wholly – the good, the bad and the ugly – who can truly be fulfilled and find and live their best destiny.

The best exercise I have learned in order to do this is to imagine my depression as a black hole. I imagine myself meditating inside the black hole and merging with the blackness – merging with the dark feelings of anger, sorrow, hatred, fear and pain. The task is to sit within the energy of depression for as long as it takes to learn what it has to teach us. When we have learned how we created this darkness and take self-responsibility and ownership for it, we will be led from within to let it go. This is basically hibernating within the cave of depression with the specific intention of allowing us to experience what we are feeling, so that these feelings will awaken us at the right time in the right way, allowing us to shine. However, it may take several attempts before ego feels comfortable and allows us access to true higher guidance from within.

Resistance, denial and avoiding pain
When we begin to feel as if our lives lack meaning, we will certainly feel overwhelmed and afraid. In the ensuing confusion, if we give in to victim-consciousness, we may be tempted to try to do something, anything, to get rid of this bewildering feeling. However, what we resist persists. Set your

intentions – be strong! Remember in the film, *The Matrix*, when Morpheus offers to unplug Neo, saying:

'This is your last chance. After this, there is no turning back. You take the blue pill – the story ends, you wake up in your bed and believe whatever you want to believe. You take the red pill – you stay in Wonderland and I show you how deep the rabbit-hole goes.'

Neo is the classic mythical hero who knows that denial or resistance blocks the progress of spiritual unfoldment. Denial may take the form of anything that increases the level of excitement we are experiencing, creating temporary escape or distraction and thereby allowing us to ignore the situation. Buying new things, taking drugs or excess alcohol, having a fling, over-eating, compulsive shopping, over-working or just watching TV are typical ways to resist or deny the process.

Shadow world

Level 1 is essentially destructive. This is a shadow world. We have all been conditioned to think of destruction as something bad. However, before we can build a house, trees must be destroyed and cut into lumber. Remember the age-old saying, 'Every cloud has a silver lining'. The hero knows that every problem or challenge also brings us a gift. The hero recognizes that the old, outworn ego defence structures and beliefs that no longer serve the highest interest must be destroyed before new, more accurate and supportive ones can be discovered and instituted. The hero knows that although this destruction may feel terrible – temporarily – ultimately it is a great gift. The hero recognizes the need to disintegrate before integrating higher, purer, more powerful, wise and loving aspects of self – best self.

Now let's take a look at the big picture in terms of the planetary shadow world.

WISDOM

The Rio Affidavit: scientists call for humans to clean up their act

Before the Rio Earth Summit of 1992, 1,500 world scientists, including 50

Nobel Prize winners, signed an affidavit warning humanity of the likely outcome of our current practices upon the environment.

'Human beings and the natural world are on a collision course. Human activities inflict harsh and often irreversible damage on the environment and on critical resources. If not checked, many of our current practices put at serious risk the future that we wish for human society and the plant and animal kingdoms, and may so alter the living world that it will be unable to sustain life in the manner that we know. Fundamental changes are urgent if we are to avoid the collision our present course will bring about.'

They noted dangerous changes to the atmosphere including ozone depletion, pollution and acid precipitation. Our water supply is being depleted and polluted. Ocean fishing is at or above the maximum sustainable yield. Rivers carry soil plus industrial, municipal, agricultural and livestock waste into the oceans which, as a result, are becoming increasingly polluted. Our soils and our produce lack nutritional minerals. Much formerly farmable land is now unusable. Tropical rain forests with all their diverse species of life and oxygen producing capacity are being destroyed at a rapid rate. By 2100, it is estimated that we will have permanently lost as much as one-third of all species of life on the planet.

Many of these changes will take centuries to correct or are already irreversible. Global warming is likely to occur as a result of increased carbon dioxide levels produced by the burning of fuels and rainforests, which may change world climate drastically. Loss of species may cause the collapse of critical biological systems with disastrous results for the whole planet. Life as we know it on earth may become insupportable.

Unrestrained population growth is putting further pressures upon the environment. If unchecked, a sustainable future for humanity will be impossible. The earth, its ability to absorb wastes, its ability to produce food, all its resources are finite. If we are to halt destruction to the environment, we must limit population. We have no other choice.

No more than a few decades remain for us to reverse these trends 'if vast human misery is to be avoided and our global home on this planet is not to be irretrievably mutilated.'

The Rio world scientists do offer a solution. It involves five areas:

- We must bring environmentally damaging activities under control to restore and protect the integrity of the earth's systems we depend on. (They recommend the development of small-scale, non-polluting, inexhaustible energy sources. And they recommend halting deforestation and loss of agricultural land to safeguard species of life.)
- We must manage resources crucial to human welfare more effectively. We must give high priority to efficient use of energy, water, and other materials, including extension of conservation and recycling.
- We must stabilize population. This will be possible only if all nations recognize that it requires improved social and economic conditions, and the adoption of effective, voluntary family planning.
- We must reduce and eventually eliminate poverty.
- We must ensure sexual equality, and guarantee women control over their own reproductive decisions.

Since the industrialized nations pollute most per capita, they have the highest responsibility to curb their excesses. And since they have the finances and technology to fight these issues and assist the developing nations, the greater burden of responsibility is upon them. Continuing to earn profit at the expense of the future of our earth is not tenable.

They continue:

'Acting on this recognition is not altruism, but enlightened self-interest: whether industrialized or not, we all have but one lifeboat. No nation can escape from injury when global biological systems are damaged. No nation can escape from conflicts over increasingly scarce resources. In addition, environmental and economic instabilities will cause mass migrations with incalculable consequences for developed and undeveloped nations alike.

Developing nations must realize that environmental damage is one of the gravest threats they face, and that attempts to blunt it will be overwhelmed if their populations go unchecked. The greatest peril is to become trapped in spirals of environmental decline, poverty and unrest, leading to social, economic and environmental collapse.

Success in this global endeavour will require a great reduction in violence and war. Resources now devoted to the preparation and conduct of war – amounting to over $1 trillion annually – will be badly needed in the new tasks and should be diverted to the new challenges.

A new ethic is required – a new attitude towards discharging our responsibility for caring for ourselves and for the earth. We must recognize the earth's limited capacity to provide for us. We must recognize its fragility. We must no longer allow it to be ravaged. This ethic must motivate a great movement – convince reluctant leaders and reluctant governments and reluctant peoples themselves to effect the needed changes...

We call on all to join us in this task.'

The Rio summit stated the case of our world very succinctly and clearly. Now what has been the result? At the summit, it was agreed that the rich industrialized nations would double their spending on development assistance. This was agreed to be a vital factor for improving world environmental conditions. The other most important factor that they agreed to address was a change in energy policy to reduce carbon dioxide emissions significantly. Five years later, they had done neither. The industrialized nations failed utterly to keep their agreements. In fact, their spending upon development assistance had fallen by 20-25%!

Many religious traditions begin with a sense of urgency, that change or repentance is needed now. Surely, this is never more true than today, with the planet in the state it is. A Hopi Elder has said, 'You have been telling the people that this is the eleventh hour. Now go and tell them THIS IS *THE* HOUR!'

Visions of angels

I bring in angels here because they can be the first and most ready source of help if we are in urgent need. They were for me, they can be for everyone.

The word 'angel' is derived from the Greek word *angelos*, which means 'messenger'. Angels can take any form, are androgynous but can appear as either male or female. Sometimes they appear as formless fields of light. Their different colours represent different fields of service and gifts to be bestowed on us. They are the heavenly messengers of the universe, sometimes called 'the Watchers'.

There have been records of 'shining ones', 'winged ones', 'flaming ones', 'golden beings', etc. visiting people on this planet throughout history; Gabriel, for example, visited both Mary and Mohammed. But there have been three main waves of angelic contact. The first wave occurred in biblical times. The second wave occurred during the medieval era. The third wave is occurring now. During this third wave, angels are reaching out to embrace us all. In the last decade or so, the whole world is talking about angels, near-death experiences and life after death. Market research in the USA and Great Britain today tells us that more than 70 per cent of us believe in the existence of angels. In ever increasing numbers, people are recognizing the 'power and the glory' of angels and archangels. The reason is simple. We have exploited and polluted our planet (and ourselves in some cases) to the brink of destruction. We are living in times of higher stress, with potentially unparalleled levels of toxicity in most everything we eat, drink and breathe. These are times of great change when we have moved out of harmony not only with ourselves, but also with our creator and our environment. So more and more people are turning their attention to the angels and asking for their assistance.

I asked the angels and received some amazing inner guidance about the state of world affairs. On the surface it looks like a gloom and doom story. What the angels told me turns out to be identical to what other highly evolved spiritual teachers on the planet are also saying. Strange though it may seem, the self-destructive pattern so prevalent today is all part of a higher plan for humanity. Having free will, it was logical that in ignorance and fear we would first create pain and destruction. This produced a wake-up call. The mess we have made has the purpose of waking us up to the quest for a better way, learning from what ails us.

True spiritual awakening evokes the realization that we are part of the same living source as the angels, guides and teachers. Upon remembering our spirit and reconnecting to our spiritual wisdom, power and love, we become empowered to create Heaven on earth. Here's one of my favourite quotes from the film, *Field of Dreams*:

John Kinsella: Is this heaven?

Ray Kinsella: It's Iowa.

John Kinsella: Iowa? I could have sworn this was heaven.

[*John starts to walk away*]

Ray Kinsella: Is there a heaven?

John Kinsella: Oh yeah. It's the place where dreams come true.

So how do we reconnect to our angelic guides to learn how to create heaven on earth? How can we open up to receive higher guidance from within? In Chapter 3 we will practise an Angel Initiation, but here are some general principles.

First of all, realize that angels, unlike humans, have no free will. They only carry out the will of God. You cannot pay the angels for their help. Gratitude is all they need. They are attracted by higher energies and do enjoy a few candles, flowers, incense and peaceful music. But all we have to do to employ them is to believe in them. Ask and we shall receive.

Secondly, angels are longing to heal the world and all of us, it's part of their job description. But in harmony with universal law, they can only do so if we first ask them. Because of our free will, they are not allowed to interfere. So talk with them often. Make it a new habit to ask for their guidance and assistance, even in mundane matters. When we are lonely and need comfort, we need to reach out to them. We will always be instantly in their embrace. They do answer our prayers. The question is: are we listening?

Thirdly, everyone has some angels around them. When we are doing good work, angels help us to be successful. When our works are in harmony with the big picture, legions of angels are attracted to assist us. When our plans and dreams come true swiftly through a series of amazing coincidences, we are observing the power of the angels at work.

Fourthly, everyone has his or her own Guardian Angel who is always with them, radiating love and light. Before we were born we made a divine contract about what we intended to achieve on earth. Unfortunately, at birth, the low energy vibration of physical reality caused us to forget our big plan. The spiritual life is about waking up and remembering why we are really here.

The angels never forget. They know what our birth plan is. They are constantly guiding us towards achieving this special destiny. Becoming conscious of their guidance is a great assistance in becoming aware of and fulfilling our birth plan.

Meditation – 'know thyself'

In meditation I asked Mother Earth for a message about meditation for this book and what to share. The answer I received was clear and to the point. 'You have learned how to know yourself and by knowing yourself you have learned how to become whole. Now show others how…' Okay, I thought, that seems simple enough, but as I pondered this, I found myself wondering whether most people actually understand what Socrates' injunction to 'know thyself' really means.

I remember when I first committed to writing my character strengths and defects list, I didn't have a clue where to begin because of course I did not know myself. My sponsor in the rooms of Cocaine Anonymous told me about the 'Spot it – you got it!' rule and the 'three fingered indictment'. Simply put, this means that when we point a finger at another person and project a judgement onto them, we only ever judge others for what we most fear, judge or deny in ourselves. If we look at our hand with the finger pointing at the other, and turn it upside down, there are three fingers pointing back towards ourselves. Hence the term 'three fingered indictment'. I practised this in moment-to-moment conscious awareness and to my horror and amazement it worked. Fairly soon I had built up a long list of character defects and strengths that I could work on. Then I found the source of this quote from Carl Jung, 'Everything that irritates us about others can lead us to an understanding of ourselves.'

Today I have a very good idea of who I am because I have worked so hard with so many spiritual and psychological disciplines to know myself... I have spent at least a minimum of 15 hours per day, 365 days per year for the last 15 years on this quest, developing mindfulness in order to know, accept and love myself.

I have long since learned how to recognize and dismantle the masks of subtle ego and sickly sweet persona. I learned how to identify and then dis-identify from universal shadow elements. I learned how to re-programme myself to replace fear with love and also how to feel the fear and do it anyway. I accessed and accumulated knowledge, developed understanding and eventually wisdom came and higher understanding... I learned that I am not my job, my car, my address, my jewels, my clothes or how I look – these are all personality and ego aspects of my behaviour but these are not me. I learned I am something much greater than these external symbols of power – SPIRIT. I found the strength, calm and focus to do this as I began to learn how to meditate and quieten all the internal mind noise.

Through learning to be still within and become the compassionate witness, I learned how to identify and dis-identify – how to let go of behaviours I repeated in ego which were out of harmony with spirit. This is called spiritual evolution. This allows spiritual involution to occur where I let go of baggage and old outworn energies, to make space for higher, purer and more powerful multi-sensory aware aspects of myself to come in and replace the released negative aspects of my personality and ego self.

When I look around I see so many people who have no idea who they truly are or what's really possible. So many wonderful people have no idea that they could be something more whole and complete. They are still asleep and many of them don't know it. They think they have been saved. Some of these people are spiritual teachers themselves who write books, talk in lectures and then run all kinds of competing, judging, attacking ego behaviour in private. This happens because they ignore their own shadow and the hard work necessary to overcome it. I feel true compassion for all those people who are still drowsy or awakening and sense that there is something missing but don't know what, and certainly don't know how to connect to it. I hope this book will help them to find the missing link and encourage them to do all the necessary work to awaken to best self, best life, best destiny!

One of the fundamental keys to finding that missing link is knowing where we got lost in the first place. It's vital that we look at our childhood conditioning. Growing up, I was directed (sometimes with care and concern, other times being admonished, scolded, shamed, and bullied), by parents, school and culture, to be a certain way.

The message was: 'Be nice, be good, be smart, be happy, be beautiful, be successful, be hardworking, be strong, be compliant, be accommodating of others. Don't complain, don't be lazy, don't be selfish or self-centred, don't pay any attention to your own wants and needs, don't pay attention to your aches and pains. Ignore them. Ignore any feelings that are not happy, helpful, and compliant.'

The emphasis was always on being more concerned with how others feel, and how my actions were affecting them. I learned if I didn't follow these rules I would be punished in some way, and if I did follow the rules I might better avoid the painful consequences. I also learned if I could somehow prove myself in the process to be 'good enough' according to these external standards, then someday there might be rewards for my good behaviour, maybe even in this world, but if not here then for sure in the next world.

So I wondered all those years ago when I was in so much pain, when my life didn't make sense – who am I? I was dutifully living life, obeying all the rules I had been given, just as some of you are probably doing now and just as likely wondering – who am I and how can I be myself when I am not sure who I am? Who am I beyond these external rules that often leave me feeling confused, less than, not good enough, angry, out of touch with my own sense of self?

These thoughts brought me to the realization that I am on a path of discovering what it truly means to KNOW and be myself, my true authentic essential self, without the heavy programming from all the rules of how I 'should' or 'should not' be, 'must' or 'must not' be.

Some of those rules I discovered were helpful guidelines to be aware of. Most of these rules, however, I discovered, were about control and manipulation, inciting me to fear, compete, win, judge, attack and stay in separation just to survive. Conversely, today, I know that genuine expressions of caring and co-operation with each other are essential in creating a peaceful, loving world.

I have come to know it is equally important for me to understand and care for my personal needs, releasing the old programmes that disconnect me from my essential self, getting in touch with my deep inner knowing, loving all my parts including the angry, hurt, fearful and confused parts (the shadow) as well as the best self parts that are genuinely loving, co-operative, happy and willing to help others selflessly with no thought of reward (spirit).

I was only able to remember best self and begin to be guided from within by this higher aspect of myself when I learned how to balance and empower my emerging mind-body-spirit connection. Such spiritual evolution was achieved through various forms of meditation, developing mindfulness in moment-to-moment conscious awareness and self-healing, but above all by being obedient to my teacher's requests to do whatever practice I was given daily, or several times a day, and to be patient; to wait, if required, for up to two years of consistent practice for any results. Thus it was that the universe revealed to me, through various teachings, the ancient secret of what the mystics call 'chakras'. This knowledge, coupled with discipline and the wisdom to work with what I knew daily, truly was the vital key to unlock all the hidden mysteries and reconnect me to best self.

Understanding the human energy system via the chakras

Chakra colour therapy

The body is an energy system and we use different energy forms to interact with the functions of this system as a whole. Understanding the human chakra system is the key to understanding how to use colour as a part of the healing process. The word 'chakra' comes from Sanskrit and it means wheel. Ideally, each chakra spins in harmony with the vibrations of the planet earth.

Chakras are the primary mediators of all energy coming into and radiating out from the body. They mediate the impulses of our energy system. Although not part of the physical body, chakras link the subtle energy fields surrounding the body to the activities of the body itself. Often perceived as hocus pocus in the past, modern technology and science has proved that in the areas of the body where chakras are traditionally located, the electro-magnetic emanations are higher.

Chakras help the body distribute energy for its various physical, emotional, mental and spiritual functions. They are connected to the functions of the physical body primarily through the endocrine glands and the central nervous system. They mediate energy inside and outside the body through the various spinal and cranial nerves. This energy is distributed throughout the body by means of the nerve pathways and the circulatory system. In this way, all the organs, tissues and cells receive these vibrational energies. This is how we stay healthy and alive...

One of the most effective means of correcting an energy imbalance is Reiki (more on this later in the chapter). However, if this is not readily available, colour therapy can be used, which is very easy and straightforward. For instance, eating and drinking foods with specific colours, wearing different colours of clothing, even surrounding yourself with certain coloured soft furnishings can be therapeutic. Individual chakras and the related organs and systems in the body will respond to the stimulation of the specific colours or energy vibrations. When we 'feed' the charkas in this way, they can use these colour energies to balance and heal the body.

Another way to powerfully balance and heal the chakra system is through the use of pure high-grade therapeutic essential oils. The science of aromatherapy and essential oils is as old as the beginning of time, although it was lost through the ages and has only begun to make its re-entry into the modern world during the last 50 years. Diverse ancient records indicate that natural elements were mankind's first medicine. Essential oils were used by Christ and biblical prophets such as Abraham and Moses, as well as by kings, priests, emperors and pharaohs from different cultures and times, to promote youthfulness and beauty and give protection from disease and plagues. Today, modern science continues to validate the many powerful uses of essential oils, including their immune-supporting properties. The oils I recommend come from Dr Gary Young of Young Living Oils in the US and you can find out more about them in the appendix at the back.

Here's an example of just one of the products I never leave home without, especially if I am flying anywhere or going on public transport… Thieves. In November 2006 the University of Manchester published findings from their extensive research on Thieves versus the hospital super bug MRSA. In every case study it was found that Thieves 100% destroyed MRSA. With rumours abounding about 'bird flu', this is a great oil to use regularly.

Thieves is a blend of highly antiviral, antiseptic, antibacterial, anti-infectious essential oils from Young Living Oils. It was created from research of a group of 15th-century thieves who rubbed oils on themselves to avoid contracting the plague while they robbed the bodies of the dead and dying. When apprehended, the thieves disclosed the formula of herbs, spices and oils they used to protect themselves in exchange for more lenient punishment. Studies conducted at Weber State University (Ogden, UT) during 1997 demonstrated its killing power against airborne microorganisms. One analysis showed a 90 percent reduction in the number of gram positive *Micrococcus luteus* organisms after diffusing for 12 minutes. After 20 minutes of diffusing, the kill-rate jumped to 99.3 percent. Another study against the gram negative *Pseudomonas aeruginosa* showed a kill rate of 99.996 percent after just 12 minutes of diffusion.

How different energies – colours and essential oil vibrations – affect the chakras

The different colour vibrations and energy frequencies interact with the electro-magnetic emanations of the body. These are transmitted to the spinal cord, which then transfers the colour energies along nerve pathways to the organs, restoring homeostasis or balance. This principle also applies to any emotional or mental imbalances that can cause or aggravate the physical problem.

According to yogic lore, there are seven major and 43 minor chakras in the human system. All the chakras are said to revolve, but the rate at which they spin is proportionate to the amount of energy in the system (i.e. the degree to which they are awakened). Many other ancient cultures were aware of these energy vortexes in the body, although they differ in the number, which they believed were of most importance.

The Hopi Indian tradition designates five energy centres in the body; the Huichol Indians of Mexico speak of energy fields which radiate from various areas of the body; and the Cuna Indians believe that eight 'spirits' inhabit the body in the chakra locations. The renowned 'siddhis,' or spiritual powers of the yogis, are the result of awakened chakras. The chakras and kundalini are really inseparable; when the kundalini rises, the chakras begin to open up. If the kundalini has not been activated, it is impossible to awaken all the chakras. As with the kundalini, the awakening or piercing of the chakras is a long developmental process. This process, however, is greatly accelerated, understood and assisted by the wisdoms shared in this book.

At different stages of our transformation, we may feel particular chakras being worked upon or spontaneously opening. Sometimes more than one chakra is being cleared during the same period. (Often, the 6th and 3rd, and the 7th and 4th, open together as pairs.) The chakras may awaken in any order.

In partial awakenings, only the lower chakras may be effected; the kundalini may then subside. In complete awakenings, the upper four chakras are also involved. Each chakra governs a particular level of consciousness. The 1st through 3rd chakras regulate awareness that is essential to ordinary functioning in the mundane world. Above the 3rd, the chakras open us to increasingly rarified states of being and levels of perception.

We can consciously invoke our genius!
The many teachings about the chakras differentiate between active and awakened chakras. Active chakras are those in which energy regularly or habitually congregates. Everyone has activity in their chakras, and each individual characteristically 'carries' more energy in certain chakras than others. However, this can be balanced – all chakras can be empowered equally and I honestly believe this is how we can consciously invoke our genius.

I once worked on a child with an inoperable cancerous brain tumour. We worked together 5 or 6 times a week. After several weeks both the cancer and the tumour had gone. Then this child told me she wouldn't be able to grow because of the amount of radiation treatment she'd had which had destroyed valuable irreplaceable human growth hormone. We continued to work together diligently every other day – during a period of about 5 months – focusing on the intentionality of growth and stimulating new human growth hormone spiritually. She grew several inches. However, she also transformed from being an average student into a student with true genius potential, illustrated by outstanding examination results.

In astrology we can determine certain basic characteristics about ourselves from knowing where our sun and moon were placed at birth and, of course, various other planetary influences define us further still. Similarly in terms of knowing the 'psychology' of the chakras we can also understand why we are predisposed to behave in a certain way. For instance, an overactive red root chakra will make us impulsive, reckless, aggressive and prone to angry outbursts. A dysfunctional yellow solar plexus chakra can induce fear and anxiety, while too much blue in the blue throat chakra makes us melancholy. A very sensually oriented, hedonistic type would have a strongly active 2nd chakra (orange), while a highly ambitious, competitive personality would be very active in the 3rd chakra (yellow). Intellectuals have strongly activated 6th chakras (indigo). Undoubtedly, we forgot about the psychology of the chakra system in our day-to-day material world existence. Yet, nevertheless, in our everyday language there is an unconscious reminder that we once knew about the psychology of colour when we refer to seeing red when we are angry for example. We also refer to yellow-bellied cowards and feeling blue when we are sad and depressed...

Fundamentally, the consciousness levels of the active seven chakras are mapped out as follows:

TRIBAL SURVIVAL ISSUES

1st chakra: (root chakra, located at the base of the spine – colour red)

Physical survival – this is the level concerned with personal and/or tribal needs, i.e. food, shelter, safety and security. Here we focus on overcoming fear of death and fear of living. This is the level of physical body consciousness. When this chakra is in the process of awakening, there may be strange sensations at the base of the spine. Itching, tingling, or much stronger vibrations, including thumping and cracking, may be felt in the tailbone. When the 1st chakra opens, Mother Earth energies (sometimes called shakti) may shoot up the spine in a spectacular way. Sometimes this can result in a great deal of pain in the spine. Intense heat may be felt in any of the chakra sites when they are beginning to be unveiled or opened.

To restore balance; work with Myrrh, Cypress and Vetiver oils.

RIGHT RELATIONSHIP TO MONEY AND SEX

2nd chakra: (sacrum chakra, located in the lower abdomen – colour orange)

Seeking pleasure and avoidance of pain (sexuality in its instinctual sense, or lust, is located at this level) – this is the level of emotions and is concerned with basic as opposed to sacred desires around money and sex. We need to balance our relationship to money, i.e. overcome greed and poverty consciousness or lack. This can be done by becoming grateful for all kinds of abundance in our lives, no matter how small. This is how we create more abundance – gratitude. We need to balance our relationship to sex – co-dependency and lust must be balanced with the opposites of isolation and frigidity in order to return to sacred sexuality practised in alchemical relationship (that's the subject of a whole book...). The 2nd chakra awakening can manifest powerful sexual feelings. I was sitting on a train in rush hour Japan when my 2nd chakra began to open. I had spontaneous orgasms, which was a pleasant surprise, but also quite frightened me because I had no idea what was going on. To restore balance; work with Ylang Ylang, Jasmin and Sandalwood oils.

RIGHT USE OF POWER

3rd chakra: (solar plexus chakra, located at the solar plexus – colour yellow)

This chakra is concerned with how we use our personal power. Do we dominate others, which is abusive, or do we allow others to dominate us – are we doormats? That's also abusive. When the 3rd chakra opens, there can be challenging emotional upheaval, and painful unconscious material can erupt. Vomiting, diarrhoea, stomach cramps, nausea and other digestive troubles can accompany this opening. Telepathy, clairvoyance, clairsentience and awareness of astral entities may emerge with an awakened 3rd chakra. The newly unfolding 3rd chakra can make one emotionally and psychically hypersensitive. Of course, if we are working with Reiki daily, these symptoms can be managed through energy mastery. Reiki is absolutely key to alleviating these symptoms of awakening – meditation and prayer are not enough. To restore balance; work with Lemon, Chamomile and Thyme oils.

DETACHMENT AND UNITY CONSCIOUSNESS

4th chakra: (heart chakra, located at the centre of the chest – colour green)

I call this the Job Initiation – The Lord Giveth and the Lord Taketh Away, Blessed be the Lord. The lessons of this chakra relate to right relations with others, detached involvement, shared experiences and cherishing others beyond the self. This is the level of compassion. When the 4th chakra is being awakened, crushing pressures are often felt in the chest. I felt as if a hippopotamus was sitting on mine, and had the typical breathing problems associated with this opening. Vibrations may be felt in the heart and chest; there may be periods when the heartbeat is erratic or races wildly. All sorts of discomfort may be felt in the chest, including acute pain resembling a heart attack. In seeming paradox, feelings of detachment from loved ones may signal the early stages of the heart chakra opening. The power to heal is awakened and arises from an open heart chakra. Wish fulfilment and manifesting ability is also increased when this chakra is opened. To restore balance; work with Rose, Geranium, Helichrysm (called Immortel by the French) and Bergamot oils.

CREATIVITY AND SELF EXPRESSION

5th chakra: (throat chakra, located at the base of the throat – colour pale blue)

Here we begin to access inspiration and self-expression through communication. This is the level of higher creativity. This chakra often takes a long time to fully open. Sensations of strangulation, constriction or tightness around the neck and throat may occur, as well as inexplicable gagging. There may be internal pressure which feels as if a growth is developing in the throat. An awakened 5th chakra produces spontaneous vocalizations. These may be unusual sounds, singing (sometimes even in unrecognized languages), or words, which do not seem to be coming from oneself. Some people call this channelling. One may also become clairaudient, hearing inner voices or other people's thoughts. The lesson here is to be impeccable with the word: speak the truth to self and others and always remember the power of the word, ceasing to harm self and others with careless words and through gossiping. To restore balance; work with Lavender, Eucalyptus and Marjoram oils.

DIVINE INSPIRATION AND REALIZATION
6th chakra: (third eye chakra, located in the centre of the forehead – colour indigo)
Abstract thought, intellectual focus – this is the level of knowledge. When the 6th chakra is awakening, enormous pressures are felt in the head, particularly around the eyes and in the forehead area. These may cause excruciating headaches. There may be twitching and vibrating felt between the brows. The eyes may roll cross-eyed or up into the head. There may be dazzling visions seen with the eyes open or closed; sometimes a huge single eye is seen staring out. When the 6th chakra is activated and awakening one gains contact with spirit guides, totems, ancestors, elders, deities and one's holy guardian angel and teachers. Incredible out-of-body experiences may occur with this opening. To restore balance; work with Rosemary, Peppermint and Basil oils.

ENLIGHTENMENT – SUPRAMENTAL DESCENT
7th chakra: (crown chakra, located at the top of the skull – colour violet)
Reverence, spiritual focus – this is the consciousness of the divine, oneness. When the crown chakra opens, there are tingling sensations, vibrations or coursing energies felt at the top of the head. For some, the skull may feel

sore. In my own experience and that of others I have spoken with, the cranial bones actually start to separate and 'float' beneath the skin. People can still see and feel this when they work on the back of my head. When the 7th chakra is awakened, there is often a transcendent experience. One may experience a spellbinding, super-conscious light flooding into the top of the head. Frequently, Samadhi (a deep trance ecstasy state) occurs when the 7th chakra is awakened. I have learned how to experience this constantly to varying degrees yet still be grounded to go about the 'Great Work' of helping others... a challenging task indeed but nevertheless possible. To restore balance; work with Frankincense oil.

How grateful I was to discover and do the daily practices and disciplines to unlock the secrets of universal life-force energy and the chakras, those secret inner doorways on the Map to God... Healing and balancing my chakras daily helped me to put my self back together again. Also, it seemed that the more grateful I became about life, the more my heart chakra opened and was healed – the more love I felt. This leads me onto another very important spiritual principle: gratitude and the power of thank you.

Spiritual principle - gratitude

The Essenes believe that gratitude is one of the most important spiritual practices to cultivate. Acts that come from an attitude of gratitude are blessed and have a beautiful beneficial effect. The simple act of saying the words 'thank you' in the right way is one of the highest forms of prayer.

Gratitude opens up the consciousness to the influx of divine light into our daily experience. Gratitude allows true wealth to manifest in our lives. When we are grateful for what we have, we receive more. When we are grateful for what we are, we become more; we become a more pure and perfect being – our best self. When we can say 'thank you' from our hearts, even when under challenging trials or hardship, we are proving our knowledge of spiritual principles and our connection with higher states of consciousness. The power of this kind of thank you has the alchemical energy to transform reality.

Truly, gratitude is a potent tool for increasing abundance. Jesus taught this principle in a parable that is quite a paradox: he who (thinks and complains that he) has not will lose what he has. He who has (and is aware of and grateful for what he has), to him will more be given.

Saying 'thank you' to a person can purify the energy or karma in the interaction or relationship. When we can see that the most challenging experiences in our lives have made us who we now are, and we love who we now are, we can say 'thank you' to them and release them. Real detachment and forgiveness are only possible from such a state of gratitude.

Those who are conscious of their spirituality will find that practising gratitude increases the intensity of their lives. It increases their happiness and the love that they receive. The Essenes teach that saying 'thank you' to the earth and all the nature spirits purifies us and frees us of both physical and psychological diseases. Similarly, saying 'thank you' to the sky (the heavens) and all the nature spirits brings awareness of our best direction in life and goals. The true 'thank you' comes from our deepest centre, unites heaven and earth, and creates unity consciousness with all life. This heartfelt 'thank you' truly has the power to change our lives.

Nature spirits

Pan and the nature spirits

'I am a servant of almighty God
I and my subjects are willing to come to the
Aid of mankind in nature if they affirm belief in us
And ask for our help.'

According to popular myths and legends, Pan, often depicted as half man and half goat, is traditionally the aspect of God who oversees all of nature and is in charge of the devas and nature spirits. Devas and nature spirits exist in the ethereal world, a hidden world which runs parallel to our own and is invisible to the unconditioned naked eye. These spirits can be seen or felt intuitively and when we begin to purify our vibration and raise our frequencies, we can learn how to see, sense, communicate and work with the 'elemental kingdoms' intuitively. The Jews call them Shedim. The Egyptians called them Afries. Africans named them Yowahoos. Persians called them Devs. Nature spirits are one way that allows human consciousness to connect beyond the physical and they help us to understand other realms of consciousness.

According to Eileen Caddy at Findhorn, and also the Theosophical Society teachings, I learned that there are four different types of nature spirits (or elementals as they are also sometimes known) that we can invoke via the devas to assist us with creating and manifesting. Devas are part of the angelic kingdom and are in direct service to the world of nature, expressing themselves as one of the four elements.

The nature spirits of the earth are called gnomes. There are male and female gnomes. In our daily lives, we come in contact with the male, because the female almost always apparently stays at home.

The salamanders are the fire spirits. Without these beings, fire cannot exist. It's impossible to light a match without a salamander being present. There are many families of salamanders, differing in size, appearance, and dignity, but usually people see them as small balls of light.

The sylphs are the air spirits. Their element has the highest vibratory rate of the four (beside earth, fire, water). They are said to live on the tops of mountains. The winds are their particular vehicle. They work through the gases and ethers of the earth and are kindly toward humans. Seers report that they have wings, looking like cherubs or fairies. Because of their connection to air, which is associated with the mental aspect, one of their functions is to help humans receive inspiration. The sylphs are drawn to those who use their minds, particularly those on creative arts.

The undines are the elemental beings that compose water. They are able to control, to a great degree, the course and function of the water element. Etheric in nature, they exist within the water itself and this is why they can't be seen with the normal physical vision. The concept of the mermaid is apparently connected with these elemental beings. The undines also work with the plants that grow under the water and with the motion of water. Some undines inhabit waterfalls, others live in fountains, ponds, rivers and lakes. The undines work with the vital essences and liquids of plants, animals and human beings. They are present in everything containing water – that's 80% of us!

As well as nature spirits, Pan also oversees the animal kingdoms and all the animal power totems. Here are some totems that could be relevant to you at this stage.

Animal totems

The last few hundred years prove how destructive we humans have become without the guidance of our animal ancestors. I was guided that it is now time to renew our ancient bonds with our animal totems, and to learn to walk once again in the protection of their wisdom and their guidance.

Native and tribal peoples call upon particular animal spirits or totems to fill them with their empowering energies. We can do this too. This is often called 'invoking.' Invocation is a form of prayer we use to call the powers of various animals or angels or masters into ourselves. When we invoke, we actually invite the spirit of the animal to live within us or be very near us for a while, so that we might share their power.

When we pray to or invoke an animal, we are actually appealing to the spirit of the entire species. For example, when we invoke Wolf, we call in the wisdom, experience, power and understanding of all wolves who are living or who have ever lived. Wolf is the teacher... and often symbolizes a new teacher in our lives.

The world is a whole, with levels of being throughout creation, and all can be accessed. It's not just angels that are appearing more frequently today. We are also seeing a recovery of the knowledge of animal spirits. We look more closely at the shamanic path in Chapter 3, but if you are more attuned to the lower levels than the higher (in descriptive rather than qualitative terms) here are some general principles.

When an animal appears to you, it is a powerful synchronicity. The message the animal has for you depends upon the type of animal. The particular species of animal holds a message for you about your current situation. The particular qualities of that animal are the qualities you will need to embody to best deal with your own situation.

To most people, animals seem to be without much consciousness, driven by instinct. However, the behaviour of animals reflects our own level of consciousness and our expectations. If we expect them to just hide from us and be rather dumb, they will appear that way. However, when our human energy level increases, the animals will appear more often to us. And their presence will bring important messages and guidance for us.

The animal totems that come into our lives represent aspects of ourselves that we need to become more aware of and express in a positive way. When a particular animal comes into our perception, it often indicates that we are both ready and need to integrate that which it represents into our lives.

Remember, our encounter with an animal need not be in real life in nature. We are not likely to encounter a jaguar stalking the streets of our town. However, we are likely to see a Jaguar motorcar sometimes. We may see a picture of an animal in a magazine or on a billboard, hear an animal's voice on the radio or see an animal on TV. It is especially meaningful when we dream of an animal. However we encounter an animal, consider its significance and possible message.

Keep a journal of your experiences as to how different types of animal totems or spirit medicines accelerate you on the path of awakening spiritual integrity. Perhaps at first you might only notice a slight change in your energies when working with animal power totems. However, as soon as you begin to open yourself more deeply to the flow of universal energies using Reiki, the difference will be altogether more tangible, in fact, it will be incredible.

Reiki (universal life-force energy mastery)

Reiki is a Japanese word. REI means: 'The invisible force of all essence' and KI means: 'That which creates, sustains and nurtures all living things.'

In a nutshell, Reiki is the science of energy, based on the language of symbols, and is related to a number of similar types of universal energy sciences from India and Tibet, such as the science of mandalas and mantras. Symbols play a crucial role in the influencing of one's own body for one's own benefit or for the well being of another who is experiencing negative conditions. Realizing that psychological problems have direct influence upon one's body temple, Tibetan Masters developed ways to correct negative states of mind and made Sanskrit symbols to remind people of the divine power ever present in their daily lives. Other uses for the symbols include protection, balance, success, power, increased vitality, healing, increasing happiness, aiding in meditation, sending prayers and absent healing.

Throughout history, humankind has often turned to spirituality in times of distress. Now, on the brink of substantial destruction of this beautiful planet, many people are turning to higher agencies for guidance. Some are turning within for answers or for more clarity. There are many ways to aim the arrow of awareness towards our own centre. Reiki is a perfect self-help system. The energies it invokes adjust themselves to the user, which provides for everyone to receive only the intensity of energy they are ready for. Regardless of whether you are a newcomer to the inner world, a hard-boiled intellectual, a body-oriented yoga student, a housewife or a spiritual devotee, Reiki will bring you into contact with the energies appropriate to your particular state of spiritual readiness. It puts us back in touch with the long-forgotten but all-pervading universal life-force energy. It teaches us how to know and love ourselves again. It helps us bridge the man-made gap between our fellow human beings, nature and spirit, so we can all live in harmony again.

Life-force energy (Reiki) is present wherever and whatever we may be, yet evades our intellectual awareness the moment we turn our head to analyze it. Every form of life-energy has its own identity or individuality, its own characteristics, but they are all made of the same fundamental material. Called 'prana' in India, 'elan vital' in Europe, 'chi' in China, 'orgone' by William Reich and 'ki' in Japan (just to mention a few of its names), Reiki is the energy that pervades everything sentient and insentient. It is ever-changing, yet always the same.

In the beginning, Reiki calligraphy was a system of meditation used by Tibetan lamas. The calligraphs were painted upon large wall hangings and were the centre focus within mantric (chanting) ceremonies performed to produce enlightenment by Tibetan holy men in the monasteries. Participants would sit upon four-legged wooden stools, positioned in 3 inches of water in the centre of an earthenware container that was oval in shape to represent the Akasa (etheric egg). The stool was composed of wood with pure silver inlaid in a channel up each of the four legs, and in turn connected with a square silver inlay upon the seat. One wall of the temple was composed of copper, polished to the highest sheen imaginable. Behind the aspirant, there was an angled wall containing the lama's prayer, and the calligraphs of the Reiki symbols. The symbols were reflected by the copper wall. The initiate would meditate upon them as he sat upon the stool in the centre of the vessel filled with water. The idea was to implant the symbols deep into the subconscious mind through concentration, thus raising the consciousness and heightening the awareness, while purification of the body and mind occurred. This was a very esoteric science passed on by secret ritual and word of mouth. It eventually disappeared. In the mid 1800s, Dr Mikao Usui rediscovered, in ancient Sanskrit texts, the symbols which were used as the catalyst for this meditation technique.

Dr Usui's rediscovered form of the system has undergone many changes. Although the calligraphs remain basically the same, revisions have been made to simplify them and to make them more appealing to the Western mind.

I have studied the Reiki system in its various forms with many teachers from all walks of life. Although the systems do vary slightly, the following assumptions and conclusions remain valid:

- Although all systems of Reiki are valid in the content of their teachings, some are more powerful in effect upon consciousness.
- Some teachers are more powerful than others, even when teaching the same system. There are many reasons for this.
- In the same way that some people are more perceptive to subtle energies, some students are more receptive to these teachings and the experience of Reiki energy than others.

According to Indian, Tibetan and Chinese philosophy (and now even modern science too), we are surrounded by an incredibly lively universe that is made up of energy. Scientists have recently demonstrated that what used to be thought of as 'solid' matter is in fact rapidly moving energy. Solidity is, in fact, an illusion created by our limited perception. Everything is energy and therefore alive and receptive to energy. Even though we are floating in this pool of refreshing, life-giving energy 24 hours a day, we have forgotten its presence. Without this awareness, we can no longer receive and enhance many of its positive effects on our physical and psychological health. Science now acknowledges that the entire universe may well be constructed from nothing but consciousness, and that material reality is created by consciousness. Indeed, science now proves that no object or being on earth is solid – all is vibration.

In the popular *Star Wars* film, Obi-Wan refers to the connectedness of all things when he talks about, 'The Force is what gives a Jedi his power. It's an energy field created by all living things. It surrounds us and penetrates us. It binds the galaxy together.'

In 1917, the father of Quantum Physics, Max Planck, stated, "We must assume behind this force the existence of a conscious and intelligent mind, this mind is the matrix of all matter." Today, Western science has refined our understanding of Planck's 'matrix', describing it as a form of energy that is everywhere, always present, and one that has existed since the beginning of time. Additionally, Planck's matrix appears to be holographic – meaning that any portion of the matrix contains the pattern of the whole.

The existence of a holographic universe suggests three powerful principles:

1. Everything is connected.
2. There is no 'here' and 'there.'
3. The past, present and future are intimately linked.

Knowing that the Planck matrix exists, it makes tremendous sense that we'd be able to communicate with it in a way that is meaningful in our lives.

I believe Reiki is one of the most powerful and fast-track ways of opening up a means of communication with the 'all that is'. Remember, energy is always responsive to energy. Therefore nothing can remain completely negative. All seemingly negative conditions can be changed with consistent positive thoughts, words and actions. We can always transform and evolve situations and heal ourselves personally in the process.

Unfortunately, in forgetfulness of the fact that the universe is holographic in nature, we have allowed ourselves sometimes to communicate in a way that is harmful to ourselves and to the lives of others. This is how we have created (bad) karma through the ignorance of the power of our words, thoughts and feelings; through forgetting that our words, thoughts and feelings transmit energies. In ego and separation from spirit we became blissfully ignorant that we could create holograms that influence the world around us. We forgot that when we project our thoughts onto another person, that person is influenced and affected by the energy that our thoughts have carried to them. If these thoughts are unkind or unjust, then the other person can be trapped into becoming the very image that we have projected upon them. The same goes for all the negative images we project onto ourselves.

We create our own experience of reality. Are we ready to change this? Are we ready to change our attitudes and how we think? Would understanding what has kept us from abundance improve our lives? Who wishes to repeat 'poverty or lack of love patterns' that are keeping us stuck in lack?

If we could be shown how to recognize and release generational beliefs that are holding us back, surely this would make life more fulfilling? We need to become 'believers'. When we believe in miracles, miracles happen. Because I know that thoughts can alter my experience, my experience changes. Because I know I will find love and abundance, this comes to me and in so many ways.

Occasionally, in the beginning, I was disappointed or hurt when things didn't turn out as I imagined (such as a work relationship, a friendship, even a marriage). However, when I took the courage to see the false beliefs that blocked my creation, and when I detached from this self-limiting perception, I set myself free from the suffering. This takes incredible determination, focus, clarity, strength, integrity, courage and above all faith. Are we willing to learn a new science in order to know how to help ourselves to do this? I am referring to the ancient science of energy – Reiki – based on the language of symbols.

Faith is needed to embrace the mysterious. Gandhi said, 'Faith is not something to grasp, it is a state to grow into'. He also said, 'Faith... must be enforced by reason... When faith becomes blind it dies'. I agree and the information in this book is balanced and enforced by reason. Finally, Martin Luther King said, 'Take the first step in faith. You don't have to see the whole staircase, just take the first step'.

Are you ready to follow in my footsteps and take the first step? If so, lets look at the Reiki symbols in more detail...

There are three main areas within which we can apply the Reiki symbols:

Absent healing

Reiki energy transcends time and space. Not only are we able to send healing over a distance, but we can also travel through time. We can address past, present and future issues. It becomes possible to explore different dimensions.

Personal growth

On a personal level, we can choose to work with our heightened awareness, listening and acting upon our inner knowing and creating personal empowerment. We may become more aware of mental and emotional processes which no longer serve us, such as judgement, lack of forgiveness and inability to accept or give love. As we connect with these layers of our conditioning, we can begin to heal ourselves at a very deep level. We can then make choices which are in line with our highest purpose.

Manifestation

As we attune our will with the Source through Reiki, we can open ourselves to the abundance which is our birthright. Universal abundance is always available to us in every area of our lives, from the bounty of nature to the love of our fellow beings. The ability to allow and to receive brings many blessings.

It's not what other people say and do that hurts or dis-empowers us, it's our attitude towards what they say and do. Failure in our lives is self-created. We self-sabotage ourselves with habitual negative patterns based upon 'victim consciousness'. If we work with energy mastery, we can raise the level of our personal energy frequency so that it's no longer possible to accommodate or hold such lower frequency, negative thoughts. True success is no more complex than that – achieving and maintaining a higher energy vibration. In my workshops, sessions and retreats, I show people how to achieve this.

Reiki is the womb that surrounds us. Initiation into Reiki does not necessarily turn us into a great healer, wealthy businessman or luminous being, yet daily self-healing with Reiki, working with psychological recapitulation and aligning our intentionality with these goals, will. Reiki brings out the best in us, intensifies our capabilities and shows us what parts of our lives have not yet been integrated or healed. Then, from that point of self-mastery, we can create our own best destiny.

Anyone can be initiated to become a Reiki channel within a day or two.

No skill and no special preparations or degrees are necessary. Energy mastery is our birthright or, as I prefer to call it, our divine inheritance.

Once initiated into Reiki, a person remains a channel for universal life-force energy throughout his or her lifetime, even if it isn't put to use. I encourage daily practice, which deepens reconnection to Source and understanding of the universal life-force. It also helps us to become a clear channel for it. There is no philosophy or religion attached to Reiki. It is pure energy! Reiki can easily be combined with orthodox medicine, as well as with other forms of alternative healing or relaxation methods. Generally, the Reiki system is divided into three or sometimes four degrees that are like building blocks. An individual does not have to complete the whole curriculum. In fact many people the world over have learned only the first two degrees. However, the sequence of the degrees has to be followed. Each degree is complete in itself. Understanding Reiki in its totality is an endless process. Energy mastery cannot be conveniently described, nor can its effects on us be determined in a handbook. As long as we live and practise Reiki, however, we will experience continuous personal growth – supramental descent. The best thing to do is go with the flow and trust that life itself will shower its blessings upon us.

Wherever I mention Reiki in this book, I should clarify that I am specifically referring to MS-REM, which I describe as a kind of super-Reiki and which forms a central tenet to the self-enlightenment work of this 'Map to God' material. MS-REM is an evolved and advanced form of Reiki that is exponentially more powerful than the violet planetary ray of Usui Reiki. The MS-REM ray is a four-fold ray, which is pictured by clairvoyants and Kirlian technology as a combination of rays, mainly gold, silver, white, opalescent and platinum in colour. The specific vibrational energies of these rays interact to form alchemical White Gold. The vibratory nature of White Gold, which balances and merges the masculine and feminine within, is crucial in this alchemical process to enlightenment.

Traditionally, silver is feminine, lunar, calming, receptive and amplifying, whereas the vibrational nature of gold is masculine, solar, stimulating and active. At a higher level of consciousness, gold and silver are directly related to the internal male/female and solar/lunar aspects of one's own subtle energies. By meditating with the specific colours of gold and silver, as opposed to other colours, the disciple aligns himself or herself with this higher alchemical principle. It is one of the most powerful fast-track ways to elevate consciousness on offer, and that is why it is being given to us at this crucial time in our evolution.

PRACTICES

Ask the angels – mindfulness meditation

'People are like stained-glass windows. They sparkle and shine when the sun is out... But when the darkness sets in, their true beauty is revealed only if there is a light from within.'

ELIZABETH KUBLER ROSS, MD

At Alchemical Level 1, one of the most powerful practices we can learn is mindfulness, how to focus in the moment we are living. Much of the time our mind is daydreaming – more in the past or the future than it is in the present. Unawareness can dominate the mind in any moment and can affect everything we do. It's like living in a perpetually drowsy or semi-awake state (another description for what I call the matrix). For most of us our minds are like employees who aren't fulfilling their job descriptions. We are living in the age of the wellness revolution and there are many health-giving benefits to the practise of staying mindful in the moment. When uncontrolled thoughts are dominating our experience, our brain waves are going very fast – beta brainwave state. I call this busy state. In this state we are producing a large quantity of stress chemicals. These chemicals are responsible for making important changes in our body, many of them disrupting important systems, such as blood pressure, heart rate, metabolism, blood sugar levels, gastro-intestinal functioning including digestion, endocrine function, and perhaps most importantly, the functioning of our neurological system. When we practise mindfulness, the brain waves slow down appreciably to alpha brainwave state – a deep meditative state. This has the knock-on effect of slowing down the production of stress hormones and the body can become balanced once again.

When we have an out of control or over-active thought process, it is very difficult to concentrate, make decisions, be highly creative and get break-through ideas. This state works to increase negative emotions and we experience anxiety, fear, depression, helplessness, hopelessness, intolerance and the like. Once these negative emotions take hold, and it doesn't take very long, the body sensations are not far behind. This can all occur in a split second. If we are not working with mindfulness techniques, we may not even notice the beginning of the build-up of tension in our body. Often we do not notice until our body is screaming with pain, perhaps a migraine headache, backache, stomach ache, or extreme fatigue. With this amount of stored tension, it is more difficult to bring the mind and body back to balance. Generally at this point, we go for some artificial means of changing the body sensations and the emotions. Some of these include food, especially high carbohydrates or pure sugar, caffeine, medications and alcohol. While one may feel better temporarily, the effect is short-lived, and a pattern of dependency can be developed. This cycle is only one step away from serious breakdown, either from a compromised immune system, emotional collapse, or the development or worsening of a serious disease state.

The tools of mindfulness are really quite simple, yet sometimes far from easy to use. The reason for this is that we seem to find it challenging to practise something called 'non-doing'. So let's turn the challenge into a mindful experience. We do this by noticing and discriminating. We simply notice negative thoughts, judgements, projections, blaming and allied emotions. We delete all negative harmful energies in the moment. We learn to discriminate and remind ourselves constantly in the moment that we are not our thoughts and emotions. Practising mindfulness we learn in moment-to-moment conscious awareness how to observe all the mind-noise and correct this instantly. If we lose our focus and discover ourselves involved in our thoughts or emotions, we can very gently but firmly notice this and return to focus on the breath and create stillness within. Learning to meditate is a great way to learn how to achieve mindfulness. Eventually, practising mindfulness, our lives can become a wide-awake meditation.

How does one enter into a meditative state? To begin with the mind must be still and free of thoughts. Slowing down the breath, breathing deeply and regularly, may calm the mind and the emotions.

While meditating it's imperative to establish a comfortable, upright posture, with your spine as straight as possible. You can either sit on a straight-backed chair with your feet on the floor or assume the Eastern position of sitting on the floor with your legs crossed.

To alchemically fast-track the desired state of emptiness and simultaneously create magical, powerful inner healing, imagine yourself inside a violet flame of purification, which totally permeates the mind/body/spirit complex. The intention is that this sacred spiritual flame washes clean everything that you are on all levels, through all times, space and dimensions. Imagine, will and intend that all imbalanced and unqualified energies are being transmuted back into love! Ask the angels for assistance – even if you don't believe in them yet, they believe in you. They'll help you, but you have to ask! So ask them to empower your will and intention that all negative, fear-based thoughts, feelings, emotions, images and projections are returned to love in the violet flame.

If you feel stiff or in pain ask the angels to violet flame the pain away and relax. When you feel the violet flame has done its work, begin to focus solely on the breath. On the in-breath when the lungs are full, do not close the air passages. Instead flow from inhaling to exhaling continuously, smoothly with no break.

Notice the immediate calm, how good you feel and know how powerful this is. Do this several times daily because the more you practise the more benefits you'll feel.

This simple meditation can produce, with time, very profound results. Eventually, you will experience the limited space that you have perceived as being within your head as vast and limitless. You may feel as if you have merged with everything that once you thought existed externally in separation to self. In advanced states of meditation, time and space may even seem to collapse...

Eventually, everywhere and every time may seem to be in the here and now. The totality of everything merges into an expanded, evolved awareness of oneness.

Also imagine any attachments to undesirable people, places and things melting and vanishing in the flame. The Tibetans gave me a very powerful affirmation to say three times to clear karma, use this now.

Tibetan karma clearing affirmations

I hereby terminate, remove and erase any and all images projected onto me by any person, or by myself, throughout all space, times and dimensions.

I hereby terminate, remove and erase any and all images that I have projected onto others or onto myself throughout all space, times and dimensions.

Use these affirmations daily. Use them in the general form given above. Whenever disturbances concerning any specific person come to mind, replace 'any person' with their name while making these affirmations. This will clear all kinds of psychic dross from your life. And remember that if we strike without compassion against the darkness, we ourselves enter that very darkness we have judged in another...

For most people, the majority of their day is spent in their knee-jerk thought processes, mainly related to past and future events. This can be compared to spending all day at the cinema, and the results are about the same – not very much gets achieved. When people mention they have problems with procrastination, you can just about guess where they spend most of their time.

Learning to have power over your thought process is a very important mindful activity. Part of this training is achieved in the formal practice of meditation, but when you continue to work with your thoughts during the day outside of your meditative practice, the results are dynamic. Command your brain to make you aware when uncontrolled thought processes captivate you. In other words, train yourself to wake up and notice this temporary loss of consciousness, so that you can begin to choose to exist in a more powerful awakened state. You can do this with the simple Tibetan mantras above and then work with the breath to let go and re-focus, breathing light in and letting go of darkness on the exhale. As you manage your thoughts, this control is carried over to emotional and body sensation management. You'll begin to feel stronger, calmer and more balanced through just noticing what you are thinking and feeling, waking up, letting go with the breath.

As you become a master of mindfulness, you'll notice how powerful and positive you become. You are much more awake, in charge of your life and able to make choices to influence growth and self empowerment. Life is no longer like being in a run away car with no brakes.

Gratitude – the power of saying 'thank you'

Inwardly say 'thank you' for everything in your life, including your own body. All of these things are gifts. Practising gratitude will bring them into their highest and most pure state of expression.

Write a gratitude list of all the things you are grateful for. Add a few things to it each day. Read the whole list to yourself often. When you are feeling a bit down, read this list and feel your spirit soar. Counting your blessings is a good way to practise gratitude.

Write a brief history of the main events of your life

Make it a time-line, year by year, starting with your birth. This will be developed in further chapters, so take time do this first part properly. Add to it from time to time as you think of other events that happened to you. Resist the temptation to analyze much at this stage, just make a sequential list of memories of your life by year. Definitely have some Reiki energy-balancing work to help you deal with toxic energies that come to the surface. See how great you begin to feel.

Working with animal totems

Animals will share their spirit gifts with us, if we but ask. Many tribal peoples consider the animals as our wise grandparents, for they evolved before us and witnessed our own evolution.

A very simple way to invoke an animal spirit or totem is to simply visualize and call upon it. For example, perhaps you need to become more adaptable, contained and clever at camouflage. You might visualize fox and say something like, 'Fox totems and spirits, I am calling to you. Live within me and fill me with your cleverness, the power to be unnoticed, camouflaged, adaptable, and to be contained.' Some people find it helpful to look at a picture or statue of the animal they are invoking.

Practise this with the animal totems I list below to help you through the particular challenges of Alchemical Level 1.

BAT: The bat is the Mayan and Aztec symbol for rebirth. Bats hang upside down in the cave, similar to babies in the womb preparing for birth. The darkness of the cave is safe for the bat, just as the womb provides protection for the child. In leaving the cave or the womb, we are forced to look at the light and at the shadows it produces. We are then given the choice to follow the dark or the light; that which furthers our growth most. Consciously confronting this duality of life is an unavoidable stage of our evolution into wholeness. Through this confrontation, we finally see that both the dark and the light sides contribute to our awareness and our growth process. Living in this higher consciousness and embracing change is the key to understanding wholeness and being at peace – with self and with all that is. Everything, every place and everyone is a test of mastery; an opportunity for growth. It all brings us great wisdom – if we know where to look, how to look, and who to ask for help.

SNAKE: Snake spirit medicine transmutes all poisons into medicines – physically, mentally, emotionally and spiritually – and awakens the deepest mysteries of all creation. Snake assists us to 'shed the skins' of the past. In times of transformation of the deepest and most dynamic levels of the psyche, snake can be a powerful friend. Snake spirit medicine facilitates initiation into the deepest, most hidden levels of the unconscious. Snake assists us to integrate new and old, positive and less positive archetypal energies, smoothing the transition between daily deaths and rebirths of this path.

Reiki Symbol 1

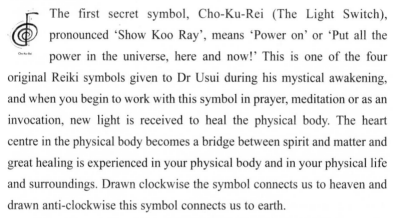 The first secret symbol, Cho-Ku-Rei (The Light Switch), pronounced 'Show Koo Ray', means 'Power on' or 'Put all the power in the universe, here and now!' This is one of the four original Reiki symbols given to Dr Usui during his mystical awakening, and when you begin to work with this symbol in prayer, meditation or as an invocation, new light is received to heal the physical body. The heart centre in the physical body becomes a bridge between spirit and matter and great healing is experienced in your physical body and in your physical life and surroundings. Drawn clockwise the symbol connects us to heaven and drawn anti-clockwise this symbol connects us to earth.

This symbol is the empowering symbol. It focuses Reiki energy on an area or issue and may be used in all aspects of our daily life. From blessing food to travelling and healing, this symbol is used as the next most powerful symbol in the Reiki system. Only the Master symbols have more power. And the Master symbols themselves are powerless unless you cover them with the first symbol.

My suggestion to you is to copy this symbol onto two A4-sized pieces of paper and laminate them. Learn what the symbol means. When you do the Violet Flame Mindfulness Meditation you could sit on one copy of the symbol and meditate on the other symbol – eyes open to empower, enhance and protect your process. Working with this symbol opens you up to become truly receptive to the light and all its gifts and blessings – the harvest.

Always remember to deeply thank the Reiki guides, the angels, nature spirits and animal totems when you have finished your practice.

CHAPTER 2

AWAKENING

'A journey of a thousand miles must begin with a single step.'
Lao Tsu

OVERVIEW

Confrontation

Alchemical Level 2 is that of Dissolution. Physically, it's when the ashes of Calcination are dissolved in water or acid. Spiritually, we break down the ego further by immersing ourselves in the waters of the subconscious, the irrational or rejected parts of our minds. Without the inhibitions and repressions of the ego, we fall into ourselves. All the walls of denial come tumbling down. All sorts of forgotten memories and denied behaviours flood into our awareness. We start to feel genuine feelings – feelings that we perhaps didn't even know we had. We learn to accept our emotions. We learn to transform our inner voice of criticism into spiritual discernment by lovingly embracing all of our feelings, including those awful feelings that accompany depression. The ability to fully accept emotions comes from a willingness to let them flow so they can be observed and fine-tuned. This involves an honest inventory of how we use or misuse our emotions. For example, do we manipulate others with our tears or anger? Do we deaden our feelings in order to appear 'sane and in control'?

We also come in touch with the 'shadow' parts of ourselves that were suppressed in our upbringing as being socially unacceptable. We learn how to stay aware, avoid old distractions and release all attachments to the status quo. We are taught how to watch for meaningful coincidences in our lives and follow up on them. Above all we learn to conquer denials, be truthful with ourselves and with others in order to escape the bondage that a life without higher purpose has become.

Within these teachings 'Psychological Recapitulation' is key. It is very much less than optimal to suppress an emotion, or to deny what we feel. If we don't know what we feel, we will never be able to fully understand the fragmented nature of our personality, nor how to challenge those aspects and those energies that no longer serve our development. Psychological recapitulation, in the form of writing down our life stories, and listing our ego shadow persona defective behaviour and energy-stealing patterns, is used to confront denials and clear unwanted emotional baggage. We learn how to challenge irrational, exaggerated attitudes, beliefs and expectations. We are shown how to replace these self-limiting patterns of behaviour with sensible (rational) ones. This improves emotions and makes for happier, easier, healthier, more fulfilled lives – and, of course, spiritual integrity. Gary Zukav taught me that, 'Humble spirits are free to love and to be who they are. They have no artificial standards to live up to.'

The irrational beliefs, attitudes, etc. are always based on 'shoulds', 'oughts', 'musts' and 'I can't stand it'. When people give them up, they acquire high frustration tolerance, which encourages them to accept (not like) in detachment life's hardships and other people's imperfections. This leads to less emotional pain and greater perseverance, patience and the ability to get along with others. We have little power to change others. But if we seriously determine to change ourselves and practise true intimacy with regular psychological recapitulation, we all have the power we need to change ourselves.

'It is foolish to see any other person as the cause of our own misery or happiness."

BUDDHA

Psychological recapitulation is a realistic approach that doesn't try to eliminate all unpleasant feelings; rather, it understands that in important areas of our lives, we are actually empowered when we can identify knee-jerk egotistical reactions and be in touch with feeling appropriately sad or regretful at failure, rejection or frustration. The most important thing to learn is to deal with this feeling in the moment and transcend it.... Thus reacting in ego is replaced with responding from spiritual integrity to any given 'challenging' situation. Thus we learn how to embrace our mistakes as teachers and we grow from them. All the pain that I suffered, the loneliness I endured, my disappointments, my compulsive obsessive behaviour and addictions, these were all paths to higher awareness. From these experiences, I was able to see beyond the illusion and grasp all the opportunities disguised as loss that served the balancing and empowerment of my soul.

When we stop to see what the pain is that we are feeling it's never normally about just what's happening now. We are clearing old toxic emotions from similar rejections or failures of the past. Clearing denied or repressed emotions is core to good health and spiritual integrity. Spiritual principles applied to any perceived feeling of loss, rejection or failure bring us to a place of acceptance and detachment. This is the work of the 'Map to God' material; it shows us the 'how to' of all this.

Psychological recapitulation aims to smooth off the sharp edges, the exaggerations that cause self-defeating, sometimes traumatising, self-destructive emotional pain. This work trains us to accept ourselves and others unconditionally, whether or not we are 'successful' in life, whether or not we behave as we 'should', and whether or not anyone else in the world loves us. Why worry when we can pray, meditate, practise mindfulness and learn to respond in mastery in moment-to-moment awareness?

My work with others affirms the value of achievement and helps people to give up their upsetting demand for total success at all times. Instead, people are encouraged to discover a more realistic and satisfying system of values: one that encourages people to work toward their goals, but never to condemn or damn themselves when they fail. All the great spiritual teachers will tell you that 'mistakes are teachers, great opportunities for learning and growth!'

The ego

What is the ego?

The ego is who we think we are. The ego is how we have been taught to see ourselves in our own eyes. It consists of the things others projected onto us and said we were, and that we accepted as true. The ego is our matrix-type definition of ourselves. When people are driven by ego they need to control others, judge others and seek approval. This all takes so much energy and drains our creative power.

Let's now look more deeply into the role of the ego. When we were children, we had to create an ego to survive. We had to learn what to eat and what not to eat. We had to learn basic rules for keeping our bodies alive and well. The ego was generated and trained through the use of words. A young child does not appear to know of itself as a separate being. A tiny baby does not even know that its mother's breast is separate from its hunger and the fulfilment of drinking. When it begins to understand that it is a separate being, the ego is born. Our ego creates our world with the words and thoughts we choose. The way we describe our world to ourselves defines how our ego perceives the world to be.

At first, others told us what was true and instructed us as to how to behave. Much we learned by direct imitation of the behaviour we observed in them. However, a great amount of the formation and training of the ego occurs through the use of words – many people told us about ourselves. What our parents, teachers, friends and others said about us did not always agree. We pieced together our images of ourselves from all these observations and judgements about us made by them. The things they said about us and what we accepted as true formed our self-image, our ego. Later on, the words we ourselves thought and said about ourselves gave our ego even more definite form.

The basic error that most of us learned is the belief that we are separate from others and from all life. It does seem as though this is true. After all, we do have separate physical bodies. However, those who have peered 'behind the veil' have all returned with the same message: we are all the same One Self. It may seem as if this just can't be true. For now, shall we just allow that thought to simmer in our minds and sink into our unconscious? Perhaps imagine a tree and relate all people to individual leaves on the same tree. All humans are part of one great being, the thoughts, feelings and emotions of the collective consciousness, just as all our cells are part of our bodies, our One Self.

In this light, Albert Einstein made a profound remark. He had been asked by a reporter something on the lines of: 'Dr Einstein, you are known to be one of the great geniuses of all time. You have explored our world from the tiny insides of the atom to the cosmos as a whole. Your discoveries have both enriched and destroyed human life and the environment. What do you feel is the most important question for humanity to ask itself today?' As he often did, Einstein stared off into space for a quite a while. Then he looked back to the reporter and replied, 'I think the most important question facing humanity is, "Is the universe a friendly place?"'

This is the first and most basic question all people must answer for themselves. For if we decide that the universe is an unfriendly place, then we will use our technology, our scientific discoveries and our natural resources to achieve safety and power by creating bigger walls to keep out the unfriendliness and creating bigger weapons to destroy all that is unfriendly—and I believe that we are getting to a place where technology is powerful enough that we may completely isolate or even destroy ourselves in this process.

If we decide that the universe is neither friendly nor unfriendly and that God is essentially 'playing dice with the universe', then we are simply victims to the random toss of the dice and our lives have no real purpose or meaning. But if we decide that the universe is a friendly place, then we will use our technology, our scientific discoveries and our natural resources to create tools and models for understanding that universe. Because power and safety will come through understanding its workings and its motives, Einstein suggests that we retrain the ego.

Another time, Einstein spoke about the nature of our ego, of how we experience ourselves. He said, 'A human being is a part of the whole called by us "universe"… a part limited in time and space. He experiences his thoughts and feelings as separated from the rest – a kind of optical delusion of his consciousness. This delusion is a kind of prison for us, restricting us to our personal desires and to affection for a few persons nearest us. Our task must be to free ourselves from this prison by widening our circle of compassion to embrace all living creatures and the whole of nature in its beauty.'

Here you see how ego creates the illusion of separation and an attitude of short-sighted selfishness. This ego attitude tells us that it's OK to chop down trees, pollute our rivers and air – all because we need somewhere to live and a car to drive. However, the selfish ego attitude doesn't take into account how we are destroying our environment and our relationships. Rather than co-operating for the greatest good of the whole, we are competing and focusing upon 'What's in this for me?' This unchecked and untrained ego attitude is destroying our lives and our planet. So we can see now that our ego is a kind of prison that distorts and limits our ideas about our world and of who we really are, and also limits how we relate to others. My intention is to assist people to overcome the limitations of the ego. Another goal is to retrain the ego to be a responsive and useful tool to serve us in a more effective way in harmony with spirit.

The solution is to stay awake, keep aware, practise mindfulness, be compassionate with ourselves and others. We need to accept all feelings that come to the surface for resolution without judgement, as we contemplate all the times we have hurt others or remember how others have hurt us. We should impartially notice what pushes our buttons and who and what 'gets us down' and when and how. The wisest advice is to cease to take anything personally, past or present and banish all future fear projections. Most importantly, we need to develop single pointed focus as we sift through all our emotional debris at what amounts to our own experience of ground zero, now that our own personal towers (ego) have crumbled. The good news is that once we have dismantled the old, we can create the new from a marvellous blank canvas.

Defeating the ego

The main challenge to this process is that the ego wants, more than anything else, to survive unchanged and remain in control. Resistance to change is a necessary quality of the ego. The ego creates order out of chaos. Without this ability we would have no order and no sense of stability in our lives. Without this ability we would likely not have survived past our childhood. However, when the order in our lives becomes too rigid, dull and structured and will not allow for natural growth, the ego becomes an insecure tyrant instead of the useful servant it is meant to be. The tyrant ego says in effect, 'We can only do things in the socially accepted manner. New behaviour is dangerous.' This attitude can stifle further growth and dilute the positive effect of this stage.

What happens when the ego's structures are questioned? When the ego feels that its boundaries are threatened, it may make quite a scene. Shock, anger, hatred, the making of wild accusations and generally issuing guilt to others – blaming and projecting – are typical ways the ego reacts to protect the status quo. The inflexible ego tells us that it is unsafe to open the heart too far or trust too much. In fact, when the tyrant ego is in control, what we consider appropriate behaviour is extremely limited. Any behaviour that is outside of our rigid definitions of that which is correct is considered dangerous.

A typical way the ego maintains its stranglehold of control is through taking offence at the behaviour of others. The personality may then imagine great damage has been received and imagine (or carry out) plans for revenge. The error here is in taking the behaviour of others personally. The immature ego is a victim and is afraid, like a 'control freak'. It tries to control everything, including other people. When our egos' control dramas are being destroyed, which does begin to occur in this level, we may feel very insecure and may cling to old behaviour like a drowning man to a life raft. Clinging to the old will delay the creation and emergence of the new. To overcome this heroes know they must practise 'No Distraction' (explained later in more detail) and commit to diligently replacing all ego-based behaviours and beliefs with spiritual behaviours and beliefs.

The persona

Whilst the ego is who we think we are, the persona is who we pretend we are. Our persona is the basis of our personality – it's our 'Sunday-best' selves that we show to others. We all create a 'perfect' image of ourselves, the way we want others to see us. This part is the persona, the social mask. The word persona in Greek means 'mask' and refers to the mask that actors wore in ancient Greek plays.

We've seen the persona in action. For example, when we go out on a date, we 'put on our best performance' and act as we think our partners would like us to act. We do this to gain acceptance. Another example of persona: we (our ego selves) may think, 'This person is hateful.' However, our persona self will act in a friendly way in order to get what it wants and to avoid what it doesn't want.

The persona does help social interaction to go smoothly. It does so by not telling or revealing any truth that would possibly be upsetting to others or self. It is basically a social lubricant and a lie. It is the pretence and the best performance we all present as 'us' at work, especially with our superiors and often with our colleagues as well. We have been trained in our matrix-type existence to present ourselves in this way in order to fit in, succeed and get what we want.

In popular language, we refer to our persona as our personality. Although we may pretend to be our personalities, even fooling ourselves into thinking that we really are this sickly gooey sweet person, our personality is not who we really are. Our personality is merely the learned false identity that we show to other people to fit in and get what we want. As we develop and perfect our personality, it may assist us to achieve success and recognition in our field of work. Yet truly, personality alone is not enough. If we live from personality and nothing deeper, eventually we will be hounded by feelings of emptiness and alienation.

Our personality has been generated and conditioned to fit in, to be nice and especially to be obedient. The vested interests of the matrix-type society prefer people who are like doormats – obedient and easy to manage. In this case, if a big corporation pollutes their water and ruins their land with toxic chemicals, doormats just stay in the group and move on with nothing to say. An authentically powerful person living in spiritual integrity is like a hero – independent, decisive, powerful, self-determining. Heroes defend their territory and never allow others to make decisions for them. Society wants doormats and is afraid of heroes. Thus we have arrived at a choice point – will we be a doormat or a hero? Will we dismantle the lie of persona and retrain ego to live in harmony with spiritual integrity?

To sum up, here is a simple definition of ego and persona:

Ego is our personal identity and who we believe ourselves to be, based on what other people have told us about ourselves. Persona is the mask we show to others. It's who we want others to think that we are so we can fit in and get what we want.

And there is still another aspect of ourselves we need to tame. The shadow, which consists of all the denied, repressed, suppressed or simply as yet unknown or unconscious (to us) parts of ourselves. It is who we don't know ourselves to be, but nevertheless we are these shadow parts too. We cannot achieve wholeness until we have brought all of our shadow aspects into the light of conscious awareness. Here's a really powerful quote from Paul Feyerabend that helped me to focus on planetary shadow and be determined to balance it:

'I say that Auschwitz is an extreme manifestation of an attitude that still thrives in our midst... It becomes manifest in the nuclear threat, the constant increase in the number and power of deadly weapons and the readiness of some so-called patriots to start a war compared with which the holocaust will shrink into insignificance. It shows itself in the killing of nature and of 'primitive' cultures with never a thought spent on those thus deprived of meaning for their lives, in the colossal conceit of our intellectuals, their belief that they know precisely what humanity needs and their relentless efforts to recreate people in their own sorry image; in the infantile megalomania of some of our physicians who blackmail their patients with fear, mutilate them and then persecute them with large bills; in the lack of feeling of many so-called searchers for truth who systematically torture animals, study their discomfort and receive prizes for their cruelty.'

Farewell to Reason
It's truly imperative that we all get to know these shadow parts of ourselves very well. It's important that we understand how inauthentic we've been conditioned to act. Only then can we awaken, become authentic and live with spiritual integrity.

Recognizing and integrating the shadow

'No matter how dark the night, somehow the sun rises once again and all shadows are chased away.'

ANONYMOUS

After understanding the nature of the ego and the persona, the next inner archetype we need to become aware of is the 'shadow'. The shadow exists just below our conscious awareness in our personal subconscious. The shadow embodies all our uncivilized, anti-social impulses, the ones that are at odds with our conscious image of ourselves, the ego. These are all the things we were taught that good people are not and that we must not be, do or even talk about.

Shadow qualities include impulses to be cruel, hate-filled, lust-filled, dishonest, deceitful, sneaky, back-stabbing, unfair, gossiping, evil, etc.

During our childhood, we may have been trained so well to be a good boy or a good girl that we are no longer aware of even having such feelings and impulses.

The truth is that everyone has both dark and light, bad and good impulses. This is what George Lucas was trying to show us via the Darth Vader archetype, one of the heroes of his *Star Wars Trilogy*. If we are not aware of all these impulses, both dark and light, they will get us into trouble. What kind of trouble we get into will depend upon whether we are more outwardly oriented (extroverted) or more inwardly oriented (introverted). Extroverts act out their repressed impulses. Introverts imagine that others have such impulses. Extroverts tend more towards being possessed by shadow impulses and acting them out compulsively. Introverts tend more towards projecting shadow behaviour onto others who they judge, criticize and attack. Clearly, it is very important to bring out shadow impulses into our conscious awareness.

When we deny the existence of our own fears, doubts and dark tendencies, they become ever stronger and more destructive. The shadow consists of the parts of ourselves of which we should be conscious, but instead we have repressed, denied; or of which we are simply not yet aware. If it is out of awareness, how then can we determine what the qualities of our shadow are? One answer was provided by the Jungian analyst, Joseph Henderson, who said, 'There is nothing easier. Ask your friends who know you very well what they do not like about you.'

Another way to become aware of our shadow is to remember our dreams. Every night, we journey into the subconscious. Our memory of these journeys is in the form of recalled dreams. Here we will encounter our shadow as a figure of the same gender and approximate age as ourselves. The shadow in our dreams will do all the things that we do not allow ourselves to do in our waking life. If we observe what this character does in our dreams, we will become aware of our repressed or denied shadow impulses. This is why it's important to have a dream journal right next to the bed. If we don't have enough Vitamin B Complex, incidentally, we will not be able to remember our dreams.

Carl Jung had a patient who dreamed that Jung was a cannibal. In her dream, Jung put her into a pot full of water and vegetables, put the lid on and began to cook her over a fire. She tried to push the lid up and escape. Jung jumped on top of the lid to keep her in the pot and said, 'Not back out. Go down through!' She looked down (between the vegetables) and saw a light below. As she began to swim down towards the light, it grew brighter. She didn't drown, and continued on her journey within.

Repeatedly, we are going to be confronted with memories of our lives relevant to all the negative, cruel, evil things we have said or done. Ghosts of the past will return to haunt us and we will undoubtedly feel guilty and ashamed. Yet this is only spirit urging us to balance our books of karma and return to love. During times such as these we have the opportunity to wake up and be the hero who recognizes and corrects past errors, breaks down and breaks through past conditioning and false beliefs. We can heal our lives. Chief Seattle taught that as each person undertakes to purify and heal himself and live in harmony with spirit, this will affect positively seven generations back and seven generations forward. The question remains, will we use these introspective times well and 'go down through' them? Or will we distract ourselves with outer interests and try to 'get back out'?

When we finally admit our fears and dark impulses to ourselves, we begin to bring them into the light. Are we ready to stop hiding? If so, embrace wholeness. I have discovered the veracity of Marianne Williamson's quote, 'Our deepest fear is not that we are inadequate. Our deepest fear is that we are powerful beyond measure. It is our light, not our darkness, that most frightens us.'

Yes, let's look at a simple example: if I walk into a room and say to a crowd of people that I have done something stupid or terrible, made a big mistake, then I have everyone's attention and sympathy. People will offer me assistance, buy me a drink, dinner – do all kinds of things to console me and feel protective of me.

However, if I walk into the same room, with the same people, and say:

'Hi, I'm Dr Susie Anthony and I've just written the most incredible, spellbinding, best-selling informative book on spirituality called 'A Map to God'; I have created and presented to the world the most powerful life-changing event to create peace on earth; I daily am capable of the most amazing healings to others; I am making the most incredible, amazing difference to life on this planet because I am powerful, loving, unafraid and courageous,' the same people will be appalled and repulsed by this POWER and judge me to be bragging or boasting (or both). Yet, if I can do all these things – and I can (and so can you; so can anyone if they learn how to) – how does it serve our world if we hide this power (light) under a bushel so that others who are less evolved and less powerful feel comfortable around us? It doesn't; and this has to change.

The shadow is the other part of us, dark and scary, that we hide from others and deny within ourselves. Best self can only emerge when the shadow is recognized as having the right to exist. Shadow qualities, when redeemed and integrated into the totality of our emerging individuality, give us dynamic will power and great ability to forge on towards any goal we deem worthy.

For example, in the eyes of the ruling government, revolutionaries are criminals (shadow characters). However, there comes a time in the lives of men when their nation becomes corrupt and no longer serves the needs of the people. Then revolutionaries arise as freedom fighters, for example Nelson Mandela. The powerful shadow qualities of righteous indignation, rabble-rousing and destruction are needed and are correct to express in such a situation. Without the power of the shadow, necessary change would not come about.

Shadow qualities live a kind of subterranean, revolutionary life within our subconscious. Until we take the time to honestly look within ourselves and become aware of our shadow, we will remain ignorant of and separated from some of the most powerful parts of our being.

Being aware of our shadow impulses doesn't mean we will then do those things. Still, knowing and feeling the true feelings of the shadow makes whatever actions we choose to do far more dynamic and effective. If we deny our shadow qualities, our actions will be wimpy and ineffective in producing change. Imagine the effect of a revolutionary who requested politely, 'Oh, mister government, you are unfair to us, the people. Please change your rules and give us more.' With no shadow punch, without the power that will not be denied, there would be no change.

When the shadow is denied and repressed, our behaviour remains immature and self-serving. We couldn't care less about others. As we integrate the shadow qualities, our desire and the emphasis of our lives will naturally change from self-serving to serving others. Selfless service is a key spiritual attribute. When a person begins to express desire to serve, the spirit in him is symbolically in the process of being born. Our challenge is to release our self-serving ways and begin to look for ways that our particular talents can better serve our community, our fellow humans or the protection of the health of Mother Earth.

When we shine the light of consciousness into the dark areas of our life, when we choose to assess our life honestly and thoroughly, the process can proceed more swiftly and with minimal stress. However, if we resist and avoid the process, life will bring us periodic 'wake-up calls' in the form of shocking and perhaps disastrous events that we cannot just ignore. One day we will awaken and become a true individual – a hero, if not in this lifetime, then in some future one. The question is, are we willing to do it now?

Understanding the subconscious, the unconscious and the archetypes

In Level 1 of alchemy, our feelings tell us that something is not right in our lives. However, we don't know what to do. We have questions, but we don't know the answers. The answers we need are not in our conscious awareness. Therefore, they must be sought somewhere else. That somewhere else is outside of what we know, outside of our conscious awareness. The answers are to be found in our other mind, the one we may not even be aware of, in our subconscious or unconscious mind.

Our subconscious mind stores the memories of everything that has ever happened to us, whether we remember this consciously or not. At Alchemical Level 2, we will remember memories that we have forgotten. Remembering can be an uncomfortable but necessary step in finding the answers we need. We are forced to think about our lives and what they are all about. Many questions then arise including 'What do we really desire or choose to experience in life?'

Prior to this time, when a situation arose in which we did not express our emotional reaction, we repressed it. These 'undigested' memories continue to exist within our subconscious. After a while, the undigested memory kind of rots and becomes toxic and poisonous. This toxic energy poisons our inner life and thereby our ability to feel and express similar emotions. Moreover, when we have these pockets of emotional poison within us, they act as a kind of magnet that attracts more of the same from others. Do we keep getting into the same kind of emotional problems with each new girlfriend, boyfriend or business partner? Might there perhaps be some experience we have not adequately processed, some lesson there that we haven't really learned?

It requires energy to repress an experience and a continuous expenditure of energy to keep it repressed. I feel this is the spiritual cause of the disease known as ME, where people seem to lack energy for no apparent reason.

After a strong awakening experience, the ego is not strong enough to keep these memories down. Repressed and otherwise unknown material in the subconscious can now arise into consciousness. We have the opportunity to get to know all that is hidden within us. We may well feel like we are in free fall in the subconscious which is symbolized by water.

If we haven't 'digested' a powerful and moving old experience well enough, we will sometimes 'regurgitate' it. When we have a strong experience, we need to reflect upon it, ask questions, and find answers within in the moment. If we haven't done this in the past, at this level we have another opportunity to do so. If we take time alone, and pay attention to our feelings, all the memories that we need to clear will come up from our subconscious mind into our conscious awareness.

Perhaps our only experience of the activity of our subconscious mind is daydreaming and in memories of our sleeping dreams. Most people's lives are so boring that the only sense of adventure that they experience is in a few of their more exciting dreams. The journey within is into the world where we dream, into the subconscious. These journeys within are filled with real adventure. At this time, journeys to outer space are only for a few professional astronauts. However, journeys into inner space are open to every intrepid soul. If we say 'yes' to these inner journeys, they can be thrilling and bring rewards beyond comprehension.

A mistake in our personal life, such as stealing or cheating and being caught, may push us into this process. However, if our erroneous lifestyle has caused us to be forced within, kicking and screaming, the ride can be quite bumpy and extremely uncomfortable! Those who enter this stage without guidance of the kind provided by this book may not know what is going on, may be scared silly and may think they are going mad.

To travel these inner highways, we need courage, self-honesty, poise, humour and great humility. If accepted and traversed consciously, with dedication to the process, these inward journeys can be extremely beneficial. When successful, we are stripped of outworn behaviours and become aware of possible new behaviours that more adequately express our true nature and our real needs. If all goes well, this leads to a rebirth process. The new best self emerging feels renewed and has new energy, hope, vision and enthusiasm.

Shamans, in so-called primitive tribal cultures, act as healers, spiritual leaders, teachers and priests or priestesses. They act as the bridge between the physical world and the so-called 'spirit world'. They are trained to safely journey into the 'lower world', into the subconscious and back again. They do so to attune to the cycles of nature, to discover why someone is sick, and to retrieve their patient's soul or fragments of it that have become dissociated. While on their inner journeys, they communicate with, receive guidance and gather 'medicine' (healing energies) from their 'totems', the spirits of nature. Some of the American Indian shamans lovingly refer to their totems as the stone people (rocks and crystals), plant people (herbs), standing people (trees) and the four-leggeds (animals). They return with information and healing energies that are often effective for the healing of their patients and for the benefit of the tribe as a whole. The medicine they gather is often effective for the healing of the body, emotions, mind and spirit of the two-leggeds – their patients.

In order to become whole and develop greater self-awareness, we need to learn to journey safely into the subconscious, contact our totems, and return with medicine for our healing. As our own shaman, we will strip ourselves of the harmful social habits we have been taught. We will discover our true needs and assemble a new self that more perfectly expresses our growing awareness of the totality of who we are. This is the process that reconnects us to spirit.

As every shaman knows, journeys into the subconscious are not made without danger. We must courageously and honestly assess our lives and accept responsibility for the current state of affairs. Feeling that we are the victim and blaming others can cause us to remain in a depressed state, in the dark cave of the subconscious. Or, if we do manage to emerge, we will not have learned the lessons or made the changes needed to upgrade our lives.

Our subconscious, by definition, includes everything which can influence us but of which we are unaware. Subconscious means under the level of conscious awareness. Let's make a graphic illustration to clarify these concepts of conscious and subconscious. Imagine you are on a small island in the middle of the ocean. You are conscious of everything you can see, everything that is above water level. You know that there is far more below the water, but you can't see it. It's dark blue and it surges with movement. Now and then you spot a fish near the surface. But you don't really know what is down there. Under the water, in our illustration, is within the subconscious.

The subconscious has two main parts: the personal subconscious and the collective unconscious. Your personal subconscious is like a bay on your island. The water is shallow in the bay and you can see many of the things under the water, such as your personal memories. Your personal subconscious contains the impressions, the memories of all that you have experienced during your whole life.

Your bay is connected to the rest of the ocean. The whole ocean outside of your bay is the collective unconscious. The collective unconscious, to which you have access through your personal subconscious, contains all the experiences of the races throughout their evolutionary history. Big fish, great realizations and new insights can swim into your personal subconscious from the ocean of the collective unconscious.

The collective unconscious has two main components that help us to survive: the instincts and the archetypes. The instincts are in-built, biological patterns of activity. For example, we have the instinct to sleep at night in a protected space. This instinct kept our ancestors alive and safe from predators.

The archetypes are built in patterns of understanding, of how we give meaning to experience. These primitive and powerful primordial images have existed in the consciousness of humans since early in the history of our species. They have a powerful influence upon our behaviour. They are the basic roles that everyone plays. In fact, they are so basic and so powerful that until we are well advanced in our personal development, it could be rightly said that they play us. Until we have made their presence conscious, their activity manifests through our behaviour with little choice in the matter on our part. These can be called the 'outer' archetypes. We also have 'inner' archetypes; the ones defined by Carl Jung. The inner archetypes include the persona, the shadow, the anima (inner woman in a man), the animus (inner man in a woman), the wise old man, the earth mother and the self.

The process of becoming a true individual involves becoming aware of and resolving the issues of each of these outer and inner archetypes. Every archetype has a positive and a negative aspect. Until we bring an archetype up into conscious awareness, try it out and become well acquainted with it, we are susceptible to being possessed by it. This means that we identify with one archetype and make the mistake of believing that we are that archetype, instead of knowing that it is a part of us and of everyone else too. When so possessed, we have little control whether the positive or the negative aspect of the archetype expresses through us, which can cause great chaos for us and for others we encounter.

Alan Watts related a relevant story concerning identification with an archetype. His brother was in a psychiatric clinic. When he visited his brother there, his brother announced, 'I am God.' Alan's response was of the nature of, 'Oh, you've discovered that you are God. How wonderful. We are all God. In India when one realizes that he is God, his family and friends gather to celebrate this awakening.' His brother said, 'No, you don't understand. You're not God. Only I am God.' Alan replied, 'And that's why you're locked in here. You won't let other people be God, too.' His brother was possessed by the archetype of the self.

Perhaps the archetype we can most easily identify with is the persona; the self that we show to others. It is not the same as our true self, which is our individuality. Our individuality represents a potential that we can realize through sequentially integrating the archetypes into consciousness and thereby becoming whole. Our individuality represents the wholeness of the true self. The person who journeys through the archetypes becomes a true individual. It is an adventure that requires real courage and dedication. These are the qualities of a worthy aspirant – the hero.

Understanding blaming and projection

We have all heard excuses to perpetuate denials of negative behaviour such as, from the drunk, 'I only drink because my colleagues drink or living with you makes me drink.' The sex addict may destroy all trust and peace in the relationship or leave the relationship blaming the other for imaginary or exaggerated problems. They might blame their partner for being inadequate, poor, boring or fat and old. They will live in denial and lie to themselves rather than admit their own inability to respect and honour one person and overcome the addictions of lust and fear of intimacy. The gambler perhaps blames a life generally lacking in excitement for his or her foray into debt, bankruptcy and sometimes suicide.

These people are all in denial of their bondage to various destructive behaviours or substances. As long as we choose addiction over truth, self-love and reconnection to spirit, we stay 'victims' stuck in bondage. The only place to go when we resist transformation and the call to spirit, is to move deeper and deeper into the black hole of self-deception, denial and self hatred. If we choose ego and resistance over transformation and spiritual maturity, we also choose separation from spirit. The amazing thing is that we have no idea we are in denial or that there could be a better more powerful way. Picture a seed in seed state. It's perfect and thinks it's perfect, but when you water it, growth takes place and it becomes something better, a beautiful flower. This is how it is with human consciousness and tuning into spiritual energy, which is like the water of life we need to transform into the best possible selves we can be. We don't need to stay stuck in the seed state without water. Choose love, strength and balance.

Fragmentation

Fragmentation is where the part of us that experiences the pain of something we are trying to deny splinters off and is buried together with the pain, deep in the unconscious. This fragmentation occurs so we don't continuously feel bad about harming others and ourselves with our negative behaviour. If we don't feel bad we can continue to harm self or others with no conscience. So fragmentation perpetuates denial. When fragmentation occurs we can literally turn off our feelings and access no pain. The part of us (fragment) feeling the pain has been filed deep in the unconscious and we can no longer consciously access any truth or more important any of our feelings about the issue. This is quite different from the spiritual principle of detachment where we learn to embrace pain and detach from the suffering by conscious choice and open honest sharing of our issues. Fragmentation is dangerous and, like denial, also allows ego behaviour – the habit, the lie, the matrix – to perpetuate itself.

The life-embracing capacity of the highly developed soul comes directly from the transformative spiritual experience of oneness, wholeness and completeness. When the best self has directly seen that its own deepest depths are absolutely full to overflowing, all existential doubt is extinguished and we are freed to embrace the life process without reservation. But even then, our conviction and our surrender will be tested, again and again and again. How much love do we have in our hearts, especially when we are being challenged? How constant and strong is our spiritual integrity, even at those times when it seems that the whole universe is conspiring to tempt us to compromise? How alone are we willing to stand in what we know to be true?

Our best self has limitless spiritual strength. Reconnecting to our best self is the ultimate source of dignity and self-respect. And it is exactly this position of unwavering conviction that we so desperately need to cultivate if we're going to change the very fabric of the emotional, psychological, philosophical and spiritual energy fields that we all share.

Learning how to remain awake

Level 2 of this alchemical 'Map to God' is the stage of crisis that catapults us into seeking solutions. Alchemical Level 1 showed us the challenges of living the lie, how we had been trained to forget our best selves and lost connection with spirit. However, in Level 1 it is likely we also realized we had neither the willpower, nor determination or sufficient life-force energy to transform anything despite great and good intentions. At the second stage, therefore, after resisting Level 1 inner stirrings to transform, life gives us a powerful wake up call. Level 2 unfolds when we experience some type of tragedy, crisis or disaster, something powerful or terrible enough that our entire sense of who we are (ego) is shattered. For many this level is like the 'dark night of the soul' we have all heard so much about. If the wake up call and resultant awakening experience has been shocking enough, our ego is devastated. When the awakening lightning strike is powerful enough, our ego becomes sufficiently overwhelmed and lets go of attempting to control everything. In all honesty, sometimes this can feel like the Disney 'space mountain' roller coaster ride... but if we just relax and enjoy the ride, all will be well.

The shocking thing is that we probably had no idea that we were asleep. Yet when we get hit by the lightning of this powerful wake-up call, we know that something profound must be happening. Forewarned is forearmed, if we can learn to just compassionately witness the whole process with detachment, that's the key to being successful here.

Thus commences the level of unfolding that alchemists refer to symbolically as the 'immersion in water'. With ego no longer driving the cars of our lives, the floodgates of emotion are opened. Bang, bang, bang... we recall and get in touch with all the events we had carefully denied and forgotten. Denial I have come to understand means 'Don't Even Know I am Lying'. DENIAL. Out pours all the most dreadful, horrible, excruciatingly embarrassing, heartless and hurtful things we have ever done or experienced from others, to re-surface into conscious awareness. To be fair, we also remember positive and pleasant memories. However, at times like this, the temptation is to be a victim and to be focused most on the negative, feeling guilty, ashamed, low, filled with despair and regrets. Well that's a good thing and it means our conscience is informing us directly in terms of where we have lived out of harmony with spirit. This is exactly what we need to encourage inner transformation. If we tend to concentrate only the unpleasant memories, however, despair is the natural outcome, together with depression and self-pity. The important thing is to stay balanced and there is nothing more powerful than Reiki healing for this.

Never surrender and never give up was my motto at this stage. Powerful, new energies surface to assist this process of disintegrating the old and integrating the new to completion. If handled well, this newly discovered power can make us fertile, and transformation is greatly assisted and accelerated. If we try to resist, however, we cause unnecessary pain and suffering both for ourselves and for others.

Partners, friends and family may attempt to medicate us at this time by trying to distract us and take us away from all this soul searching. After all, if we wake up and soul search and transform our lives, the pressure is then on them to wake up and get to work too! They may try to entertain us, divert us, but if we go along with them we'll likely notice that what we used to consider as fun, no longer is. We no longer choose to do such empty, vain and superficial things because they are so empty, vain and superficial. When all attempts to distract us fail, friends tell us about anti-depressants and other pharmaceutical medications, yet statistics show these don't work – they only dull our senses so that we cannot feel anything at all. More than anything we need to be brave at this stage and commit to the journey of the hero and keep on keeping on. Two quotes come to mind relevant to this alchemical level.

'Difficulties are meant to rouse, not discourage. The human spirit is to grow strong by conflict.'

WILLIAM ELLERY CHANNING

'Every calling is great when greatly pursued.'

OLIVER WENDELL HOLMES

Only a rare few in the Alchemical Level 1 have the courage or personal power to actually put insights into action, raise awareness and transform. There are usually just too many attachments – people, places, things, status, creature comforts, continuing addictions. Thus when at first we resist the clarion call to wake up, we attract Level 2's dramatic lightning bolt of awakening, which shunts us in the desired direction back to balance and harmony. Repeated with increasing intensity, this divine intervention eventually creates enough destruction to reach us. Some of the people, places, things we have so treasured, perhaps esteemed ourselves from, are taken away from us. Our lives are changed forever and very much for the best.

What next? There is a distinct danger that if we try desperately to recreate our lives, to be a copy of what went before, we risk making the next awakening even more severe. It's much easier if we can learn to heed divine guidance and allow the process of awakening to proceed with acceptance and willing participation.

Pay attention – no distraction

'During the spiritual growing up period the inner conflict can be more or less stormy... The self-centred nature is a very formidable enemy and it struggles fiercely to retain its identity. It defends itself in a cunning manner and should not be regarded lightly. It knows the weakest spots of your armour and attempts a confrontation when one is least aware. During these periods of attack, maintain a humble stature and be intimate with none, but the guiding whisper of your higher self.'
FROM *PEACE PILGRIM*

In Alchemical Level 1, we wondered what our lives were all about. A nagging and unrelenting sense of meaninglessness interfered with our usual activities. We tried to think about it, but didn't come up with much. We tried to change, but our less than admirable habits still continued. Acting out of harmony with spirit is not wrong or bad, it just means that we are incomplete. It is precisely the way we learn important lessons and gradually realize a higher purpose in life. The word 'sin' literally means to miss the mark. It is an error, but is not all that bad. The lesson is that we need to keep aiming and practising until we do hit the mark. When we constantly hit the mark, we can make our mark in life.

Human free will allows us to go in directions counter to our instincts and to what's most optimal for us. Later, the repercussions of our actions bounce back and figuratively smack us in the face. This feedback is instructive. It shows us the effects of our actions. Then we have the opportunity to reflect upon what happened, take a new aim and start again.

Our errors bring corrective experiences that, step-by-step, destroy the false patterns of the immature ego. But for the repercussions of our experiences to have a positive effect, we have to think about them. We have to make time to reflect and ponder upon what it all means and what we should do. How many of us take the time to really think about what happens in our lives?

Most of us are so distracted by the business of our lives and by ten thousand outer stimuli that we don't go within at all. Advertisements, TV, radio, driving a car in traffic, people telling us what to do – there are so many outer stimuli demanding our attention that it is the rare person who withdraws from it all and attends to their own inner world of visions, memories and feelings. If we avoid, deny or resist these natural periodic times of introspection, life will force them upon us with increasing intensity. They may then be precipitated by some great loss or disaster in our personal life such as a major disease, the death of (or separation from) a loved one, or the loss of a job.

The tragedy or crisis forces us to reconsider our values and to ask ourselves if what we are doing is really important or not. In the case of major disease or bereavement, we are forced to consider that someday we too will die. Most of us live as if we are going to live forever. Unless we are really avoiding the facts and are very successful at fooling ourselves, major disease or losing someone near and dear to us will make us think about our own mortality. The awareness that we are going to die, and only have so much time until then, is very sobering. It provokes us to consider and do that which is really important to us – and to live each day as if it were our last. When we keep in mind the knowledge that death is stalking us, we make amends to those we have harmed, forgive those who have harmed us, and tell those we love that we do love them.

When we stray too far from the path of our soul, we attract these awakening experiences just like a lightning rod attracts bolts of lightning.

Each time the lightning hits, for a brief moment we have an opportunity to see clearly something of our true identity. It could be that when the lightning flash occurs, we realize that we are part of and connected to all that is. In these moments of 'enlightenment' we may experience that there is no personal separate will at all. Gone is the desire to strive for anything. We feel like we are a part of a greater whole. We feel at peace, blissful yet at the same time invigorated. Then, suddenly we are back in the darkness, but have at least glimpsed a guiding light and perceived a different reality. The question is, can we remember it? And can we integrate this perception into our lives? Are we willing and able to make the changes necessary to live this new realization in all our relationships?

Even after we have a flash of this new awareness, when the darkness closes in again, we may not be able to relate to it. It is so different from anything we have ever experienced before. Perhaps we imagine it was some kind of dream or fantasy, nice but impractical. Our ego will struggle to maintain the old beliefs and behaviours. It will take many flashes before the old ego is sufficiently humbled to allow the new worldview to arise and exist in our daily lives. The capacity to remember more than a cartoon image of what we experienced in the flash of awakening may be still beyond us. We may only be left with a vague feeling that somehow our lives could have and need to have more meaning than before.

We cycle through these phases again and again, hopefully learning a little and making a few more changes each time. Each time, the ego is temporarily knocked out of its stranglehold on control.

Seeker be aware – single-pointed focus
Upon seeing the mess we have made of our lives, our regret may be so strong that we don't want to be confronted with all this. When Oedipus realized that he had killed his father and married his mother, he had seen 'too much truth' and put his own eyes out in a vain attempt to blot out the vision of what he had done. Alchemical Level 2 can seem like too much truth to bear. We may try to flee from its revelations by frantically seeking

outer stimuli. We may indulge in more TV, more films, more sex, more alcohol, more anything out there to block the inner confrontation. If intense enough, such activities may distract us from our inner process. We can't drown our problems in alcohol, but we can make them swim for a while. At all costs we need to avoid the temptation to distract ourselves or our inner situation will return ten-fold to plague us like a hangover.

Another block to this process is rationalization. For example, when we remember having hurt someone, we may give ourselves many excuses as to why it was the right thing to have acted thus. The words we say to ourselves can keep us in bondage.

To stay on track at this stage, we will need to temporarily 'stay in' and reflect upon our lives. However, we need to be very aware of the things we are saying to ourselves and choose our words wisely. To help the process along, make a list. Writing everything down ensures we are not tempted to deny or forget anything ever again. As we get started on this personal inventory, it's important to have single pointed focus and be determined to list all life events in a balanced way.

Depression

If our condition is given a medical diagnosis such as depression, physicians typically will want to prescribe a psychoactive medication. However, the medications such as the tricyclics prescribed for depression and similar 'mental illnesses' may prevent the necessary inner work to complete the process. These drugs dull the senses and suppress our natural ability to sort things out for ourselves. They do mask the symptoms so we may not seem so disturbed and may feel some relief from the inner pressure. However, the pressure is good pressure and is there to motivate us to make needed changes in our lives.

Drugs may be temporarily helpful; for example in cases of suicidal depression. They may give us a pause, a new position from which to sort ourselves out. But in the long run, drugs generally fail to provide a lasting or complete solution. They may help us to temporarily come out of the cave without having learned or changed anything at all. That's madness, doing the same thing twice and expecting a different result!

If this stage should take the form of depression, the key is to look into the darkness of depression without judgement and especially without self-criticism for being depressed. Judging ourselves because we are feeling depressed does not help. That is like adding insult to injury. Rather, we need to ask ourselves what the depression is, what it does and how it makes us feel. Then the depression can be a fine teacher. This is the difference between victim and victor consciousness and anyone can learn this new type of thought construct, with much to gain.

Depression can be compared to being in the womb. The baby stays inside in the dark until it is ready to emerge. If we have been in a deep depression for a long time, that which we now bring to birth is as large and wonderful as the depression has been dark and long. The new us needed a long gestation period. Be eager to meet, greet and live the new best self emerging. Something and someone wonderful is on the way. When we have the courage to go within and face our fears, we find hidden treasures and rewards to help us live our dreams.

Sky Dancer's story

Sky Dancer was a Princess born in eighth century Tibet who became Tibet's only female Buddha. Buddhist teachings say that before she departed this life, she predicted times of grave crisis in earth's future. Out of immense compassion for the pain and suffering of the life process, she hid many treasures of various kinds in different sacred caches throughout the world. The treasures were called termas. Some were hidden within the earth and rock and some termas called 'mind treasures' were hidden internally in the vastness of inner space – to be accessed in meditation or other types of energy mastery enlightenment. These treasures were hidden for the benefit of all sentient beings in the dark years that were to follow Tibet's final downfall. Each of the termas was destined to be revealed by an intuitively guided person known as a terton, a treasure finder. I only discovered this story about Sky Dancer after many years of conscious disciplined alignment to the alchemical path. I immediately recognized that it was at Level 2 that I had first been opened up to my own particular 'mind treasures'. This opening to higher levels of understanding was both terrifying and sad yet, all at once, blissful, peace-filled, awesome and magnificent. This is how it happened.

Finding our termas

As described in the previous chapter, I came to realize I was 'in bondage'. I knew I was living a life without any special purpose or true meaning. I was intelligent yet when it came to life and making it work for me, or being happy and peaceful, I didn't know how to accomplish these simple things. Looking back, I can see that I was completely lost on what the Hopi call 'the path of comfort, profit and greed'. This is also known as the path of ego. The stresses of being in bondage to ego were overwhelming. The pain of resisting the call to spirit and doing nothing about it was even worse. I felt torn between two realities. The continual tension of this dynamic inner conflict fuelled denials and led to fragmentation.

I believe that everyone on earth today has within them an aspect of the legendary Sky Dancer treasure, a gift which is wholly/holy and unique to that individual and which only they can determine to find. Through re-discovering or remembering this treasure and experiencing the revelatory nature of our true self or spirit, we are then able to heal and empower ourselves. Reconnection to a higher aspect of ourselves simultaneously precipitates the potential to right relationship with all creation. Suddenly we have a real reason to be, a divine purpose and we can feel our connection to the earth, the sky, angels and nature. This is ecstatically blissful. Unfortunately, the reason many of us never experience this mysterious state is due to denials and fragmentation.

Understanding denial and fragmentation

'At the approach of danger there are always two voices that speak with

equal force in the heart of man: one very reasonably tells the man to consider the nature of the danger and the means of avoiding it; the other even more reasonable says that it is too painful and harassing to think of the danger, since it is not a man's power to provide for everything and escape from the general march of events; and that it is therefore better to turn aside from the painful subject till it has come, and to think of what is pleasant. In solitude a man generally yields to the first voice; in society to the second.'

LEO TOLSTOY, *WAR AND PEACE*

Most of us deny our negative self-sabotaging addictive behaviours. We rationalize – tell ourselves rational lies that we only have a few drinks or whatever but we can control it or stop whenever we want. Witnesses on the other hand, see someone, us, slurring our words and making a fool of ourselves, saying things we'd never dream of saying if we were sober, quite possibly passing out, vomiting, and so on. The sex addict tells himself he sees a beautiful woman and appreciates her like a fine thoroughbred racehorse. Yet, onlookers see someone consumed with lust, eyes fixed on sexual body parts, lost in the cheap thrill of lust and sexual excitement with no risk of intimacy – incidentally, this is why pornography is so popular. The sexual pull is so powerful, it doesn't matter who gets in the way or suffers for this cheap thrill, and the ultimate pay off is that there is no risk of intimacy or all the noble challenges this brings, like sacrifice and responsibility.

I remember myself in full-blown cocaine addiction. I was about 40 lbs underweight and looking like a walking dead person, yet telling my friends I was fine. When tackled about my problems I would arrogantly reply, 'Addiction? Huh, that's only a problem if you cannot afford it and of course I can.' In order to perpetuate denials and stay in our comfort zones of illusion, we blame others and project. In this way nothing is ever dealt with. Nothing is ever our fault and we don't have to take responsibility to change, grow and transform.

In my own personal Level 2, fifteen years ago, part of me knew the truth of my addictions to many behaviours and substances. The part of me that could own the addictions and desired transformation hated the other part of me that still sometimes watched vain vacuous empty films and read fashion magazines, feeling totally convinced again that I needed the big job, big money and glamorous lifestyle to esteem myself and be loved. The trouble was I had achieved all this and it didn't work. I didn't feel happy. Yet I didn't want to change or give anything up. Better the devil you know than the devil you don't! I was in denial and fragmented into all sorts of distracting behaviours where I became so frantically busy I could hide from all the pain. Thus the powerful alchemical friction intensified. Something had to give.

In the years leading up to my near death experience, I did all kinds of 'geographicals' believing that my problems must be about living in that particular place with those particular people, that culture, those rules, those beliefs. In ignorance and denial that the problem was me and seeking always to blame someone or something external to me, I felt convinced that the relationship or job problems were related to which country I lived in. Yet as I moved around the world, the same problems seemed to follow me, no matter where I lived. Eventually, I had nowhere to go but within. Surely we have all experienced changing partners, jobs, homes, countries, yet the same problems soon re-emerge with different faces? Amazing!

Avoidance

Denial, fragmentation and geographicals are all types of avoidance I later learned, and are typical of Alchemical Level 2. Eventually in the deep, very dark black hole of being unable to leave my home without drugs, with no distraction, God found me. I became totally isolated in my addiction and although this led to my near death, it also led to a new beginning. The Destroyer archetype became its more positive aspect, the Change-Maker. Later when I became familiar with the path of the shaman and the power gifts of animal totems as guides, I realized that bear totem was calling me to go within. I was being guided to practise no distraction and find the message of all this pain and the gifts of such suffering.

I wasn't looking for God because I didn't feel worthy and I'd been programmed not to believe, yet something divine found me. Eventually, when I knew I was dying, I began to ask for help from something out there. What if God existed...

Divine intervention

Looking back on the first of my near death experiences, resulting from a 72 day (and night) cocktail of class A drugs, prescription drugs and alcohol, I now believe that in some way these highly toxic mind-altering substances 'accidentally' opened a gateway into my own 'inner sky' and although totally oblivious to its existence, I found my mind treasure. In retrospect it's clear that this was my lightning struck tower experience so typical of Level 2 and true awakening.

What I experienced at the time was a feeling of incredible power and energy, a truly all-encompassing, all-consuming, overwhelming sense of unconditional love, forgiveness, understanding, immense peace and tremendous compassion. It was almost beyond human comprehension. This is the kind of love I somehow remembered existed somewhere and had searched for all my life. Now I had finally found it and the joy I felt was beyond measure. Words are somewhat inadequate to describe this my first of many direct experiences of great mystery and divine intervention.

The divine message was that there was great work to be done – a planet needed to be healed and the only way to do this was to heal the consciousness of its caretakers, one by one. Of course I was guided that I had to begin with myself. I was shown that everything in my earth walk so far had been a necessary part of my training. My healing began immediately in the form of psychological recapitulation and my life inventory. I was gently yet most insistently guided by Michael through a spiritual review of my life.

Enfolded in this blue ray of divine power, love and wisdom, I was opened up to a new level of understanding. It was suggested to me that when our outer lives (in ego) move too far out of harmony with our inner selves or soul, we are forced into a state of introspection. I had resisted this all my life. Now I was dead, any resistance was dead too. I felt like Indiana Jones who had found the Ark of the Covenant, Parsifal who had found the grail… It felt awesome. This is a word I use a lot these days to describe how I am feeling.

When I had been alive on earth, I had been too afraid to show people my inadequacies and pain and too afraid to ask for help. Yet in this sacred, mysterious space of absolute love, purity and truth, I was finally able to break down and break through denials, confront myself with my own shallowness, with my immature behaviours, with how I was not being true to myself. It felt fantastic and oh so liberating. The shame had gone.

Why me? Why not!

Now why would an archangel bother to rescue and RESURRECT 'poor me' – the ultimate self-created OD suicide victim? That was my question too. Michael revealed to me that I was filled with so much despair, hopelessness, fear, anger and self-hatred, that no mere mortal could ever reach me! That, I know now, is why I was having this conversation with Michael – an archangel, a shining pillar of royal blue light who informed me that he would 'lay my foundations with sapphire!' Sapphire is the energy of unconditional love, wisdom, peace, loyalty and devotion. A quote came to mind, 'If you have built castles in the air, your work need not be lost: that is where they should be. Now, put foundations under them.' Henry David Thoreau.

Michael was able to persuade me that if I could create such a destructive living hell culminating in this premature experience of death aged 32 then surely, armed with the gifts and wisdoms he was bestowing on me, and with his continuing protection, teaching and guidance, I could quite literally in truth create a true foundation for 'heaven on earth'. Somehow I knew *this* being could never lie. I believed him and with courage I didn't know I possessed, I agreed to come back to give it my best shot.

Today I know many others to whom similar things have happened and seemingly we all had thought one thing 'Why me – I'm not special?' What I have come to know is that we are all special, but we fell asleep and forgot or we have been distracted by the glamour of life on earth. I trusted this being, Michael, who couldn't lie and I knew that what I was seeing was the reality and not some drug induced illusion. Michael has stayed with me ever since and will remain with me into eternity. It took a little longer than I expected, but now I AM aligned with creating 'Heaven on Earth' everywhere, everyday, and showing others the 'how to' of all this! What is more, I am now connected to other guardians and warriors of light, both in and out of embodiment. This is 'Heaven on Earth' indeed.

Of course, there are those who prefer to stay stuck, resist, deny, blame and project, and I have learned to walk away from such ones. This is what the Sufis say about sharing spiritual enlightenment:

There are those who don't know but want to know;
and the job of the Sufi is to teach them.

There are those who know but don't know that they know;
and the job of the Sufi is to remind them.

And there are those who don't know but don't know that they don't know;
and the job of the Sufi is to walk away from them.

A new job description

Michael shared sacred knowledge and wisdom with me; he revealed who I truly was – a divine being of light and love. As, indeed, we are all spirit enjoying physical manifestation here on earth. Michael told me that I had made a sacred agreement before being born on earth to be 'a light unto the darkness.' I was assured that my essence or unified self was a powerful creator, a transformer of energies.

But I had a choice to make. I could go back into my healed physical body through this experience of divine Grace or I could choose to embrace the light there with Michael, once again without a physical vehicle. Yet, tempting as it was to stay in this cocoon of love and perfect peace, I would not have completed my sacred agreement. In personality self, I had become an achiever and the thought of not being able to achieve this divine contract was more than I could bear.

Moreover, in realizing I was spiritually powerful, that I could help others heal or deal with their own pain and then knowing without doubt that divine guidance and GRACE really existed, I chose life. Suddenly, instantly, I was alive again, but in a miraculously healed and enlightened physical vehicle, with no adverse affects or outward signs of the ravages of my damaging path of total self-annihilation through drugs. You can well imagine this was very truly a life transforming experience and countless 'synchronicities' have since proved to me and others I have met, that it was totally authentic.

Opening to higher awareness

When I use the word 'enlightened' this is how Michael communicated through light, colour, sound, impressions and pictures – not words. Different emissions of light seemed to trigger activations or openings within me and suddenly I just knew things, things about which I had possessed no previous knowledge and, moreover, no previous desire to recognize, in what I now refer to as my former personality/self life. I had found my mind treasures and all kinds of gifts I didn't know existed.

This sense of just seeming to 'know' things was repeatedly proved to me each time I tested my new 'knowing' in order to satisfy the 'Doubting Thomas' within. Through synchronicity, I was guided to books by eminent scientists, doctors and healers on quantum physics, consciousness and energy healing with light and colour, which all corroborated and further explained what I had so simply and quite divinely been 'given'.

I can recall that as I looked down at my dark blue 'dead or vacant' physical body, I was enlightened by Michael to embrace the concept that the divinity which we have been looking for all these centuries is actually within us, within the 'electrical' energy circuitry of our own bodies, which universal life-force energy we share with the planet and all sentient beings. Michael conveyed to me through this experience, an incontrovertible belief in the power of the human body to regenerate itself through connection to spirit.

The interesting by-product of this experience, and indeed the new emerging worldview, is that it finally lays to rest the myth that only 'special' people can heal. This is reinforced experientially by way of the three degree traditional Usui Reiki attuning process, wherein we also evolve new ways of communicating with higher aspects of ourselves, with nature and all sentient beings. Because these are consciously learned skills rather than the results of exotic ancestry or celestial blessings, they are transferable. Anyone can do this, or more to the point, BE authentically powerful, if they choose to reconnect to spirit. I know this is true because in the last ten years I have worked with hundreds of clients, who keep coming back to share their own miraculous life changing stories.

The law of attraction

A universal secret was shared with me – the law of attraction. Inherent in every intention and desire, good or bad, conscious or unconscious, is the mechanics for its fulfilment. Intention and desire in the field of pure potentiality have infinite organizing power. And when we introduce an intention into the fertile ground of pure potentiality, we put this infinite organizing power to work for us. I was shown how my own faulty, fear-based thinking and self-limiting false beliefs had ultimately created a death wish. Although this death wish was at first largely unconscious, nevertheless the law of attraction had given me what I feared and secretly desired – death, an escape from the matrix-type of consciousness and all the pain.

I saw how I had come to hate myself and my life. What I truly loathed was the 'personality self' behaviour I was misguidedly exampling and the negative victim consciousness experience of life this negative energy attracted and created. What I learned is that we are not our behaviour. In ego, I had been unable to give or receive love. I hadn't been able to access any real feelings. I just thought I was having feelings. I had become like an automaton performing a lie of a life in the matrix that had no joy or love. Yet deep down inside there was an ancient longing within me for something better. Because I was so busy doing, having, consuming, I had ignored this call to spirit. As long as I strived for false symbols of external success, the longing couldn't be discerned, because all my energy was caught up in hard work, the hustle and bustle and the striving.

I felt disgusted and ashamed that I had ignored the inner call to awaken. I had forgotten my passion, stopped following my bliss, fallen asleep, then quite willingly helped to perpetuate the structure of the lie here on earth – the matrix. I was part of the problem. Through ignorance and fear, I had forfeited my truth and spiritual integrity – all because of a strange compulsion of needing to fit in and to do what everyone else was doing. Thanks to divine intervention, I was set free from bondage and illusion. I was being freed from the trap of self-limiting beliefs. I was being shown how to use my termas and free my mind from bondage.

Becoming a 21st century shaman

I was guided that this going within is a natural cyclical process, where inner aspects of higher or best self call us to go within, understand ourselves more deeply and unfold new qualities. If accepted and lived consciously, these inward journeys generate higher self-awareness and empowerment. When successful, we become aware of possible new behaviours that more adequately express our true nature. This leads to transformation and spiritual integrity. We feel renewed and have new energy, hope and enthusiasm. This process is sometimes called shamanic death and rebirth. Normally it can be achieved without actually physically dying. However, I was so terribly stuck in denial and so incredibly afraid, so filled with pride, I was unable to reach out and ask any human for help. I once asked for guidance as to why I was experiencing divine interventions – I wasn't important or special; far from it, I was a mess. Society called me a junkie – ready for the junk heap. The answer was not what I was expecting. I was advised that in practical terms, according to my birth contract, Source knew that – no matter what – I would always get the job done; the task of healing the planet and raising planetary consciousness. It was right.

I learned I had to become a 21st century shaman. Like a shaman, I had indeed entered sacred no-time and no-space. I was rediscovering the wisdom of the Ancestors, those wise ones who trod this path before us, some of whom had paid the price. Here I am talking about the Gnostics, the Knights Templars, the Cathars, the Bogomils and the Rosicrucians, in fact all those who were referred to as heretics wherever 'Orthodoxy' existed. These brave men and women were tortured and put to death by virtue of false statements given under extreme duress. This was done, incidentally, largely to preserve the lies of traditional fundamental religions. The heart love and wisdom of these wise ancestors was guiding me to go within to my inner core and find out what truly motivated me, to find truth, especially the truth about our own creation story. They were showing me how to honour my passion and follow my bliss. I had already done the hard part, realizing that superficial desires could never satisfy. I looked at my body and it was glowing with golden light...

I was told that I was being 'called' and if I 'chose' I would be trained by my spiritual guides and teachers to remember and perform this kind of magical work to help others. I remembered a line from the Bible, 'Many are called and few are chosen.' I later realized that this meant everyone has at least one call to spirit – the quest of the Holy Grail, yet it is we who choose whether we listen, respond and transform. I knew what I would do. I chose the path of love, strength and balance, the path of the soul.

As I agreed to serve, I was shown billions of others like me, here on earth, who had lost their light. Suddenly, the penny dropped, it was clear to me that addiction was NOT a disease. Addiction, I realized, was only a symptom of a much larger disease called separation from spirit. I was shown that this is the disease that most of us on earth are suffering from. I was shown what I can only describe as a dying planet in virtual darkness, where most people had lost heart in forgetting or denying this magical connection to spirit. I was given to understand how we lost this connection through our programmed personality pursuit of external symbols of power – fool's gold.

As all these revelations sunk deep into my heart and soul, I knew I was being called and had to make a choice. Would I choose to awaken and help empower universal intelligence and creative force to heal the disconnection between personality and spirit, to orchestrate a return to love? You bet I would. And now I am.

Spiritual involution versus spiritual evolution

It was made clear, however, that there was much work to be done on healing myself first, mentally, emotionally, physically and spiritually. I needed to learn how to re-establish and purify the mind-body-spirit complex connection. I learned that I needed to get rid of old self-sabotaging thoughts, feelings and emotions – all the old planetary programming that had led to this physical and psychological death. This I was given to understand is called spiritual evolution. Spiritual evolution is like clearing out our old software programming, which has been infecting all our thoughts, feelings, emotions, attitudes and behaviour with a virus called fear. Fear teaches us to seek security and to fear change or loss. Germaine Greer once said, 'Security is when everything is settled. When nothing can happen to you. Security is the DENIAL of life.' I agree with this entirely. What we need to learn is how to become secure even in times of great insecurity. This requires faith. Faith comes from love.

Love is the most advanced software programme that we all need to upgrade to. The reception of new software being installed and programmed is called spiritual involution. Here we learn how to clear and purify space within us for new higher spiritual aspects of self and creation to merge back down into the physical. This I was told is how we create heaven on earth. Out with the old and in with the new. I was later shown how to do this and that's what this book is all about. It was made very clear to me that I couldn't transmit something I didn't embody. I was told to focus on purity so that I'd truly be able to embody divine love, wisdom and power. Much later, I learnt that my name, Susie, in Tibetan means purity. Coincidence? I think not. In Chapter 4 we will find out how words and 'names' do indeed carry power and influence our reality.

Conditioning

So it was that I was shown and came to understand what had gone wrong for me. I knew I had become lost in the matrix – doing, having and consuming – and this is how I had forgotten spirit. Having broken through all my denials, with realization I was able to forgive first myself and then others, completely, and return to love. This was Grace and I felt one with love. I realized that even the pain and suffering had been necessary and had been, ultimately, a blessing. After all, I reasoned, how could I go back and help others if I didn't know about or hadn't personally experienced all that I had. Ultimately, realizing the blessing in the pain was how I was able to let it all go.

How had I become so lost? It was made clear to me that our conditioning in early childhood and adolescence defines our beliefs and behaviours to be only those acceptable to our parents and later on to our society. We are trained to conform to their idea of social norms. The realization that I had learned to desire that which I had been conditioned to desire was one of the biggest revelations of this divine intervention.

This conditioning or programming came from daily TV, magazines, Hollywood. Mainly these desires were centred on money, sex, image, things, status, power, control. I had been taught or programmed to give my real power to others and to outer things. I had allowed my personal values to be determined by possessions, status and appearances. I had been programmed to do, have and consume. TV and films had told me what to think. Suddenly in death I was awake. I knew I had to retrain my thoughts and free my mind. I didn't know what a big job this was going to be – almost too big.

Dying to learn how to live

'In the night of death, hope sees a star, and listening love can hear the rustle of a wing.'

ROBERT G INGERSOLL

As a result of my near death experience, a new understanding was being born in me. This new awareness created a higher consciousness. On Alchemical Level 2, we are all of us given lessons that can shake the foundations of all that we have held to be true. Old belief systems must die to new sacred insights. This is a gradual yet continuous process of death and rebirth until first-hand experience hones shaky new thoughts into inner knowing that is real. Many are called yet in fact few choose to open their hearts and stop giving away their authority to people, places and things. We need to commit to going through all the experiences that give us authentic wisdom, love and power. This is what makes us strong and pure. What makes us great is then using this power for the greatest good and to serve others. This is what I am teaching by example in my spiritual community in England.

In actual fact, addiction and this near death experience was a gift. Dying is perhaps one thing to be sad about, I discovered. Living unhappily, I knew, is quite another. To know that we are going to die and to be prepared for it at anytime is a true gift because then we can learn how to live. That is how from the experience of dying I came to discover we can actually be more involved in our lives whilst we are still living them. Once we learn how to die and can accept unexpected transformation, no matter how painful or frightening, we can know how to really live.

'Do not seek death. Death will find you. But seek the road which makes death a fulfilment.'

Dag Hammarskjöld

In my life I had suffered so many great disappointments, and in embracing death at such a young age it was totally clear that there was no point in holding onto vengeance or stubbornness. Pride and vanity had isolated me in ego and denied me the experience of true love. In death, I found true love, Grace. To love is to receive a glimpse of Heaven. I was given a choice which I grabbed like a drowning man grabs for air. I awakened to spirit. I truly realize that so many people walk around with a meaningless life, disconnected from the full majesty and power of their life-force and, having forgotten spirit, they seem asleep – even when they are busy doing things they think are important.

Walking the talk

In dying, I woke up and devoted myself to creating real meaning and true purpose in my life – that's the gift. This was the opportunity disguised as loss. All I had to do to receive the gift and give it to others was to learn to walk my talk, in total integrity and truth aligned constantly to spirit, free from ego. This is simple but not easy. I had to learn how to conquer the programming of the lie – doing, having and consuming. Finally my true good character was being given a mission to shine through like a radiant light. Because of this, I was able to die to my negative ego, shadow and persona behaviour. I was able to do this with all the power and all the courage gained from facing my innermost fears. Practising mindfulness was also vital, every hour of the day. This is my legacy NOW to all, that we can all take this time to ponder our reason for living, find greater meaning and discover our own purpose for being here. Love life and it will surely love you back – tenfold!

WISDOM

Toltec

Based on Toltec teachings and Don Miguel Ruiz's interpretation of Toltec Wisdom outlined in his best-selling book *The 4 Agreements* (*The 4 Agreements* are Ruiz's interpretation of Toltec Wisdom – just as *The Four Winds* are Alberto Villaldo's interpretation.)

1. *Before speaking, ask yourself why you want to say that now*

We need to create a new discipline of mindfulness that before we begin to talk, we ask ourselves why we wish to say what we are about to say to this particular person in this particular moment. What is our intention? It's vital we become clearly aware of why we wish to say anything at all. Is it usually because we are so insecure and lacking in self-esteem that we are asking the other person to agree that we are good, intelligent and caring to give us some kind of energy, attention and validation?

When we become conscious or mindful enough to realize that verbal banter and chitchat is actually approval seeking, we will gradually become so uninspired that we will eventually cease to do this. This lack of inspiration (energy loss) will short-circuit our desire to speak before we begin. If we do this practice faithfully, very likely we will find we won't speak so often. And we won't speak at all unless we have a good reason for doing so. Then what we do choose to say will be truly meaningful. The effect of our words will then become a blessing to us and to others rather than an energy drain.

2. *Stop taking anything personally*

Nothing anyone does is because of us. They are in their own waking dream, acting in response to their own self-created reality.

If it's NEVER about you or me personally, how can we explain how others respond to us? Perhaps we resemble someone who was once cruel to them or cheated them in some way. In response, they may be fearful or abusive towards us for no other reason than this passing resemblance triggering unconscious negative energies. Perhaps we have some personal feature or tone of voice that reminds him/her of someone who was nice to them in the past. He or she probably doesn't remember any of this, but as a result, immediately trusts us. These reactions don't have anything to do with us personally. It's just that something about us in particular or our behaviour has triggered and released some automatic behaviour in them.

Just as others have triggers that we provoke, others will trigger automatic behaviour in us. Begin to impartially notice such triggers. Remembering this sets us free from experiencing repeated automatic behaviour reactions. This will help us to release ourselves and others from the negative effects of our own thoughts, feelings, emotions, words and deeds.

Thinking that what others do is because of us is a kind of negative egotism. It is very egotistical to assume that we are so personally important that what others do is caused by or has anything to do with us. Let's come down from our ego pedestal and realize that others are reacting not to us personally but rather to their model of the world, their dream and their prior experiences. We may 'push their buttons', but the behaviour we observe as a result of our interaction with them has very little or nothing to do with us. When we realize this and cease to take anything personally, we will be immediately freed from much needless pain and suffering.

Then we will cease to react to others' behaviour without reflection, but rather have considered responses. A spiritual warrior never acts rashly. He or she first gathers information and internal feedback on what has been and what is right now. Free from preconceived opinions, he or she just observes what is.

3. *Listening to the internal voice*
Remember that voice in our heads, the one we hear when we talk to ourselves? The internal voice we hear is the 'judge'. We, the listener, are the 'victim'. The judge makes these inner statements based upon our own 'book of the law' – the rules we learned (and accepted as true) from those who domesticated and trained us, i.e. parents, teachers, religion,

corporations, governments and cultures. Do the work necessary to conquer this false programming and reconnect to guidance from best self.

4. *Recapitulating our lives*

To encourage and accelerate total personal awakening, the Toltecs teach that it is imperative to remember the events of our lives. They call this psychological recapitulation. It's a shamanic process to begin to heal forgotten or suppressed memories of traumatic events, which are often the cause of great challenges in our personal lives. Recalling, processing and healing (releasing the emotional charge) from such memories is absolutely necessary for our psychological sanity and general spiritual unfoldment.

The Toltec wisdoms give us a powerful confirmation that to 'know yourself' is key to enlightenment. Let's now learn how Tibetan Dakini can assist us further to fulfil this injunction.

Tibetan

The word 'dakini' in Sanskrit means 'celestial woman', 'space goer' and 'cloud fairy'. In Tibetan, dakini is *kha'dro*. *Kha* means sky, celestial space or emptiness. *Dro* refers to a sentient being moving about dancing. My favourite translation is 'sky dancer'. The dakinis have attained the 'clear light' and embody the enlightened spirit of wisdom and compassion in female form to assist all beings.

Dakinis appear in the visions, dreams and meditations of humans to assist them in their search for wisdom and enlightenment. They inspire and help us to overcome all physical hindrances and spiritual blockages that hold us back from our awakening. In appearance, dakinis are calm, wrathful or fierce. The wrathful and fierce forms assist humans to overcome obstacles on the path of spiritual awakening. They assist us to fire up our aspirations. They reveal that it can be very useful and effective to be fierce with those habits that prevent us from gaining enlightenment.

In the spiritual life of the aspirant, the dakinis represent the sacred meeting of the body and mind in meditation, the sacredness of the body itself, and the quiet expanded consciousness of the enlightened mind. The Tibetans teach that the mind of the enlightened lama is pure dakini – an inseparable union of wisdom and emptiness. The dakinis represent the ego-shattering wisdom of blissful emptiness. Some of their forms are macabre and terrifying, which serves the purpose of stopping our conceptual thinking (internal dialogue) and our incorrect perception.

In the Tibetan wisdom teachings, the male principle on the relative level is represented by the five qualities of perception, corresponding to the five senses. The female relative qualities are the five elements: earth, water, air, fire and space. On the absolute level, the male principle expresses as skilful means and compassionate action. The absolute female principle is wisdom-emptiness, the absolute principle of expansive, timeless, serene 'suchness'. Our spiritual goal is to achieve, with the help of the dakinis, the wisdom of emptiness, which purifies our perception of the five elements. Then our work is to embody this wisdom skilfully in compassionate acts to assist others towards their liberation.

Dakinis are the companions of Buddhas and spiritual aspirants. When we are ready, willing and able, they bring us special teachings and wisdom. The Tibetans teach that spiritual practice (sadhana, also meaning 'vision') liberates powers that the dakinis assist us to integrate. When we have accomplished this integration, the dakinis grant us their four enlightened actions: pacifying, enriching, magnetizing and subjugating.

The Tibetans teach that there are many kinds of dakinis. There are dakinis of wisdom and activity, as well as mundane dakinis – some enlightened and some not yet so. In esoteric Buddhism, enlightened dakinis are the third 'root', the matrix, the source of all enlightenment and auspiciousness. A good example of an as yet unenlightened dakini is a female aspirant that has achieved a level of insight, but is not yet free from the suffering that accompanies incarnate existence.

Wisdom dakinis have achieved enlightenment and liberation from all sorrow. These enlightened dakinis have the role of protecting wisdom. A traditional way the dakinis protect wisdom is to hide spiritual energies, communications, texts and other objects for future generations to find. These wisdom objects are called terma. Dakinis have hidden terma in all of the elements. Physically, texts are written and hidden, for example, in clay pots in temples. Subtle terma are to be found in the wind, in water, in fire, in space and in the mind itself.

Dakinis create the written and subtler termas using a mysterious code. You need their assistance to recover and to decipher the meaning of termas and other forms of revelation including signs, omens and prophecies. In the termas, The Queen of Great Bliss, Yeshe Tsogyal, is referred to as the human incarnation of the principle dakini, embodying primordial wisdom and emptiness-bliss. This text was discovered by the eighteenth century terton, Jigme.

Many termas still remain to be discovered. We are also tertons, the treasure finders. These treasures are to be found not only in the physical world. Many of them are subtle treasures. We can discover them within the mysteries of our own awareness. Of course, we have to train ourselves to be aware, and working with the universal laws of attention and intention will greatly assist.

Attention and intention

True healing is simply the recognition of wholeness (holiness). Energy mastery and psychological recapitulation, combined with living in spiritual community with like-minded others practising wholeness, are the tools and the structure we need to embrace and undertake in order to achieve wholeness and perfection.

No one can truly heal another until they have committed fully on all levels to take self-responsibility to restore themselves to wholeness. Remember we cannot transmit what we do not embody and live. Moreover, please remember that ultimately in truth there is no 'another'. What we do for another we do for ourselves and what we give to others, we give to ourselves. Everyone is merely 'part' of our own 'reality'. If we are to truly heal and once again truly know our divinity, then we must claim our own perfection right now and detach completely from the illusion of imperfection as we progress spiritually on the path of spiritual completion. In order to grow, we need to create and demonstrate the perfection of this new image in all our 'words, thoughts, feelings and actions' constantly and consistently.

I quote the Course in Miracles: 'Give me your blessing, Holy Son of God, for I would behold you with the eyes of Christ and see my perfect sinlessness in you.' By recognizing the divine in others with this model, we reconnect to our own divinity, and by acknowledging our own divinity, we are able to see the divine in others.

Healing is based on two sacred premises: attention and intention.

Attention – I give you my undivided love and attention, knowing that you are God and I AM God.

Intention – I offer you the recognition of perfection that you may once again reconnect to soul and spirit and release all that is preventing that remembrance of wholeness and authentic power. Draw whatever you need through me rather than from me. Healing is instant, working on the perfect time for you. It could be a brief second or a lifetime. I will only know and see you as perfect. My most fervent prayer is that you see yourself as perfect, divine and already healed.

So how did we come to lose our connection to spirit and forget that we are already healed? It's rather a long story…

Religion versus spirituality

'Your religion is where your love is.'

HENRY DAVID THOREAU

Before we go any further on the path, it's very important to be totally clear on the difference between religion and spirituality. My experience is that not many people do understand the difference, and this causes great confusion, slowing down the alchemical process of enlightenment. I tend to agree with Abraham Lincoln that, 'When I do good, I feel good. When I do bad, I feel bad. That's my religion.' Just because we may have read lots of spiritual books does not mean we are spiritual. It just means we are doing lots of spiritual reading. I have read many murder thrillers in my previous personality days, but this does not make me a murderer!

Developing and adhering to a daily spiritual practice that deepens our connection with the 'all' or the 'one', and conquering negative ego through developing mindfulness in every word, thought, feeling and action, is the only way to truly expand our consciousness and lead to higher awareness. The Buddha said, 'All that we are is the result of what we have thought. If a man speaks or acts with an evil thought, pain follows him. If a man speaks or acts with a pure thought, happiness follows him, like a shadow that never leaves him.' Ralph Waldo Emerson said, 'Nothing will bring you happiness but the triumph of principles.' This is the true key to enlightenment in this lifetime – living the principles rather than just simply knowing them. The first is real wisdom (knowledge lived) and the latter is the conceit of wisdom, which is a burden to all society.

I feel it is vital to have a clear perception of how spirituality has evolved and how consciousness continues to expand on this planet. If we pledge our allegiance to just one particular religion with such tunnel vision, we sometimes deny ourselves the chance to grasp the bigger picture and experience the oneness. Most religions, including some of the more evolved and new aged ones, tend to lean towards separation and tell us not to mix disciplines. This can be seen, for instance, in their policies of 'This is right and this is wrong. This is sinful and this is holy'. Wars are even fought over whose God is the real God. There's almost no mention of Goddess!

Thanks to all the divine dispensations of Grace on this planet in these times of great shift, the veils are thinning and there are people who have developed the ability to intuit and channel spiritual insights. In ancient times these people were called oracles. Suddenly we are open to hearing a much more inclusive history of this planet straight from the horse's mouth – from disincarnate holy beings, spiritual teachers, ascended masters, angels.

Thus now more than ever, we are able to build a much clearer picture of how teachers from all the great religions have in fact been from the same soul groups, simply re-incarnating over and over to bring through and learn/teach different aspects of God's message. This in fact is the theme behind the teachings of Helena Blavatsky's Theosophical Society. The basic message of these soul groups is that of wisdom, unconditional love and power – and living these qualities daily. These are the divine attitudes embodied by Masters like Buddha/Christ/Maitreya.

Whereas religions traditionally tell us what to think, spirituality teaches us how to think for ourselves. Religions teach us to fear the shadow. Spirituality teaches us to bring out all of our feelings into the open for sharing and transmutation to higher expression. This is how we learn to live in constant connection to, and therefore in expression of, the vibrations of unconditional love. This book and my workshops expand on this and teach us how to align our thoughts and feelings to the highest aspects of our best spiritual selves and divine intelligence.

At the higher Levels of the map, I teach daily practices which go beyond prayer and meditation. Yet we need to do the psychological clearings before we are ready to work with these higher esoteric processes, which really empower our connection to higher aspects of ourselves. We learn to become channels and to receive and transmit spirit constantly on a daily basis. When practised daily, we can learn to create and manifest from the higher mind, exactly the life we choose, for the greatest good of the 'all'. Learning to guide our own thought processes is truly the key to creating heaven on earth.

Spirituality is a living, breathing thing. It has the capacity to grow within a living creature, without limits. Religion by contrast is a body of codified forms that have been agreed upon by a society and usually used for the purpose of controlling the masses. Religion is like a school. Spirituality is the education, which is supposed to occur in it. Spirituality is what matters, not the particular religion. Religion is only valuable to the degree it serves the evolving needs of our spiritual elevation. Having said all this I agree with Gregg Braden that religion, like conventional medicine, is not bad or wrong – just 'incomplete'.

For the past 5,000 years, we have lived in the period known to the Hindus and the Tibetans as the *Kali Yuga*. *Kali* means chaos. These times are considered to have been a profoundly dark age. The whys and where-fores are not only beyond the scope of this presentation, but it is likely that few humans could fully appreciate them.

The important point is that we have moved beyond the darkness now. A whole new world of possibilities is dawning for mankind as a result of the higher light quotient that the people on the planet today generally have access to. It's time for mankind to wake up to the depth of the grandeur and antiquity of our spiritual tradition. The great scientist, Einstein, when talking about consciousness and spirituality, once said, 'The rational mind is a faithful servant, the intuitive mind is a divine gift. We have created a society that worships the servant and has forgotten the gift.' Today there is a ripple of awakening throughout the scientific community, which is beginning to remember the gift...

Consciousness

Rupert Sheldrake has proposed a most promising theory of the evolution of consciousness, from matter to spirit. He contends that each species of life has a unique 'morphogenetic field'. This field exists everywhere on the earth. It guides the alignment of atoms and molecules in the development of the individual member of the species (whether plant, bacteria, insect, animal, human, etc.)

The morphogenetic field is responsive to the needs of the species. Thus, if a species of bird needs a longer beak to survive, this need will cause a change in the morphogenetic field and subsequent generations of the bird will be born with just such a longer beak. When a species reaches the limits of development within a certain form, the morphogenetic field can make a 'quantum leap' and generate a whole new species. Thus could be explained the exodus of certain fish from the form of a water-breathing sea creature to an air-breathing creature that walks the land.

Sheldrake's theory also provides an explanation for unusual facts of human history. How is it that so many scientists living in far-flung parts of the world, working with no knowledge of each other, often make scientific breakthrough discoveries almost simultaneously? Here the minds of humans, striving to understand the same bit of knowledge, are connected through the morphogenetic field. This field defines the current limits of both physical ability and of knowledge. When any one person makes a breakthrough, the morphogenetic field is changed. Subsequently, the same breakthrough becomes more easily accessible for all other people. For example, soon after Roger Bannister was the first runner to break the barrier of the four-minute mile, several other runners did so as well. This also provides an explanation of how it is possible that great inventions were created at nearly the same time by people far apart from one another.

Research on the effectiveness of prayer and affirmations support the idea that we have a far greater influence upon our environment than was formerly believed. What we think and what we expect do much to define the reality that we experience. We are not a victim of life, we are co-creators.

It appears that the evolution of humanity on earth has not been a random process. Throughout evolution, the Source has been evolving ever more complex species of life on earth. The goal of evolution seems to be to create beings that can 'wake up' in consciousness. In humans, consciousness awoke from the instinctual animal level to self-consciousness, the awareness that allows you to say, 'I am'. Though the scientists are not yet in agreement about this, it appears that dolphins and a few other species of animals are also self-aware. Self-awareness means that we can do things that we think up ourselves. This means consciously choosing how to act rather than reacting instinctually.

Remember, what we visualize and expect has a powerful effect upon the world we experience. Our vision will assist all of us to grow in consciousness. One wonders, however, if there might be some effective way to accelerate the maturation process of the nations and governments of our planet. The need is large. If we continue in the direction we are currently headed, we may well destroy much of the life on earth and make it, for our descendents, more of a dead planet than a lovely place to live.

Dharma and science

> 'Science sans conscience, n'est que ruine de l'âme.' (Science without a conscience is nothing but the destruction of the soul.)
> Rabelais

Science is essentially a compartmentalization of all the knowledge humans have gained about the external world through our senses. Dharma is the compartmentalization of all the wisdom gained by humanity. Therefore, science and dharma complement one another. As the Isa-Upanishad puts it, 'He who has both spiritual wisdom (Dharma) and secular knowledge (science) together keeps death at bay through the latter and experiences immortality through the former.'

> 'Dharma without science is superstition. Science without dharma is intellectual madness.'
>
> SWAMI CHINMAYANANDA

> 'Science without religion is lame, religion without science is blind.'
>
> ALBERT EINSTEIN

Meditation, scientific studies and brainwave patterns

Through well-designed research projects, it has been determined that ALL types of meditation, but particularly that combined with life-force energy mastery, Reiki, produce the following benefits:

* provide a deep physiological state of rest
* are more effective than relaxation techniques

* increase energy
* lower blood pressure and cholesterol levels
* reduce atherosclerosis (hardening of the arteries)
* increase happiness and improves relationships
* reduce stress and anxiety (decreases stress hormones)
* improve marital happiness
* improve sleeping
* reduce the symptoms of asthma
* increase creativity and intelligence (IQ)
* give broader comprehension and improved ability to focus
* improve perception and memory
* improve students' learning skills and intellectual performance
* increase orderliness of brain functioning
* increase self-actualization and self-concept
* reduce the use of cigarettes, alcohol and non-prescription drugs
* improve general psychological health and well-being
* lower healthcare costs
* result in more positive health habits
* increase life span and reduces effects of ageing
* increase levels of DHEA, a hormone described as the elixir of life
* improve job performance (productivity) and job satisfaction
* improve relationships at work
* improve health in the work place
* help in the treatment of traumatic stress
* are effective in the rehabilitation of prisoners
* improve quality of life in society
* decrease violent fatalities
* in group practice, decrease crime rates

Brainwave patterns appear during different activities. Alpha occurs when we are relaxed and not thinking about anything in particular. Alpha waves are also associated with a calm and focused mental state and meditation.

Alpha waves oscillate between 8 and 14 Hz.

Theta is a state of deeper relaxation and is often associated with bursts of creative insight, sleep learning and vivid mental imagery. It is also found in more advanced meditators. Theta waves oscillate between 4 and 8 Hz.

Delta is the slowest of brainwave activity and is found during deep, dreamless sleep and sometimes in very experienced meditators. Delta brainwave activity has also been recorded in states of transpersonal awareness such as open visions. They oscillate between .5 and 4 Hz.

Scientists have known for years that when individuals listen to binaural beats at specific frequencies, the brain begins to 'entrain' or follow that frequency in a very short time and meditators have been studied using EEG equipment. Japan's leading neurophysiologist, Dr Tomio Hirai reports that Zen meditators are able to alter Alpha/Theta frequency according to their depth of meditation. According to Dr Hirai: 'Meditation is not merely a state between mental stability and sleep, but a condition in which the mind operates at the optimum. In this condition the person is relaxed but ready to accept and respond positively to any stimulus that may reach him.'

Scientists monitoring individuals experiencing expanded states of awareness (telepathy, visions, etc.) have determined that each experience is consistent with different brainwave states. For example, during open visions when an individual is awake and alert, the brainwave pattern is often found in the Delta range. Delta is normally associated with deep sleep and should not appear while an individual is awake and alert!

Benefits of accessing the various states:

Alpha – 8Hz

* good attention focusing, meditation and awareness of balance
* an increase in serotonin (feel good chemical) levels
* a decrease in blood lactate levels
* an increase in beta-endorphin levels
* enhances the immune system
* reduces stress

* quick pick-me-up at the end of the day

Theta – 4Hz
* deeper states of attention focusing and meditation
* expands problem solving, gaining insight and new concepts
* travelling the perinatal matrix to resolve life issues
* flashes of deep insight into paradigm issues
* increased intuitive and creative ability
* increased psychic abilities

Delta – 1Hz
* deepest states of attention focusing and meditation
* expanded awareness
* out of body experience
* open visions and transpersonal experience
* deeper insight and understanding
* gaining a sense of Oneness

The Bhuddist approach to meditation

In Zen, meditation has two objectives: stopping and seeing. Stopping nurtures our minds, releases us from compulsiveness and brings calm. Seeing engenders intuition and inner knowledge, clears confusion and brings enlightenment.

One without the other is imbalance. Too much calm lacking the balance of seeing creates dullness. We fall asleep... Many meditators belong to this category. They are very calm but rather unstimulating. The pitfall to overcome here is to ensure we are never using meditation to find bliss to deny pain. Too much seeing conversely, without being able to stop, is also imbalanced and creates inner tension, where possibly the desire to achieve is out of balance and has become obsessive. We have to beware of the temptation to channel high inspiring energies and perform worthy acts of service. We need to remind ourselves that without the balance of stopping, we might lack calm and peace, exposing ourselves to high levels of stress and tension.

In the Buddhist conception of meditation, these two (stopping and seeing) are known as Samatha (the development of mental and physical poise and calm) and Vipassana (awareness, sensitivity, mental clarity). The Buddhist ideal is to embody a combination of these two, which might well be called 'calm and clear awareness'. When developed deeply enough, we penetrate through our daily concepts and self-definitions and discover a deeper state of being, a new life perspective, a freedom which is not dependent upon any circumstances.

Samatha and Vipassana are tools for achieving enlightenment or Nirvana. Literally, Nirvana means 'extinction'. In this state, the usual personal ego perspective is extinguished. It is a state of 'no self'; a state that is selfless rather than self-centred.

In Nirvana, the three klesas, the 'afflictions, which prevent happiness', are extinguished. These three are raga (the desire to repeat that which is pleasant), dveas (the desire to avoid that which is unpleasant) and moha (mental confusion and unclarity). Buddhism teaches that it is moha that is responsible for our sense of personal identity. Through meditation, we become calm and see clearly and this illusory sense of personal identity melts away and we experience a state of 'no self'.

Buddhists practice compassion and service. However, it is very helpful to first achieve that state of 'no self'. In the state of calm and clear awareness, we can best serve. Then, even if our attempts to help others are less than successful, we remain balanced, enthusiastic and keep on keeping on.

Feel the force – the power of prayer

In recent years, many studies have demonstrated conclusively that prayer has many novel, useful and health-benefiting effects. Since many such studies were criticized because of the problem of suggestion with human subjects, research was performed on the effect of prayer upon bacteria, fungi and germinating seeds. Seeds that received positive prayer germinated faster and produced hearty, faster growing plants. Many seeds that received negative prayer failed to germinate at all or, at best, grew slowly and produced weaker plants. Similar results were produced when prayers were sent to fungi and bacteria from a great distance (miles) away. The effect of prayer seems to be independent of distance.

The results (increased growth or inhibited growth) depended upon factors of consciousness of those praying – factors such as caring, love, empathy and compassion. Negative caring (destructive, hurtful thoughts) produced negative results.

Since plants, fungi and bacteria are not assumed to be susceptible to suggestion, these experiments do indicate that prayer can have a profound effect indeed. Similar results have been obtained in the research of prayer upon humans, as well.

To whom shall we pray?

A dear friend who I love very much and who is a very successful businessman, objected to my advice to invoke and pray to wise beings such as Melchizedek, the archangels, ascended masters, Elohim, etc. He said, 'Look. If I have something troubling me, I just go straight to God. Why do I need all these middlemen?'

I answered, 'If you were buying a computer from Microsoft, you wouldn't wait several years until you could get an appointment with Bill Gates, the president. Bill Gates has created dealerships with chains of management and service to deal with all known types of requests. And so it is with God. There is a living God who I prefer to refer to as 'Source'. And just like any big corporation, Source has created a hierarchy of command, an executive service to deal with all different kinds of requests. Besides that, if you succeeded in going to God direct, the vibration is so powerful that you'd explode.'

He then tested me. He said, 'While you are doing a hands-on energy mastery session with me, I'll secretly invoke Melchizedek several times.

Tell me each time I do so.' I thought, 'Oh, thank you, God – a nice easy nut to crack.' The saying came to mind, 'For those who believe, no proof is necessary. For those who don't believe, no proof is possible.' However, in this case, proof was possible. Each time he called in Melchizedek, I sensed the increased energy presence and told him so with accurate timing.

According to the Jewish and later Christian stories (Hebrews 7:3), Melchizedek is a divine being who appeared on earth without being born and did not die. Hebrew traditions say that Melchizedek, incidentally, taught Abraham (Qabalah). He is referred to as the 'teacher of teachers' and stands to Moses, Jesus, Mohammad, Buddha and the like, just as they stand to us.

In Chapter 1, I wrote that we are constantly surrounded by angels and other invisible helpers who wish to help us. But, because of our free will, they are not allowed to intervene unless we ask for help. They can comfort and guide us. They do answer our prayers.

The archangels of the four directions are favourites for prayer:

East – Raphael – God has healed – the angel of healing, prayer, love, joy and light.
West – Gabriel – God is my strength – the angel of annunciation, resurrection, mercy, vengeance, death and revelation.
South – Michael – Who is as God – the angel of repentance, righteousness, mercy and sanctification.
North – Uriel – Fire (Gold, light) of God – angel of the presence, discloser of the mysteries, angel of salvation.

Mahatma (literally 'great soul') is a relative newcomer as a holy name. The Mahatma energy is said by American author Brian Gratton (deceased) to have recently (since the Harmonic Convergence in 1987) built the first bridge from the highest levels of Source all the way to the physical. To connect with deity on the highest levels, to clear out suffering and learn to truly create, invoke and pray to the Mahatma.

The ascended masters are also popular objects of prayer. These include El Morya, Kuthumi, Serapis Bey, Paul the Venetian, Hilarion, Jesus Christ (Sananda is said to be his soul name according to the Theosophical Society teachings) and St Germain. These seven are known as the chohans or ascended masters of the seven rays.

The whole group of Gods, Goddesses, archangels, angels, enlightened ones and ascended masters can be referred to or prayed to as 'the Rainbow Masters'. So when we wish to call in the whole lot, we can pray to the Rainbow Masters. Clearly, if we are from a different culture, we will have different names for Source, God and the various angels. Experiment and see which names bring the greatest inner contact and blessings.

Modes of prayer – why worry when we can pray?
1) The most basic type of prayer is petition or supplication – asking for something we want or to be rid of something we do not want. Asking God or the angels to do something for us implies either that we know better than they what ought to be done, or that they will get to it faster if we ask them to do so.

The unconscious assumptions behind this kind of prayer are:

We are separate from and not personally responsible for the conditions we choose to change.

We feel helpless and unable to change the undesirable conditions ourselves.

Some greater power that is separate from us can change the conditions.

We can ask the greater power to do so and sometimes it will.

Supplication is the typical kind of prayer that we perhaps learned as children from our parents or in church. Much research has demonstrated well that this type of prayer often does work to generate the desired conditions. Prayers of intercession, asking deity to help someone else, belong to this category.

2) 'Thy will be done' is practised by those wise enough to know that they don't know what God should do. This more advanced sort of prayer

says, 'I don't know what the divine will is, but I submit to and invoke it.' This leaves the outcome wide open and up to the divine agency to figure out and direct. It still implies the existence of a separate, outside deity that we can affect and get to act on our behalf.

3) The practice of thankfulness is a higher form of prayer than supplication and 'thy will be done'. Most of us are familiar with the homely form of this kind of prayer through prayers of thanksgiving or 'saying grace' before meals. In this type of prayer, we practise gratitude for what we have and a way of insuring that we remain in grace. Truly, gratitude is a potent tool for increasing abundance.

4) Feeling-based prayer/prayer is a feeling. There are higher forms of prayer that are accessible to us when we have discovered and experienced that there is no 'other', that we are a microcosm of Source, a co-creator with God, a hologram of the One that is all this. Then we may 'invoke' and become one with the various aspects of our greater life. We come to understand that there are various possible outcomes to our current situation and learn to 'invite' the outcome we prefer by becoming one with the reality of it now.

Feeling-based prayer is prayer as Jesus taught the disciples: thank God for the good things that we would have. This is really paradoxical to the conscious mind. In general, we thank someone after we receive something, not before. Thanking God before implies that we are absolutely sure that we will receive that which we are praying for – a kind of super positive thinking. In fact, this kind of thinking acts as a kind of magnet that invokes the desired result, provided we can practise patience and detachment from that which we desire.

In 1948, The Dead Sea scrolls were found. Among them was a complete book of Isaiah dating from about 400 BC. This version of Isaiah is substantially different to the edited and shortened one still in our Bible today. It includes specific instruction in feeling-based prayer.

The familiar American Indian Rain Dance is an example of feeling-based prayer, complete with movement, costume, music and singing. The Indian performing the rain dance is not 'praying for rain'. He is stamping his feet in imagined puddles of rainwater! In his imagination, he is singing and dancing in the rain! He is feeling how it is to be in the rain, remembering the gifts of rain and feeling deeply, intensely grateful for all this.

When Gregg Braden, the scientist and spiritual teacher, visited a Tibetan monastery at 18,000 feet altitude, he asked a monk there about his form of prayer. The monk replied, 'You cannot see our prayer. You can only see the outer rituals we perform to enter into the feeling. Our prayer is not the words we are chanting. Prayer is a feeling state that occurs within us when we perform our ritual activities.'

Similar cultural prayer practices exist in the cultures of the Hopi Indians, the Mayans and the Egyptians. It appears that in ancient times, there was a widespread awareness and practice of this type of prayer.

Modern quantum physics indicates that there are many potential future outcomes that effectively co-exist here and now. Which of them comes into existence depends upon the conditions we evoke, through our expectations, intentions and actions. Modern science seems to confirm the principles upon which this ancient mode of prayer is based. Using feeling-based prayer, we have the opportunity to generate the most positive outcomes that we are capable of imaging, for self and for all living beings upon this planet earth.

5) Mantra, the chanting of words of power, is a very effective form of prayer. In India, a practice of Bhakti Yoga (union with God through devotion) is the singing of the names of God. The Indians believe that by singing names of God, we can become aligned with their particular qualities.

The Essenes developed this concept into a precise spiritual science. They chanted names of particular angels when they needed specific assistance. Thus, for example, when they wished to heal, they chanted the name of the archangel Raphael which means 'God has healed.' When they required protection they chanted the name of the archangel Michael which means 'God is my protection and he who is like God.' For strength they chanted the name of the archangel Gabriel, which means 'God is my strength.' For purification they chanted the name of the archangel Uriel, which means 'Fire of God'.

I once talked with a man called Tony Payne who complained of terrible pain in his toe and knee. At first I could find no real cause for this energetically, but then I looked at his name badge and saw the mantra of his name he had chanted all his life – Toe Knee Pain. It's so important to remember the one spiritual truth that where we focus our attention, energy is magnified. I hope this little story will remind you of this.

PRACTICES

Working with Toltec wisdom

Stop taking anything personally. Before you say anything, ask yourself, 'Why do I wish to say this now?'

Listen to the internal voice and change the language to best reflect who you are becoming. Practise mindfulness...

Recapitulate your life.

Stop all gossiping and meaningless conversation.

Make a list of the things you say regularly to yourself that are disempowering. Define something better to say instead. Establish the new habit. Every time you hear the inner voice say something disempowering, immediately say: 'Delete, delete, delete'. Say this with the intention of cancelling out the effect of what the inner voice said. Next reformulate the idea in a positive, empowering way. State this aloud if you are alone. If you are with others who wouldn't understand, think this new thought with great mental intensity. The key to success in this process is this: whether you state the empowering idea aloud or just think it, really mean and intend it. And repeat it until it becomes the new habit.

Calling upon the dakinis

Open yourself to the assistance of the dakinis and enlist them to reconnect you to your own mind treasures. Ask them to guide you to their termas.

Working with effective prayer

'To stand on one leg and prove God's existence is a very different thing from going down on one's knees and thanking Him.'

SOREN KIERKEGAARD

Learn to pray effectively. Practise and find out which kinds of prayer suit the new you emerging.

No distraction

This process of looking or going within may be compared to a bear hibernating in the winter. It's a natural process of ignoring the outer world for a while and turning within to rest, reflect and renew. It's your inner self, calling you to go within, to understand yourself more deeply and unfold new qualities. Insights create awareness and awareness leads to transformation.

Do a 'home retreat' where you practise the art of 'no distraction'. It's a simple yet powerful way to reconnect with spirit. You can do this even if you are at work. Simplify your life for a whole month! Make time for introspection, for retreating into your personal 'inner sanctum'. Get to love being with yourself and keeping your own company.

When you get home every evening, start your retreat. Disconnect the telephone. In order to free yourself from the influence of prior and current 'programming', avoid reading newspapers and magazines. Also, stop reading and listening to advertisements. Have you noticed that what people call 'news' is only the bad news? Neither listen to nor read the news. Allow yourself no TV. It's interesting that television (tell-a-vision) shows are called 'programmes' and the arrangement of shows by the hour is called 'programming'? Do you know what you are being programmed to believe and do? Stop watching TV. If you were in the habit of watching TV every night, make a first step to watch only carefully selected videos that provide positive programming. A glossary of selected videos is included in this book in the Resources section. Cancel all social engagements for a month, and don't engage in heavy-duty household chores, which could be a distraction.

Light a fire if you have one. Light candles and incense. Play healing music to relax and inspire you. Have a candlelit bath with either uplifting or calming Young Living therapeutic-grade essential oils. Do some Reiki, meditate, pray, dance, paint, sing, and eat good healthy wholesome organic food from local producers – or fast. Walk in nature. Do an unsolicited act of kindness for a stranger or someone at work and see how great that feels.

Power journalling – expanding your life history
The teachings of Meister Eckhart inspired me to keep unravelling all the onion skins of ego. This great teacher taught, 'A man has many skins in himself, covering the depths of his heart. Man knows so many things; he does not know himself. Why, thirty or forty skins or hides, just like an ox's or a bear's, so thick and hard, cover the soul. Go into your own ground and learn to know yourself there.'

Continue reviewing your personal history and now start to look at the history of your family. Then consider the history of your culture and of humanity as a whole. Look at the social injustices on all these levels. Include all memories of those who hurt you and those you have hurt. Review and write down your shadow behaviour and that of your family members, your culture and all of humanity. Stay centred as you review all your mistakes remembering what Einstein once said: 'A person who never made a mistake never tried anything new.'

Start paying more attention to the coincidences in your life. These seemingly chance occurrences may be veiling meaningful synchronicities. Follow up on these synchronicities and you will be led along your spiritual path. For instance, when you meet someone and then bump into them again unexpectedly, take the time to talk. Tell each other your stories. Give your total attention and listen carefully with your heart while the other is talking. Never be preparing your response but rather, just really listen. After your stories are told, stay in the energy, wait in the silence until you are inspired to say something. In this way, deep messages will be given to one another. You will be guided to say just what the other needs to hear and vice versa.

In later chapters, you will find much use for this information, so earnestly commit yourself to writing in your power journal now. Be thorough, honest and tell the whole truth. Tell your secrets. Write all this down on paper. Keep your story in a safe place where no one will find it and read it! Avoid grandiosity and victim-consciousness. Stay balanced and always be the compassionate witness knowing you are not your behaviour. Behaviour can be changed. Remember too, 'When we know better we can do better'. (Oprah Winfrey)

Working with animal totems

SALMON: Salmon spirit medicine helps us to achieve greater awareness of life as a cycle of initiation on the journey home to the divine. Salmon lifts us above the mundane and cultivates a stronger and clearer connection to the deeper spiritual meaning and purpose of our lives. If you need to strengthen your ability to move forward with perseverance towards your happy and unavoidable destiny of enlightenment (whilst trusting completely in the unknown – the hero's journey), this is the spirit medicine required. Salmon spirit medicine will enhance total surrender to the great mystery of life and greatly accelerate you on your journey back to oneness.

BUTTERFLY: A great catalyst for transformation, attuning to this spirit totem energy supports one in times of emotional and spiritual transformation. It is excellent for letting go, for moving forward and trusting to be carried by the universal flow. It encourages feelings of lightness, grace and a gentle fluidity in both giving and receiving. Butterfly creates an harmonious balance of vulnerability and strength within oneself. It is also good for nurturing feelings of peace, calm and stillness in the heart. It quiets the mental body and allows one to experience the power of now. Butterfly spirit medicine brings about a sense of the divine feminine. It opens us to honour and appreciate the simple things in life.

Let Go and Let God
Reiki Symbol 2

Symbol No 2, Sei Hei Kei (Mental/Emotional Body Balance), pronounced 'Say Hay Kay', is primarily used for healing rigid entrenched mental and emotional energetic patterning, but is also used for protection. Again, one of the four original Reiki symbols given to Dr Usui, this symbol is especially useful to assist us to 'Let Go and Let God' – to relax and release negative energies that perpetuate stress and tension. Above all this ancient magical shamanic symbol helps us to balance and reconnect right and left brain hemispheres so that, to quote Christ, 'The two become one.'

The use of this symbol can bring us into contact with who we really are. Even before birth we begin to put together a 'survival kit' based on the impressions received through our mother and her environment during pregnancy. After birth, we continue to build up behaviour patterns that will ensure that we get our basic needs met. This early conditioning is based on our response to our original wound. The resulting false associations can lead to patterns which replay the original wound scenario, causing pain in our relationships and hardship in our daily lives.

Some of these patterns may be limiting belief systems, habits, addictions (which are habits to which we are particularly devoted!) or other stresses. As we change some of these patterns, we find that our relationship to the world around us changes completely. We become able to take on new projects in our lives. We form new, more appropriate relationships, or clarify and enrich the scope of existing ones.

The second symbol can be used to clear on many levels. When we begin to incorporate this symbol into our now daily 'Violet Flame Mindfulness Meditation' practice from Chapter 1, in addition to the first symbol, we can step onto a higher path and begin to live our dreams.

CHAPTER 3

BUILDING NEW FOUNDATIONS

If you think you can, you can and if you think you cannot, you're right.'
HENRY FORD

OVERVIEW

'Do or do not, there is no try!'
Master Yoda
(GEORGE LUCAS – STAR WARS)

At Alchemical Level 3, our ego is awake again but rather subdued and no longer interfering. Now is the time to use this helpful aspect of our ego to sort through all the memories, impulses and images that arose in Alchemical Level 2. We decide what liabilities to junk and what talents to keep. Going within to meditate and self-heal daily is vital and greatly assists this Level. We need to separate ourselves from people, places and things that no longer support the new us about to be born. I remember a great teaching on this came to me in the film, *The Matrix*, where Morpheus explains to Neo:

'The Matrix is a system, Neo. That system is our enemy. But when you're inside, you look around, what do you see? Businessmen, teachers, lawyers, carpenters. The very minds of the people we are trying to save. But until we do, these people are still a part of that system and that makes them our enemy. You have to understand, most of these people are not ready to be unplugged. And many of them are so inured, so hopelessly dependent on the system, that they will fight to protect it.'

Agent Smith, from the same film, talks of human activity in ego (in the matrix): 'I'd like to share a revelation that I've had during my time here. It came to me when I tried to classify your species and I realized that you're not actually mammals. Every mammal on this planet instinctively develops a natural equilibrium with the surrounding environment but you humans do not. You move to an area and you multiply and multiply until every natural resource is consumed and the only way you can survive is to spread to another area. There is another organism on this planet that follows the same pattern. Do you know what it is? A virus. Human beings are a disease, a cancer of this planet.'

Is humanity behaving like a virus? If so, then now is the time to go beyond striving for comfort and greed, and discover our higher purpose. Cease being a victim and stop making assumptions. Know that whatever others do, it's always about them, it's never about us. Visualize the new self powerfully emerging with all the good parts put together and fully function-ing. Now is the time to focus all the energy of our attention upon that which we choose to experience, rather than what we fear.

About 15 years ago, when I lived in Japan, I remember listening to a friend telling me a story. He said that when his career was really booming as a major league baseball star, chat show host and singer, his agent had asked him to go and see a little boy who was in hospital. The small child was a devoted baseball fan and suffering from leukaemia. My friend and his agent both saw this as being a great PR opportunity. They could milk this story with the Japanese national press to maximum potential and get lots of free publicity. It sounded like a good idea, but he was too busy training for the next baseball season, too busy rehearsing his TV shows etc. So he declined the invitation. He didn't want to refuse but had felt trapped by his demanding schedule. In hindsight, he confided that he had also felt afraid to be so close to something so painful. This was all too real and would involve authentic feelings and commitment. As he continued with the story I began to feel powerful energies all around us in the room. I got goose-bumps as he was speaking… some people call these truth bumps!

My friend, the baseball star, told me he then experienced a bewildering synchronicity. His game suddenly went off and he was dropped from the team. His TV show was dropped. Suddenly, his thoughts were about the little kid. He made enquiries and discovered that the boy was still in the hospital and still battling with leukaemia. The athlete decided to go and see that seven-year-old baseball expert. This time it wasn't a PR stunt. He felt the child calling him and felt that he needed to respond to this *crie de coeur*, this very real call of the heart. Since he'd been dropped from the team, he'd had time to think about life and how it wasn't working. He knew he needed to give something back. He felt that a visit to the sick child was a good start.

This man received much more from the innocent little child than he imagined possible. He regained his own innocence and purity. This unlikely pair built up a great bond and a genuine deep friendship. The small Japanese boy inspired the great baseball star to regain his magic touch. As a result, he made it back on the team. He knew his little friend was really sick and promised him a home run. He gave him a secret signal to watch for on TV. When he tipped his hat at the camera just before the pitch, that would be the signal to the child that this was the time he was just about to hit the home run, all especially for the boy.

As planned, he made the signal, tipped his hat and hit the home run. There was massive applause. He was back on form! However, the athlete felt something much more than this. He felt some invisible force or energy field enveloping him. He felt the child's love and gratitude. He felt touched by his little friend's powerful spirit and was deeply moved. He subsequently found out that just after this incredible sporting rebirth, his little pal had died. However, he later heard the boy had seen his home run on TV and had been joyous in that moment.

As I listened to this incredibly heart-warming story, I felt something I had seldom felt before. I could feel something touching me. Was it the spirit of the child? Was it my friend's spirit? Was it my spirit? Do we all share some kind of spirit connection? I was filled with questions. This incident had certainly changed my friend's life. Now it was changing mine.

This big shot athlete whose only focus prior to this event had been fame and fortune, suddenly became concerned for others. As he started giving and caring for others, he found new meaning in his life. He found his passion and his joy in living. I looked at my life; a life spent pursuing money and status, avoiding pain, and seeking selfish pleasure. I knew it had to change, but how?

With tears in his eyes, my friend told me he had reconnected to spirit after that experience. I didn't doubt that for one moment because I could feel spirit all around us in the room. I felt sure it was a sign to get back in touch with the divine magic in my own life that I experienced as a child before being wounded by my father's behaviour. I needed to find my own joy, my own sense of inner worth. I knew that I needed to live my life in a way that was more meaningful. I knew it was time for me to start giving back.

As the energies in the room continued to build, I suddenly remembered times in my past when I had felt this strange power. Normally it was connected to sensing danger in advance. I recalled a particular incident where a boyfriend was driving like a crazy man on the winding, twisting country lanes of Swaziland, Southern Africa. We approached a blind bend and I yelled for him to slow down and stop. Luckily he did, because as we skidded round the corner to a stop we encountered a herd of cows and would probably have killed ourselves at the speed we were going! How on earth could I have forgotten about this kind of power? Luckily it hadn't forgotten me; it was there, all around me in the room, and it was growing stronger.

Inspired by this incredible story and this unusual man, I considered my higher purpose for the first time ever in my life. Suddenly I knew that I needed a real purpose for living. Even though I didn't have the spiritual vocabulary to describe this so succinctly then, I just knew that if I could connect to my higher purpose, my life would improve and anything would be possible. Don't ask me how I knew this, I just knew! I wondered how I had become so cut off from what I really felt. Worse still, how on earth would I sort out this mess? A mixture of fear and panic began to emerge. Why were all my relationships about competing, fearing, judging and attacking? It seemed to me that my personal life reflected the global state of conflicts and the warlike behaviour of nations. Who was mirroring whom, I wondered?

This strange new witness-self kept the revelations coming, showing me visions of what I truly needed. I needed to reconnect to aspects of myself that I had lost in the corporate corridors of power and in my jet-set party lifestyle. What had happened to inner qualities such as love, kindness, co-operation, discernment, compassion, loyalty, integrity and honesty? Where was my courage to move beyond fear's stagnation and inertia, my ability to listen to my heart, my ability to balance work and play, and to live simply? I needed to stop approval seeking and people-pleasing, to find quality time for myself and my awakening spirituality.

I felt ashamed and guilty. I had lost touch with the hero inside me and thus disconnected from my true passion and bliss – helping others. I had traded my inner purity and truth to fit in, conform and people-please. Instead of considering how many Chanel handbags and what the season's colour was, I really needed to examine why my health was failing. Why I was running out of energy and physical vitality.

What I had really desired all my life was to put down roots. I longed to find a lovely home, a sanctuary where I could feel safe and sheltered from the world's dark, corrupting influences. I needed to learn to love myself, self-nurture and find self-acceptance. I had no peace in my life. I couldn't relax unless I was socializing, the centre of attention, drinking or eating; or after sex when I fantasized that this new man was the real love I had always sought. I used all of these behaviours to ease the tensions, suppress the stress, and convince myself that life was OK. After all, I was doing everything in the Martini advert, so my life must be OK!

I realized that my entire life was a sham. I didn't want any of it any more. I realized I had made all my life choices based on images of comfort, profit and greed that society projects onto everyone. Admittedly, my life choices were fuelled by a determination never to repeat the pain and humiliation I suffered in poverty as a child. I had stopped being able to trust people, to be open and to share. Instead, I misguidedly trusted money, looks, success and the high life.

I was a good performer. I should have received an Oscar! I performed the lie in order to fit in, conform, and get attention and love. However, now I could see that I never did fit in. The kind of love I was then capable of giving and receiving in ego, co-dependency, didn't last. It never brought happiness, because I knew there was always something missing. Was that missing thing spirit and higher spiritual values? Surely these would give my life more meaning, wouldn't they? However, I knew, 15 years ago, that I would certainly be the only one with these higher values in my surrounding environment.

Sadly and tragically, the more I lived the lie, the more my heart closed down. I couldn't feel any real love at all. Eventually, I couldn't feel anything. I looked to big cars, big jewels, bigger and better anything, anyone, anywhere, to give me excitement. At this point, even this didn't work any more. I had had it all and I was left wanting and deeply lost in the matrix.

At Alchemical Level 1, we realized that we had been living the lie. The awakening in Level 2 stopped us in our tracks rather dramatically – the tarot card depicting this level is the 'lightning struck tower'. Suffering great loss and in pain, driven into the cave of introspection, we had no option but to admit our hidden parts and suppressed memories. The reward now is that there is some time of calm following the storm. The guidance now at Alchemical Level 3 is that it's time to make a new plan and create a new best self.

In Alchemical Level 3 we delve even more deeply into the psyche. We begin to carefully reflect on all those things that we were told were wrong, bad, dark and socially unacceptable – those things we were taught to hide and to pretend didn't exist. Yet it's these very things – dark and frightening impulses – which hold the keys to unlock all the power required to reconnect to best self. Therefore, pay attention, commit to review courageously that which was hidden; all that we have been ashamed to admit we must now own and accept so that we can dismantle the lie and create the new best self.

I discovered that when I finally broke through all the veils of denial using radical self honesty, as I came face to face with all my fears, they no longer paralysed me and caused inertia and stagnation. I developed a new understanding that if I could face my fears, I could live my dreams. I began to sort out who I was not and mould myself into who I wished to be. This birth process requires surrender, and the words of the 12 Step Fellowship kept coming to me: 'Let Go and Let God'. I had to learn to separate from, and give up, all that was holding me back – people, places and things. Giving up doesn't always mean we are weak; sometimes it means that we are strong enough to let go. I completely surrendered to what I knew were higher, noble spiritual principles. In doing so I found Grace…

In moment-to-moment conscious awareness, practising the miracle of mindfulness, I made constant sacrifices to ensure I lived these principles, even when nobody was looking. Incidentally, the root meaning of the word 'sacrifice' is to make sacred our relationship to a person, place or a thing… Most importantly, I realized I had to retrain myself to make sacred my relationships to money, people, sex and power. This required purification on all levels, physical/mental/emotional/spiritual. It was all really so very simple! All I had to do was to let go of all that was out of harmony with spirit in my life. Yet, because of attachment, routines and habit, it wasn't easy to allow all that was impure to leave my life.

At Alchemical Level 3 we are learning how to create and manifest to become conscious creators of our own best destiny. We decide what we will detach from and we choose what to create in its place. We are beginning to balance thoughts and feelings, our inner male and female.

Albert Einstein said, 'We should take care not to make the intellect our god; it has, of course, powerful muscles, but no personality.' Our focus is on putting ourselves together in a new way that honours and unites male and female, the mundane and the divine. Spirit guides ego to step out of the driving seat of our lives and become the passenger. Ego doesn't know how to drive the car of our lives and this is why we have so many crashes. Conversely spirit knows how to drive and is fully licensed for the life journey. Remember – all the king's horses and all the king's men could not put 'Humpty' back together again. I can show others how to do this and share the knowledge about powerful tools for transformation, yet no one else can actually do the transformation for us. It's about total vigilance and diligence to recreate the new self, which is equally masculine and feminine, mundane and divine. We must visualize who we are becoming, by imagining all the good parts together, functioning in balance as the new best self. Thus we create what the ancients referred to as the birth of the divine alchemical child within and rebirth – reconnection to best self and spirit.

Alchemical Level 3 is very much about building the right foundation for the inner marriage of the conscious and subconscious that takes place in Level 4. Consequently, all relationships must be reviewed. It's vitally important especially to review any current or past relationships we have had with members of the opposite sex. All too often, we leave one relationship, feel lonely, and begin a new relationship without taking the time needed to analyze co-dependent behaviour and what went wrong with the last relationship. Unless we commit to do this self-inventory work properly, we are destined to repeat the same errors with the next partner and the next and the next. That's hell – these days I prefer heaven. With these simple teachings anyone can learn how to create heaven.

Our external relationships mirror the inner nature of the relationship between our conscious and unconscious minds, between our thoughts and our feelings, our inner male and female. When we purify within and restore harmony and balance within, then and only then will we enjoy powerful, passionate, alchemical relationship with another. How to create alchemical relationship is the subject of a whole book in itself.

As we commit to spending more time to reflect upon what we have remembered in the work on our life story in Level 2 and deepen our process, more will arise. It's like fishing, and in order to 'land the fish' we need to remember, write down and really deepen the revelations that come to us. After all, these are the raw materials for the creation of the new best self.

Through a daily discipline of Reiki self-healing and chakra-balancing work, we learn how to balance the inner male and female, the mind and the feelings, the mundane and the divine. We become empowered from within. Suddenly without knowing how we know or needing to know, we just simply know how to live our best destiny. The more Reiki we do the more pure and positive our energy becomes. This attracts all the most positive people, places and experiences into our lives.

To purify still further, we sift through our lists, discarding character defects and all behaviours that are less than love. We begin to live this new template for best self in our everyday actions in moment-to-moment conscious awareness. Reiki daily helps us to practise mindfulness in order to stay focused, centred and aware. Without Reiki daily, we'll get lost, distracted and fall asleep again. We can also use affirmations and visualizations to create the new best self. One favourite affirmation of mine was, 'My best self is authentic, powerful, loving and courageous'. This worked well and today I have become authentic and embody those qualities all of the time. However, I could not embody these qualities until I admitted I fell short of them, until I was prepared to own and accept all my worst shadow defects and commit to change my thoughts, feelings and actions to something more positive.

Alchemical Level 3 is the stage of revelation, separation and filtration of the contents of consciousness.

Level 2 initiated personal disasters and loss. Perhaps we lost our jobs, our health, a loved one or a relationship failed. Perhaps we lost all our money... Perhaps we lost everything... Our ego plans of how our lives should be, according to the matrix, simply crumbled to dust. I call this 'opportunity disguised as loss'. When we complete Level 2 successfully, the ego gives up its control and becomes still and silent waiting to discover what's going to happen next. I can remember a friend lovingly telling me, 'Hold your head up or you might fail to see what's coming around the next corner.'

Co-dependency

One of the most powerful revelations that I experienced at Level 3 was that I realized that I was responsible for creating all the unhappiness in my life. I had heard of the saying, 'You reap what you sow.' I realized how profound this saying was. I feared intimacy and I was superficial. It was no coincidence, therefore, that the men I attracted were all afraid of closeness and commitment. Just like me, they too were all terribly shallow and feared true intimacy. I was only getting out of life what I had put into it. I was withholding and feared taking risks in my most intimate relationships, so that's what I reaped – shallow relationships with no real communication. Like attracts like, I realized. My relationships were not about love at all. What I experienced was co-dependency. This is also a type of addiction where the fix is attention from another person. I had always unconsciously feared rejection, abandonment and betrayal.

Over and over again, my life had given me exactly what I feared. As each attempt at relationship or love failed and floundered in co-dependency, I blamed myself and felt inadequate. My life was about ever striving to be more perfect in a desperate attempt to find and keep love. The challenge was that I didn't love myself unless I had a powerful job, lots of money, designer labels and lots of jewels. Naturally none of the men I attracted, as partners, could love me for myself either. I realized I had become 'arm candy'. That's how one American comedian described those empty bimbo airhead women. I wasn't empty-headed, nor was I empty-hearted. This all hurt so much.

Another revelation came to me. Could it be that my life was always going to be such a terribly bad dream and so painful because that's what I expected and believed? I knew I had to change myself and find some different beliefs or this nightmare would continue forever. Again, the dilemma was that I didn't know how to do this or who to ask for help. Again, I was looking for answers outside of myself. In actual fact the guidance I needed was always within me. How could I deny this? I had physical proof in the form of the fantastic and incredible experiences and feelings of the evening I had spent with my baseball star friend. What else could explain these uncalled for, profound insights, and the energies in the room? This was spirit calling me from within. At the time, though, I just couldn't understand any of this.

The insights kept coming. How much do you have to dislike or mistrust yourself to live like this, giving away your power to external things, people and places? I knew the answer – a lot. I realized that I had been subtly and not so subtly programmed by the media – Hollywood, magazines and advertising – to be obsessed with power, money, work, sex (which I mistook to be love), designer clothes, expensive jewels, compulsive shopping, and the frivolous restaurant and jet-set nightclub lifestyle. With the help of the new witness-self, I could clearly see that I had used this compulsive, obsessive, addictive behaviour to escape and avoid.

A powerful revelation kicked in… I wondered if what I was experiencing – addiction – was the symptom of a much bigger disease, namely lack of self-love! How could I love the 'personality' me I had created in order to fit in and get on in life? I had lost my true values in this process. I had lost my spirit. I had traded the purity and power of the hero within me for some kind of fantasy, cardboard cut-out, bimbo image. The personality me just got used, recycled and used again.

The insights kept coming… If I truly loved myself, how could I possibly be influenced to continue to do something that I didn't choose? For instance, why did I compare my looks to those of a super-model and feel less than what I saw? Why did a beauty magazine make me feel ugly? Why did I believe thin is beautiful and fat is ugly, dieting is being good and eating is being bad? This was all programming urging me to consume products (diet pills, make-up, plastic surgery, fashion) in order to feel better about myself. Others were getting rich, feeding off our insecurity.

What a sick truth! I admit that it seemed to have worked for a while. Yet now I was experiencing a higher truth. I realized the real me had been consumed by all the advertising and Hollywood images. Without knowing it, I had been brainwashed.

The stream of revelations and insights didn't only come from within. A friend gave me a fairy tale by an anonymous author (in the 12 Step Fellowship, USA), and the similarities with my true-life story and behaviour were startling. I learned so much from this fairy tale, I'd like to share it here and give thanks to the unknown author for the understanding the little story brought about within me regarding addiction.

A tale of an armadillo

Once upon a time there was an armadillo who lived in the Great Desert City. The armadillo was adept at making friends easily. She was friendly and outgoing and always eager to help out. Wherever she went, she seemed to be accepted, but the armadillo always felt 'different'. Because she felt so different, the armadillo was very lonely. She never felt that she 'fitted in', but she thought that was because she was an armadillo and her friends were rabbits or squirrels or lizards or snakes or Gila monsters or scorpions.

She was a very smart armadillo and she used her intellect well. She knew about a lot of different things. In fact she'd even been told quite frequently that she was a beautiful armadillo. The rabbits and the squirrels and the lizards and the snakes and the Gila monsters and the scorpions admired her and sought her advice. Knowledge, thought the armadillo, that was the way to 'fit in'. So she became a Knower and for a long time the armadillo found comfort in knowledge.

One day the armadillo was scouting around the Great Desert City when she came across a Magic Pond. As she sampled the pond water, she found that she didn't feel so out of place any more. The loneliness went away and she felt good – really good.

The armadillo was a very hard worker. With her knowledge, she became an Achiever. As time went on, she had greater and greater success, eventually the greatest success you can imagine. She had Power and Influence. She moved among the Powers That Be in the Great Desert City. But the armadillo felt inadequate. She was recognized and rewarded time and again, but the armadillo never believed that what she had done was good enough. She was afraid that her friends would find out that she didn't deserve their praise or their respect, that she wasn't good enough to really belong in their world.

By now the armadillo was visiting the Magic Pond more frequently. It had become her escape from the pressure of her work. It helped her to relax and feel good. It helped her to laugh and to play. The Magic Pond made her forget her fear, her inadequacy and her loneliness. Her friends didn't know how the armadillo felt inside or how much she liked the effects of the Magic Pond. The armadillo was afraid to tell them. 'I'm so different,' she cried. 'They don't understand.' And, of course, they didn't and this continued for many years.

The armadillo had always been very, very responsible and very, very dependable. One day she began to feel guilty because she saw she was starting to neglect her responsibilities. Sometimes when she visited the Magic Pond, she played too long and forgot her commitments. This really bothered the armadillo, so she decided to STOP visiting the Magic Pond for awhile and work harder, and she did.

She worked very, very hard for a very long time. Her friends continued to be impressed with her skills and capabilities and knowledge. Then one day, for no particular reason, the armadillo stopped by the Magic Pond. While she was there she ate some of the plants that grew in the pond. Once more her feelings of fear, inadequacy and loneliness were eased. The Magic Pond and its special plants became a regular part of her life again.

Of course, none of her friends knew about her feelings because the armadillo was afraid to tell them. She couldn't talk to them about the wonders that happened to her at the Magic Pond. 'They aren't like me and they wouldn't understand,' she reasoned. And so it continued for several more years.

One day the armadillo was overwhelmed by a Terrible Fear. She was still working very, very hard and visiting the Magic Pond and eating the special plants more frequently, but she could not make the Terrible Fear go away. 'I will leave the Great Desert City,' thought the armadillo. 'Then things will be better.' So she filled her canteen from the Magic Pond and stuffed her picnic basket full of the special plants and set out for the Big Country. 'Surely things there will be better and I'll find a Magic Pond there eventually.'

But when she reached the Big Country things were not better for the armadillo. The Terrible Fear was still with her. No matter how often she visited the New Magic Pond or ate the new special plants, the Terrible Fear would not go away. The armadillo grew very tired and very sick and the Terrible Fear haunted her – day and night.

One day in hopelessness and despair, the armadillo cried out, 'Oh God, what am I going to do?' And a Voice said, 'Find the Fellowship of Love.' And a Messenger appeared to direct her. The Armadillo went to the Fellowship of Love and looked around. She saw rabbits and squirrels and lizards and snakes and Gila monsters and scorpions. 'Oh no,' she cried. 'They'll never understand.' But the armadillo was very, very sick and very, very tired. She just didn't care anymore. She sat down and closed her eyes. The armadillo was dying.

The Fellowship cradled the armadillo in their warm Hugs. They nurtured her with their Love, encouraged her with their Acceptance, comforted her with their Experience, sustained her with their Strength. They fed her with their Hope that the fading spirit inside her would be sparked to New Life. And so it continued every day for 90 days and more.

Then one day the armadillo gave a great sigh and opened her eyes. She looked around – the Terrible Fear had gone. This time she did not see rabbits or lizards or snakes or Gila monsters or scorpions... she saw dozens of armadillos who smiled at her and welcomed her and said, 'WE UNDERSTAND.' And the armadillo knew that they truly did. She joined with the members of her own kind in the Fellowship of Love and began to walk with them, step-by-step, down the Road of Recovery.

To all those who have no idea what drug addiction could be like, I feel this modern-day fairy tale will explain it in a way that perhaps no real-life story could. That's the power of fairy tales!

When I first heard the fairy story and reached the parts where the armadillo heard The Voice and where she knew she was dying, I felt tears flooding down my cheeks. In truth, thankfully for me, there are no longer any tears of self pity. These were tears to ease the pain I felt for all the armadillos who are still suffering out there, clean and sober or otherwise, because most of them are truly unaware that there is such a thing as total recovery in mind, body and spirit, where self-love, self-mastery and a feeling of total ease with self and others any time, any place, anywhere can be very simply achieved, maintained and empowered.

At Alchemical Level 3 if I was to experience freedom from my addictions, I knew I had to separate myself entirely from most of the people who'd been part of my personality life. A crack cocaine addict does not get or stay clean by hanging out in a crack house! Similarly, if we truly wish to reconnect to spirit and live this connection daily, we need to find like-minded others to be with to support our transformation.

Separation

The focus of Alchemical Level 3 is separation and filtering. Physically, the unnecessary material is discarded. Spiritually, we rediscover our essential self, reclaim our ideals and dreams. At this level we discern whether or not we are truly ready, willing, able and deserving to separate ourselves from habitual patterns and beliefs that limit us. We develop our new gift of discernment. We decide to become who we choose to be, who we really are. Our ego is awake again but reformed; subdued and no longer interfering. Now is the time to use this helpful aspect of our ego to sort through all the memories, impulses and images that arose in Level 2. We decide what liabilities to junk and what talents to keep. We start to separate ourselves from the habits, places, people and things that do not support the new self who is about to be born. We make sure that we learn our lessons before separating so that we don't have to repeat mistakes in the next relationships.

If we no longer resonate with the beliefs, attitudes or behaviour of the people around us, we begin to search out others who reflect our newly formed, more positive beliefs. If, for some practical reason, we still have to be with people whose beliefs no longer resonate with us, it is perfectly OK if they don't behave the way we like. We didn't die before, so we can stand it now. Calmly and without condemnation, we will do our best to convince these people to transform. If we succeed, fine. If we don't, fine and we are still alive... It is really just unpleasant or irritating, never terminal or harmful to our overall health. Moreover, what these people do has no real effect on us. We can all learn to live happily ever after and successfully in a world where this attitude, and many people's behaviour, is not as we like it or believe it should be. AND in detachment we are OK because we no longer take anything personally! Furthermore, if we don't take what others say or do personally, we can still love them. This is heaven on earth!

Synchronicity

It is at Level 3 that we might become more aware of synchronicity, and willing to follow where it leads. I used to have a strange, recurring dream in which I witnessed myself walking along a road or a path. In the dream, the journey, the scenery and people were all very unremarkable, mundane and ordinary. None of this was what one would normally deem to be particularly inspirational or incredibly dream-worthy stuff. However, what was unusual was that the dreams always ended in exactly the same way. The voice of an unseen narrator would loudly declare, 'And suddenly...' Always at this point, I would wake up. Normally, I was startled, in a perplexed state, wondering what I was missing. In the dream I never knew or saw what was going to occur, an event seemingly so unexpectedly and out of the blue.

Remembering the dream, I knew that I usually felt filled with excitement, anticipation and sometimes trepidation and fear when I heard the words, 'And suddenly'. I remember being really puzzled about the repetitive dream and all the mixed emotions I felt. I had a strange feeling – an inexplicable inner knowing – that the dream must have some deeper meaning. However, I was either too busy or too afraid to find out what that could possibly be. Again, I experienced a strange inner knowing that if I could access the part of my dream after the narrator made his announcement, what came next would alter my life beyond all recognition. Without understanding how it would alter my life, I knew that I simultaneously welcomed that change and feared it. I wondered if perhaps, on some deep inner level, I was blocking the message of the dream.

One astonishing day, in the midst of all the 'busy-ness' in Japan, the dream overlapped into my reality. I was walking along a street on the way to meet my friend, the baseball star who, apart from being a major league baseball star and a TV celebrity chat show host, was also a famous singer in Japan. I too sang a song as I walked down the road to meet him at his hotel. There was nothing very remarkable about the song except that at that time it was already very old and out of date. It was called 'Rescue Me'.

Bearing in mind that for over ten years, I had not watched TV at all or listened to the radio, I don't know how that song got into my head. Perhaps it was my unconscious wish at the time to be rescued. I remember feeling a strong sense of déjà vu when I entered the room and, at first, didn't know why. Then I got it. The same song was playing in the room! Upon realizing this, I began to sense the energy in the room and the dynamics of this meeting. It all seemed so extraordinary. With hindsight, I realize that all these strange phenomena signified that I was opening up to higher invisible levels of guidance from spirit. I later discovered this kind of amazing coincidence is called a synchronicity. A synchronicity normally portends something of great importance in our lives.

Looking back, this synchronicity was one of very many strange signs, signals and omens that something supernatural was beginning to happen in my life. Unbeknownst to me, my life as ego had created it was about to change beyond recognition, quite literally in the twinkling of an eye!

Unfortunately, I was far too busy with personality pursuits, far too unaware and spiritually asleep to look for or notice signs, let alone begin to ponder on what they might mean. In retrospect, however, the synchronicities were like neon lights illuminating a map of my spiritual journey. They were all pointing me in the same direction – to find and live truth. They were guiding me towards the path of healing myself, others and our world.

Is what you want, what you need?

That night in the hotel room with my athlete friend, I remember he remarked to me that I had one of the most amazing lifestyles he could imagine in terms of the work I did, the money I earned, the powerful people I knew, the excitement and the glamour of it all. As usual when people flattered me in this way, and it did happen frequently, I began to puff up with false pride and ego. I fiercely believed the old adage, 'Show me who you are with and I will tell you who you are'. I was constantly with the most beautiful, powerful and richest people on earth and felt this reflected my own worth and status. Because I couldn't access these feelings inside of myself, I wanted the confirmation from others that I was successful and powerful.

As always, when so flattered, I automatically began to agree that my life was brilliant. And suddenly, right out of the blue (the recurrent dream again entering my reality), I had a revelation about my life. I felt a profound sadness. Compared to my normal ego reaction to such flattery, this feeling startled me. Suddenly, my perspective changed and I was the witness to my own life. I saw that I was bored and unfulfilled. I most certainly did have everything I had ever wanted. There didn't seem to be any thing or experience that I still desired. I was astonished at this realization. Although I had achieved all that I ever wanted, suddenly I was aware that I felt totally empty inside and unloved.

The witness inside showed me how my personality was still striving to keep what I had achieved and that with which I was comfortable. I saw myself desperately wishing to perpetuate the lie of how wonderful it all was. But it was as if a wall had come down. A veil had lifted and a volcano was erupting deep within me. Truth just spilled out like a lava flow. I confided to my friend that my life seemed superficial and meaningless. I was bored. I felt confused, afraid and let down. In this instant, I saw through the big lie that my life had become. Films, magazines and TV had conditioned me to believe that if you look like a film star, drive this car, live at this status address, do this powerful job, date this rich man, amuse and entertain people, be the centre of attention, dress this designer way, and so on, then you have made it. I was at the top of the ladder. I had made it. Yet suddenly, quite literally out of the blue I realized that I was very unhappy. This wasn't IT.

My friend's interest in my pain and confusion inspired me to be courageous enough to begin to examine the emptiness that I felt. With great wisdom, my friend then asked me a question that would begin to change my life forever. He said, 'Maybe what you want isn't what you need?' I had never thought of that before. I thought that what we want is what we need. Typical of Level 3, all these sudden revelations and insights were leading me to a higher state of awareness – ready or not! Something inside me was indeed determined to rescue me.

Awareness

'Let us not look back in anger or forward in fear, but around in awareness…'

JAMES THURBER

One of the levels of our experience, which must be healed, has to do with what we call darkness, and what I prefer to call unawareness. The darkness is unawareness. The task of evolution as I see it is to expand awareness so that it is all encompassing and becomes incorporated into all of our being. The processes, the circumstances and the events that are occurring here on this planet at this time are of such an intense nature that they are activators for those feelings and beliefs that live in our underworld.

The pivotal point of experience, the strength of the moment-by-moment experiences of life are the initiatory gateways or choice points allowing us to move into an awareness and understanding of the depths of ourselves. Never doubt our nature is profoundly capable of this task for our consciousness includes the light, best self/best potential destiny, as well as the dark demonic worlds of ego, shadow and persona.

To hold these two opposites in compassion – conscious awareness and love – is to balance them and to heal the darkness through the power and light of awareness. This is the task of evolution as it has been shown to be and as I see it. What has helped me to evolve personally is something I learned from the teachings of Confucius, 'When you meet someone better than yourself, turn your thoughts to becoming his equal. When you meet someone not as good as you are, look within and examine your own self.'

Our earth is evolving, arising into a higher level of awareness, vibration and consciousness, and so are we. Our choice is: do we balance and integrate this on all levels or do we risk the danger of imbalance unrecognized, which puts us back at the bottom of the ladder again?

And, just how do we manifest our best potential self?

Manifestation

What is Manifestation? In *The Laws of Manifestation*, David Spangler states this principle well:

'Manifestation is a process of working with natural principles and laws in order to translate energy from one level of reality to another.'

Manifestation is a change of form or state of condition or being; it is not the creation of something out of nothing. The dictionary defines it as 'making clear to sight or mind, making visible'. The implication here is that the thing manifested was already there but it was not clear, not visible. It was in a different state of being.

For manifestation to work, we must recognize that that which we wish to manifest does already exist, even if it is invisible or separate from our immediate environment. What we need to do, therefore, is to open a route via the chakra system from head to root to start a process through which it can enter our environment and be 'clear and visible' to us.'

Perhaps it's becoming more obvious now exactly why it's so vitally important to heal, clear and balance the chakra system daily, if we are to learn how to manifest effectively.

Wish lists – using our best self co-creative power to manifest

I'd like to remind readers now of something I've already touched on... creativity. There's no harm in repeating this because it's so vitally important. Creativity is a fundamental part of being human. To many philosophers, this is one of the most important reasons for being here on planet earth: to create! Some will argue that we are always creating every minute of every day and this is correct. However, there is a big difference between creating unconsciously and creating consciously. This is why we need to wake up. Let me explain.

At the unconscious (un-awakened and unaware) level of creating we are unknowingly using our creative powers to re-enforce a reality and lifestyle that is less than satisfying and has few rewards. It can be said with great certainty that the majority of people everywhere are creating unconsciously through the filters of unawareness and unrecognized self-defeating thinking and behaviour. This is why it is so important to identify and then DIS-IDENTIFY from denied negative self-sabotaging thoughts, feelings, emotions and behaviour.

Whether spiritually unawakened or drowsy, most people spend the vast amount of their creative energy repeating patterns of thought, behaviour and actions. Even though the outside form may look different in each situation, it's the same film just different actors. An example of unconscious creation is the person who repeatedly gets involved in abusive relationships and just cannot seem to break the pattern. Such a person (through their inability to recognize their patterns and through their inability to change their thinking and habits) continually 'creates' and unknowingly attracts the reality that their unconscious mind is most familiar with, most fears and probably most denies. Simply put, the above example reinstates: if we fail to love and respect ourselves, we will attract people to us who also do not love and respect us. Believe me, I have learned this one well! How do we know we don't love and respect ourselves? Well, usually, we will be afraid to stand up for ourselves and what we believe in, and to ask for respect. Or worse still, we will be afraid to leave the job or the relationship if respect isn't coming.

The awakened person has come to recognize that what they believe about themselves has drawn in the matching experience. The truly awakened person then makes the effort to change their thinking and behaviour, which automatically begins to change their life experiences. This is the secret of the law of attraction. Little by little, or sometimes in great quantum leaps and bounds, the person who once attracted abuse or disrespect is now attracting a different reality and creating a different way of dealing with these situations: either by standing up for themselves in a more self-respecting way or by finally being able to walk away and end the unhealthy interactions quicker than before. Believe me the feeling of power that comes from being able to create healthy emotional boundaries is profound.

Let's take it further…

What about creative expression? It has been said that once we awaken from this 'sleep' or lack of awareness, that we can now step off the 'wheel of karma' (unconscious and habitual patterns) and no longer be controlled by the influence of past lives or by the events that happened earlier in this current life. By moving into a more awakened state of awareness and living life more fully, we begin to consciously and willingly direct our thinking and behaviour into purposeful manifestation: creating and attracting more of that which we prefer and is more natural to who we are becoming – best self.

If we were born to be writers, artists, singers, actors, architects, dancers, entertainers, liberators, healers, teachers, athletes, musicians, gardeners, and so on, but were instead encouraged, pressured, coerced, manipulated, threatened or intimidated into becoming something else to satisfy or gain the approval of say a parent, teacher, employer, lover, spouse or anyone else we've been fooled into believing has power over us, we've fallen into the world of the unconscious and the un-awakened state because we are no longer following our natural inclinations.

As very small children, most of us are still unbound by the prison of family expectations, social acceptance and peer pressure, and we freely express those natural inclinations in our play. It isn't until we are taught out of our natural inclinations that we fall from grace, so to speak.

We need to take time to remember what we did easily and freely as a child, all things that we used to love to do and did effortlessly. If we are not currently expressing in some way, shape or form, an evolved and developed form of those natural inclinations, then we know that this is where we're missing something important in our lives.

Christ Jesus stated: 'Seek ye the Kingdom of Heaven first, then all else will be added unto you'. What did he mean by this?

In honouring what I really wished to do with my creative abilities, I discovered that spirit, God/Goddess and my natural creativity are all wrapped up in the same 'package' so to speak. Ask anyone who has been inspired to teach, heal, paint, draw, sing, write or perform something extraordinary that touched their lives deeply as well as the lives of others. They will often tell us that it was like becoming one with God or becoming one with an amazingly beautiful power that worked through them or was channelled through them effortlessly. It's like being touched by the divine and enjoying every minute of it. I've experienced this so many times that I just have to continue expressing my creativity through my natural inclinations.

In order to create and manifest we need to be awake and aware, powerful and wise. Initiation, I believe, is the key to fast-tracking our progress from being asleep to drowsy to a fully awakened state. The

Essenes have a credo: 'Give healing to the sleeping, awaken the drowsy and initiate the awakened'.

Initiation

'Very few, only a handful in each country, are prepared to take the secret Path to self-mastery. Only the Few will search deeper than the narrow margin of investigation which merely brings comfort to some thwarted aspect of the personality. We search only long enough or deeply enough to find some balm for the wounds we have received from the slings and arrows of outrageous fortune or for the pangs of despised love. Too many use the occult as a sop for frustration at a personality level. But there are some who do not lose themselves in the savannah of person-ality which surrounds the deep forest of all wisdom. There are some who tread so deeply into the unknown, into the occult, that they no longer look for comfort and indeed could not turn back if they wished. For them there is only the Path and their personality interests become sub-merged in the more poignant anguish of treading an ever-steepening and narrowing pathway to the summit of the mountain of initiation. To the likes of these, the few are given the powers of synthesis and for them was written the Secret Doctrine, was fashioned the psychology of the Seven Rays.'

DR DOUGLAS BAKER FROM *THE SEVEN RAYS KEYS TO THE MYSTERIES*

At Alchemical Level 3, having made the choice to separate, we are ready to think of ourselves as initiates. On my journey, I learned that most spiritual traditions use ritual initiation to stimulate the awakening of their students. In fact, I have been taught (and through experience have come to believe) that initiation is the chosen method to elevate consciousness upon this planet. In effective initiation, the initiator connects with and embodies high spiritual energies and then channels them into the aspirant, the student who aspires to divine wisdom. If prepared to receive these energies, the aspirant will experience, at least for a short time, a state of enlightenment and personal evolution beyond what he or she has yet attained. This experience serves as a guiding light to inspire the contender to carry on with his spiritual work. More importantly, this experience initiates. It brings the spiritual forces to bear upon the consciousness of the aspirant. These energies speed his or her spiritual unfoldment, much as a hothouse speeds the growth of plants.

Initiations aren't always part of a formal sacred ritual aligned to some religious sect or secret society – more usually they are the result of higher, invisible 'formless' energies or some kind of divine intelligence teaching us about life, offering the opportunity to grow and become authentically powerful.

At first, we don't always feel powerful enough to change or grow, but at least we can begin to discover just how afraid and unhappy we truly are, trapped in a rut. That's a good start. Later as I became more conscious and aware on my own path of self-discovery, I was to learn that life is actually a series of initiations.

'Many are called and few are chosen' is a phrase from the Bible that kept coming to mind when I considered initiation. I didn't know what that meant previously. Now I realize that we are all called to reconnect to spirit when we experience some kind of awakening (initiation), but not all of us choose to respond to it. In fact only a courageous few take action to change and actually become spiritual.

Each and every one of us has at least one life changing event, be it the death of a loved one, divorce, redundancy or something that causes the personality to meet the spirit, and at this time we are given the opportunity to choose which voice we are going to listen to in order to live the second part of our life in a much bolder more powerful way, embracing greatness.

When we choose spirit we will find an unfoldment of a life much greater than we could have anticipated, which we definitely, in the ordinary scheme of things, didn't see coming or dream could ever be possible. Loss, pain and suffering are, therefore, ultimately gifts. They put us back in touch with others and their pain and loss and suffering. That's where our greatness is. Martin Luther King said, 'We are prone to judge success by the index of our salaries or the size of our automobiles rather than by the quality of our service and relationship to mankind.' Greatness isn't fame and fortune. True greatness is serving others.

Spiritually, I learned that initiation means transformation through purification of the mind, the emotions and the body – lead into gold is a most apt metaphor. Specific initiations occur at specific stages in the alchemical levels.

Initiations are tests of self-mastery on the alchemical path, which lead us out of bondage and into liberation. Throughout our history, steps and tests of physical, mental, emotional and spiritual progress have been called initiations. This is true most especially in the 'Mystery Schools'. These schools are the higher orders of learning established by and for the high elite inside normal religions. For instance, the mystery school of Judaism is Qabalah. Sufi is the Mystery School of Islam, the Gnostics are the keepers of the mysteries of the true higher Christ consciousness teachings. However, the early Catholic Church forbade Gnosticism, excised most of the Gnosis from the Bible, disbanded groups of Gnostics and had any further followers of Gnosticism, let us politely say, disappear.

There are three levels of religious teachings. I'll use Judaism as an example. In Judaism, the outermost level of religious belief and practice is embodied in the Torah, the five books of the law at the start of the Old Testament. This level is for people who can read (or hear), believe and follow the rules. These beliefs made a working social life, civilization, possible for the Jewish people. But this is not enough for all. Thinkers want to know why they should follow the rules. In Judaism, the thinkers study the Talmud, a series of learned interpretations of the Torah. Here they learn, for example, that they shouldn't kill because 'As you sow, so shall you reap', the law of action and reaction applied to morals and ethics.

And there is another level of religious person. These are the people who aren't satisfied to read of another's experience of God on the mountain, or by knowing how and why the laws work. These people desire to experience

God for themselves. These people are sometimes referred to as mystics. They seek the mystical experience of personal contact with 'the ground of all being', with what I call Source. These are the people who seek and treasure experiences of true initiation.

Seldom does the main body of the religion regard these people as more than madmen, at least while they are alive. After death, they may become officially holy or be canonized as saints. But while they are alive, they are most often a disruption, an embarrassment for the official temple, mosque or church.

Unfortunately, the orthodox leaders of the three main world religions generally find their own mystics and mystical teachings unacceptable and disruptive. The leaders of orthodox religions generally prefer that only they seek personal contact with deity. They believe that the congregation shouldn't even attempt it. Perhaps their motivation is to prevent individuals from being overwhelmed by direct contact with deity. More likely, they prefer to keep a monopoly upon contact with the divine. Their doctrine is if we wish to know what God (best self) desires for us, we have to join the church, mosque or temple, submit to their rules and give them our energy and our money.

The orthodoxy often regards the teachings of their mystics as blasphemous and even dangerous to those who practise them.

In terms of the alchemical path mapped out within this book, initiation refers to embracing a new way of living, becoming a conscious expression of our higher spiritual selves. This means we change our personality beliefs and limited expectations to integrate the higher spiritual values as we begin to learn them.

Initiation is much more than acquiring spiritual knowledge. In its fullest sense it's about understanding, exemplifying and living these new spiritual principles. This means hard work in a more down-to-earth manner to change false and rigid core beliefs and ego-control patterns. However, powerful tools exist to bring about this purification.

Once we learn how to strengthen the physical, mental, emotional and spiritual bodies, change can be accomplished more easily. Initiations must be passed, mastered and integrated in all our lower bodies (physical, mental, emotional and spiritual.) Many people prefer to ignore the more down-to-earth work of psychological healing, including the embracing of the shadow. This is because it appears to be mundane compared to the more glamorous mystical practices.

As the circle of life continuously turns for us all on this earth, no one can escape the lessons of initiation. Everything in life is about initiation and everyone is dying to some aspect of the personality self every day. Here are the basic initiations that we need to complete successfully in order to ascend or become enlightened. Remember, every minute detail of our daily lives is an opportunity to demonstrate mastery on the path of enlightenment.

At Level 1 of initiation, we learn to purify our physical body and to balance work, rest and play. At this first level, the challenge is to resolve and rise above basic survival issues. It's time to re-examine our true needs. The relevant question to ask ourselves here is not what do we want but rather what do we need.

At Level 2 of initiation, we purify our emotions. Buddha taught that all suffering results from the emotion of craving. Here we conquer craving in the form of greed for money (poverty consciousness) and lust (sexual desire).

At Level 3 of initiation, we work on the purification of our thinking. Thoughts blended with emotions create feelings. At this stage, our work is to recognize and correct our fear-based thoughts and feelings. Unless resolved, these can cause self-doubt and self-sabotage. A basic issue to confront and resolve at this level is any desire to control or dominate others. We learn to use personal power with integrity. We also learn to stop people-pleasing, being a doormat and giving away our power to others.

At Level 4 of initiation, we learn to master attachment. This freedom from craving or attachment is the initiation of the heart in which we trust to let go and let God. This detachment does not mean that we do not care. At this stage we learn to have strong preferences without being attached to specific outcomes.

To illustrate what I mean there is an ancient story that Tom Kenyon tells that I really love and would like to share with you.

This story is from the days of the Temple of Hathor in Egypt and is about an initiate who goes to the masters and says he's ready to initiate to the bliss, love and ecstasy levels. The priests and priestesses send him away to the underworld saying he is not ready. Nevertheless this person is very cunning and sly... he keeps coming back in different disguises, but the priests and priestesses recognize him and each time they turn him away directing him to the underworld. Yet he refuses to enter the underworld and learn the very lessons which would have eventually earned him his heart's desire. The point of this legend is that we cannot bypass our own underworld. I think this is what the great teacher Hariharananda Paramahamsa was referring to when he said, 'If you put nectar in a poisonous cup, you get poison'.

We must be prepared to descend into the deepest darkest recesses of our own unconsciousness before seeking the higher spiritual mysteries. We must understand that the higher we go in consciousness, along the path of the soul, then the harder we must work on transcending ego, shadow, persona to remain in balance. If we go too high in consciousness without balancing the hidden depths of our shadow worlds, including our own unconsciousness, then we are unbalanced, out of harmony with spirit and potentially dangerous. Why is this so? Because then we are acting without true awareness of vitally important aspects of ourselves that exist in our own underworld – those aspects that are not evolved, such as anger, hatred, fear, lust, jealousy, our fantasies and even our death wishes. All these things that we resist and deny and try to keep out of awareness are part of our human nature. When we begin to reconnect to best self our job is to integrate and to heal all levels of our experience. Remember Darth Vader? Vader achieves wholeness. He is the greatest ever Jedi warrior, who succumbs to temptation, falls to the darkness and all its glamour and vices, but then chooses to return to the light. This is wholeness.

Shamanic initiation

A tradition that has helped me further along the path of initiation is that of shamanism, the oldest and most widespread of all traditions. From walking the path of the shaman, I came to learn that as each lesson of initiation is learned, we die to that old aspect of ourselves. The ego or shadow side of the self is constantly forced to die again and again. These deaths are generally not as horrific or terrifying as my own dramatic 'physical death' experiences. Furthermore, they occur every day. Eg. when we choose to give up chocolate, the part of us that craves and loves chocolate – uses it as a temporary crutch to feel love, must die. As we become conscious and choose to expand our spiritual nature fully by means of the path of initiation, we gradually die to all our bad habits, negative thoughts, fears, doubts… More simply, I call all these unregenerate aspects of ourselves 'the negative ego'. Remember: God equals man minus ego.

In authentic shamanic training, we undergo all sorts of gruesome death rituals where we are forced to endure incredible humiliation, degradation and fear nearly beyond human endurance! The idea behind this is incredibly clever. When a person succeeds in transcending the fear of these insane and horrific ordeals, our mental body energy is powerfully strengthened. Then, in this empowered state, our minds can no longer be deluded by our own negative ego or worse still, by external forces of imbalance (demons) in the lower psychic regions. Similarly, we become immune to people who are controlled by dark energies who seek dominion over everyone and everything.

English philosopher Edmund Burke said, 'The only thing necessary for the triumph [of evil] is for good men to do nothing.' Our best protection is to realize that indeed negative ego, demons and evil people do exist. To pretend that forces of imbalance do not exist and to fail to use adequate protection is foolhardy indeed. Psychic attack is not only projected by great powers of evil. It can emanate from anyone who is ruled by negative ego and is still unconscious of the power of their own negative thoughts, words and feelings. This occurs, for example, when anyone is aggressive and judgemental towards others. We are indeed now beginning to see where this is all leading and why it is so vital that we embrace ancient spiritual wisdoms to strengthen and protect ourselves.

Here is an example of initiation from Mother Nature: let's consider the pain-filled process of the life of a seed. First of all, it's a seed and it's perfect. Then someone comes along with some water. The seed swells up and bursts open. If nourishment and light are present, it grows and changes into something different, something equally perfect, a flower. Then it dies and changes again to something equally perfect but different. Its spirit nourishes the earth.

The process of the growth of a seed can be likened to the spiritual unfoldment of human beings. Before I had energy mastery skills and spiritual wisdom, the matrix told me I was already perfect and that's all there was. Then life watered me with new nourishment. I wondered how I had ever felt so perfect knowing and experiencing so little of my real self. We all need to tune into nature as often as we can, watch seeds growing, seasons changing, and learn from the spirit of everything. Learn how to be at one with all that is. As we re-enter the universal flow, we begin to grow. We realize that change is all there is. Nothing remains unchanged. This is how we evolve. It's such a simple truth, but not always an easy one.

A series of shamanic deaths must be experienced and conquered at the start of this path. This is where we learn about protection, discernment and strengthening self. Normally these battles are fought with the help of gifted healers and shamans, rather than my somewhat solitary process. The finest shamans in our world today are those repaired 'wounded' healers who have walked the path of death and rebirth, destroying all the shadows that block inner clarity. Once a person has experienced and triumphed on this hard-fought road to wholeness and wellness, it becomes easy to assist others in doing the same. Having recognized and healed the darkness within ourselves, it becomes simple to see this darkness in others and diagnose it accurately. This has been my path. My willingness to confront 'anything' in myself that did not and does not serve the highest good, and my willingness to go through the cleansing process daily is my greatest gift and the one that I now lovingly share with everyone in my workshops, events and one-to-one sessions.

12 Step Fellowship Teaching

It's apparent for all to see from this story how important it is to free ourselves from the socializing influences to which we have been subjected. Yet in order to ignite our desire for freedom into a blazing fire of truth, we have to undergo a long process of transformation. Many of the tools for transformation I learned came from '12 Step Fellowship' teachings originally the work of famous recovered alcoholic and attorney, Bill W.

This 12-step programme is a process of personal transformation in which we are able to change our negative feelings about life into positive feelings. Remember it's not what people say or do to us that hurts us, it's our attitude to what they say and do. It's the same with life in general. My own personal experience on working with this 12-step programme was that I progressed through four stages of growth on what I now realize is a journey of the soul.

Unconscious incompetence

This is characterized by our actions under the influence of our obsessions, compulsions and attachments. Here we are very much in 'victim consciousness' taking everything personally, blaming others and being in a negative emotional state most of the time.

Conscious incompetence

This is characterized by the beginnings of reconnection to spirit, what I term loosely as best self. This is when we discover that our primary obsession, compulsion, addiction or attachment was not the only problem we had. Here we are beginning to connect to higher aspects of self and discover God, Great Mystery, Source, but we are still fairly negative and blaming in our patterns of behaviour.

Conscious competence

This is characterized by continued and consistent efforts to incorporate spiritual integration into our daily lives. Here we begin to experience self-responsibility and self-acceptance. We begin to work through and transform negative emotions into positive feelings with no blaming. By identifying old negative habitual patterning we can substitute more positive patterns.

Unconscious competence

This is characterized by our ability to practise integrated spirituality and all its principles without thought or effort. This leads to harmony and empowerment, where although we can see external negativity in life around us, we are unaffected by it. Now we are living in positive emotions all the time. This is self-mastery. This is also heaven on earth. We do begin to experience this fairly consistently at Alchemical Level 4, which is Christ consciousness.

Moving from unconscious incompetence to conscious competence requires humility, self-honesty, dedication and commitment to higher ideals and values, and a spiritual way of life through learning the process of co-creation. Moving into unconscious competence and staying there requires weeks, months and years of practice, acting 'as if' and practising devotion. Eventually, practice and acting 'as if' suddenly becomes being. Then you are 'there' and you are creating heaven on earth in moment-to-moment conscious awareness.

But, how do we get there?

'Rock bottom is good solid ground, and a dead end street is just a place to turn around.'

BUDDY BUIE AND JR COBB *ROCK BOTTOM*

Initially we surrender and admit that our lives aren't working, that we are powerless over our own particular set of habitual, negative life behaviour patterns. These might be, for example, co-dependency on people, substances, food, compulsive shopping, gambling, overworking, overachieving, over-exercising, excessive risk taking, or whatever. We realize that our lives have become blocked, hopeless, unmanageable and unfulfilled. In this first step, we surrender all our personal power. Personal power is what I call negative ego. Surrender goes against all we believe. Normally it seems to be easier to surrender when we are hopeless and at rock bottom. As soon as we admit that our lives haven't worked out so far, along the lines we have lived them by society's rules, we experience a sense of relief, followed by mild excitement. We are ready to commit to restructuring our lives in a more positive way. We will experience more joy, peace and love in our lives. However, you don't have to hit rock bottom in order to be successful in this process. Some people can surrender through a gradual process and still experience great transformation.

Reconnecting to spirit

All of us in separation from best self (spirit) have spent most of our lives in negative dependencies and in denial of them, too. Whenever we give our power away to the negative ego in order to fix ourselves, we are 'worshipping false gods'. These false gods could be money, sex, jobs, education, relationships, food, drugs, etc., or anything we thought would bring us happiness. Yet there is an authentic power in the universe we can align ourselves with and could turn our lives over to for higher guidance. This is reconnecting to spirit. This moves us away from the hopelessness, pain and despair of the first step towards the possibility of a solution. This brings in spirituality – the part of a human being, which is the essence, the life-force, or the intuitive best self.

Transformation takes place when we can access this personal power within ourselves permanently. The power that needs to be found is spirit and our job is to search diligently for best self, best self beliefs, attitudes and behaviours that invoke spirit. The 'coming to believe' is a process and can sometimes be a long one. But getting plugged in to Source really does change a person's perspective, especially when we practise Reiki energy mastery to self-heal and balance our energy system daily.

It is easy to determine if a person has reconnected to spirit. There seems to be an unshakeable sense of peace and contentment, an ability to accept what is happening around us without judging or needing to be the victim of life's hardships. When we finally reconnect to spirit, we have access to our own wisdom, compassion and oneness with each other. This is the crossroads where reforming old ideas really begins. In short we surrender our false gods, find power within by reconnecting to spirit, and commit to a new way that will restore right thinking. Then, even when we become challenged by life and suffer setbacks, we no longer focus on the negative or similar past negatives. We no longer feel ourselves to be victims of circumstance. We can turn the negative past experience into a powerful teaching resource to empower us. Then, current negative experiences can be viewed as a teaching to test our new-found wisdom. And remember:

'Wisdom is knowing what to do next; virtue is doing it.'
DAVID STAR JORDAN, *THE PHILOSOPHY OF DESPAIR*

In our life story we commit to examining our beliefs and ideas. As we evaluate these we begin to know who we are and who we are not! At Alchemical Level 3 we commit to changing our past thoughts and actions. Intuitive perceptions become possible and productive. We now commit, take action, and find out something we had never realized. We are all spiritual beings here in a physical body to enjoy a physical experience and grow. All that is required of us is to commit to our own values. Normally, these are values we have had all our lives; to which we have given lip service but never actually tried. We take the opportunity to become honest rather than being honest when it suits us. We become loving, patient and tolerant rather than just saying we would like to be that way and continuing in the way we have always been. This step is really where we begin the change from reforming to transforming. This is where effective living truly begins. In short, we transform ourselves to embrace more spiritual values. We live a spiritual life, in service to higher ideals and for the greatest good of the whole – not just self. We awaken and learn to develop total spiritual integrity.

The first part of awakening spiritual integrity is to find out what needs to be changed. Alchemical Level 3 is designed to allow us to outline a character profile of our old self. We list all of our self-defeating ideas, which produced beliefs that created the reality which 'didn't work' in the past or in some cases brought us to our knees. We examine a written account of our whole life to date with regard to areas of resentments, behaviour in our most intimate relationships and fears, all of which have caused us to wear masks or adopt destructive or non-productive behaviour patterns. We honestly examine the harms that we have done to others or even to ourselves, which perhaps do not fall into any of these categories. We find out what has motivated us in the past to act, feel and think the way we have (in a less than spiritual way). Through this process, we discover our defects of character. Then, almost invariably, we find that pride and selfishness are the roots of all our problems. (I realize that fear is the strongest negative emotional force, but the cause of our fears is generally pride or selfishness.) We now accept responsibility, stop blaming and move into conscious competence. We can also write a list of character qualities too. Nobody consists of just their defects. This will help us to create a new balance and to fill the two vital prerequisites for awakening spiritual integrity – 'Know thyself' and 'Nothing in excess'.

We are here to save far more than ourselves. We are all here for a divine purpose. Life becomes much easier when we have faith in concepts such as these – when we believe in a sacred life contract. Then we can tell ourselves, 'I have purpose and by connecting to spirit I am remembering this purpose. I live it as best I know how and life will take care of itself!' Take a look at nature, you don't see birds flying around with stress and tension worrying about worms and paying for nests. They trust in the universe and know that all their needs will be met. By reconnecting to spirit and discovering our sacred life contract, the daily business of living becomes free and easier. Then synchronicities start to occur and guide us. It starts with a tiny inkling that there is something sacred in everything. Then we begin to search. A day-by-day process commences, revealing more synchronicities. Then we begin to just see without searching. Revelatory experiences shift our consciousness and suddenly we don't recognize the powerful person we have become. We reconnect to spirit.

Ultimately, in its purest form, Reiki –on a daily basis – greatly assists to fast-track and create within us simultaneously spiritual evolution and spiritual involution.

Prayer is talking to God. Meditation is listening to God. Reiki is becoming and being God.

WISDOM

The Hopi path: soul versus ego

The path of the spirit versus the path of destruction

The Hopi have a prophecy, preserved in the form of a picture carved in the prophecy rock of Oraibi. The city of Old Oraibi in Hotevilla, Arizona, is believed to be the oldest continuously inhabited settlement in the US, occupied since as early as AD 1150. The prophecy concerns two possible outcomes for the human race. The Hopi say that the meaning of this petroglyph is very clear: either humanity will follow the Path of Spirit or the Path of Destruction.

The Hopi told us what action we need to take… They left us a map carved in stone.

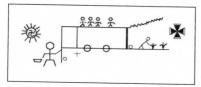 In the *owa'veni*, the rock writing or petroglyph, the Great Spirit is the large human figure to the left. His left hand is putting down a bow,

symbolizing the instruction from the Great Spirit to the Hopi to put down their weapons. In his right hand is the reed through which, according to Hopi legend, humanity entered this, the fourth world that the Great Spirit has created.

After entering this world, each member of humanity chose either one of two paths. The upper path represents the path of materialism. The four people on it have their heads separated from and floating above their bodies. This symbolizes that they are separated from their spirituality and live 'in their heads alone'. The line they are on turns into a diagonal zigzag line rising up and ending nowhere. The lower line remains horizontal and strong. The Indian upon it to the right is tending his corn, and lives a long, healthy and fruitful life. This line is said to go on forever.

The Hopi say that humanity has the chance to try out both lines and go back and forth between them along the vertical lines in the diagram. However, there comes a time symbolized by the last vertical line at which point the irrevocable choice is made. Either one goes on the upper path of comfort, profit and greed, or one chooses the lower path of the soul, the path of love, strength and balance.

The prophecy says that there will be three 'great shakings'. Hopi elders say the first two world wars are the first two of these. Some believe that the symbols on the prophecy rock of the swastika (Germany) and the red sun (Japan) refer to the perpetrators of these two wars.

The two circles on the lower line represent the first two shakings – the two world wars. After the last vertical line, there is a small circle that represents the great purification. The nature of this third shaking remains a mystery but the Hopi say it will involve a great dividing of the good from the bad. They say that how it appears upon the earth and its outcome will depend upon how we are living.

The prophecies also say that just before the great purification there will be many signs. These include trees dying, man building a house in the sky, major changes of climate, earthquakes and famine. Many consider that we are very near the time of purification. We must choose which path we are on. So which path will we choose and what are the tools and understandings we need to support our choice to separate from the path of ego, comfort, profit and greed?

The record-breaking extremes of nature witnessed in our world today suggest to the Hopi that the time of purification is upon us. The severity of our cleansing is being determined, as our individual responses to life challenges create the collective outcome. The nature of the prophesied third shaking 'will depend on which path humankind will walk: the greed, the comfort and the profit; or the path of love, strength and balance', i.e. the path of the soul. This petroglyph illustrates how important it is that we recognize the difference between the path of comfort, profit and greed versus the path of the soul.

The Hopi leave us with a message of hope. Their vision of our future concludes by admonishing us to be responsible in the way we use the powers of our bodies and our machines.

Rejecting comfort, profit and greed and embracing the path of the soul
When my self-medication with drugs and alcohol had escalated and was totally beyond my control, I was like a time bomb waiting to explode. My health was deteriorating rapidly and I would have seizures quite frequently from all the brain damage. Little did I realize that the impending loss of life was also to bring great opportunities for growth and transformation. Without realizing it, I was on a collision course with my higher destiny and a return to what the Hopi call 'the path of the spirit'. This is the path where love, strength and balance replace comfort, profit and greed – 'the path of destruction'. Unwittingly, I was soon to discover, as the master of my own destruction, I was also evoking my own salvation.

Much later, I was able to identify that I was unconsciously running the archetypal pattern of the 'Destroyer'. This dark and dangerous archetype ultimately heals us if we are strong and humble enough and brave enough to suffer the total destruction of ego and all it has mis-created in our lives. If we are willing to surrender, accept and co-operate with pain in all its guises, alchemy can occur. Rebirth is possible and what is reborn is always better than what died or was lost. Thus the Destroyer is alchemised in the transformational cauldron of our lives, transcends and then becomes the Change-Maker. We find the courage to change. When we know better, we do better; we become better and our world becomes better.

The other gift I was given by virtue of my addiction concerned losing everything. Addiction caused me to isolate and turn away from everything and everyone. Initially I suffered and was deeply hurt to lose so much financial and social status. The self-imposed material sacrifices, such as selling diamonds for drugs and then homes for drugs, didn't come easily. Yet each time I lost something, or someone, I was able to go within and feel if this job/ person/ thing had any real value in my life. Usually to my surprise it didn't. It meant nothing.

Addiction was a powerful teacher in that it enabled me to destroy my attachment to everything superficial and inappropriate that my personality had created as a result of social brainwashing and cultural programming. Eventually, in total humility, with a blank canvas, from absolutely nothing, I was able to begin life with new higher values and to start to embrace 'the path of the spirit'. I was being called to learn the true meaning of the word sacrifice, which is to make sacred all my relationships especially to money, love, sex and power, etc. I was being called to learn to create from recon-nection to spirit with an evolved ego in harmony with love, strength and balance. I chose spirit and to live in spiritual integrity. I always laugh when I hear the spiritual saying, 'Out of chaos comes order'. Yet I know this is perfectly true and so will we all if we are brave enough to go within and clear away our own programming, identify and transcend our own denials and fragmentation, projection and blaming. For sure there's a lot to lose, but it's always opportunity disguised as loss.

The sad thing I finally learned about the addict generally is that of all the personalities, he or she is the one most in need of love, yet by virtue of their behaviour is most unlovable. Normally addicts have to lie, cheat and steal to both feed and conceal their habit. This is hardly socially endearing and I was no exception to this terrible behaviour. The only way I was able to overcome all the shame about less than optimal behaviour in addiction, was that whenever I felt overwhelmed with self disgust or despair about my past, I'd say to myself, 'Today, I, Susan Anthony, no longer lie, cheat or steal. I am honest and trustworthy!' And then I'd allow myself to move into a profound state of gratitude for all the good character aspects still unfolding. It works – try it.

Cherokee teaching

Something that really helped me to understand the simplicity of what I needed to master in order to free my mind came to me from another Native American Indian teaching:

The story of two wolves

One evening an old Cherokee told his grandson about a battle that was going on inside him. He said, 'My son, it is between two wolves. One is Evil: anger, envy, sorrow, regret, greed, arrogance, self-pity, guilt, resentment, inferiority, lies, false pride, superiority and ego. The other is Good: joy, peace, love, hope, serenity, humility, kindness, benevolence, empathy, generosity, truth, compassion and faith.' The grandson thought about it for a minute and then asked his grandfather, 'Which wolf wins?' The old Cherokee simply replied, 'The one I feed'.

Clearly, such traditions recognize a direct relationship between the way we address the challenges of our world each day and the kind of world we experience in our future. The chaos of change is our opportunity to refine our beliefs, honouring the portions that work, and gracefully releasing those that may no longer serve us. It is our new, finely honed worldview of the present that will carry us gracefully through the times of future challenge.

Shamanic death

Traditional shamans undergo what they call shamanic death. Drums, chanting, rattles, dancing about the sacred fire, soul retrieval, stalking and shape shifting – these images jangle when we juxtapose them against the complexity of our information technology age. As we move now through the 21st century, shamanism will become increasingly important. It is the shaman who understands and uses the inner senses, and positively affects daily life through navigating the various dimensions beyond the physical universe. Through developing multi-sensory awareness and using these inner skills, we too can enter those worlds of extra-ordinary reality, alter the course of events on those inner levels of consciousness, and thereby change the outer reality of our lives forever.

The successful 21st century shaman will have learned and mastered the skills needed to receive and use intuition, imagination and creativity. As we increase our personal awareness of self and the worlds around us, especially the higher worlds, we become the spiritual warrior/adventurer of the future. This is what I teach. To do so, I initiate my students to crystal, plant, tree and animal power totems; the spirit medicine guides from Pan's nature kingdoms. I thereby lead participants on a journey into non-ordinary reality. There, they learn to create new realities in all their environments – work, family and play – and increase their self-awareness.

As the circle of life continuously turns for us all on this earth, no one can escape the lessons of initiation. Everything in life is about initiation and everyone is dying to some aspect of the personality self every day. I first came across this concept or this particular type of consciousness for spiritual growth in 1992 after my first near death experience, when I was blessed enough to be guided to meet Dr Credo Mutwa, spiritual leader of the Zulu Tribe in South Africa. Credo is a Sanussi – which is beyond even the rank of 'shaman'. It's a kind of 'King of the Shamans'. He gave me a new, shamanic name – Bonisiwe – which means 'The One Who has been Shown'. And this is the poem he gave me:

To thee, woman, to whom the star-gods came
Borne on bright wings across the deeps of space
This is my prayer and this my fervent wish

That you see more, more mysteries of the worlds
And know the wonders that our eyes have known

DR CREDO MUTWA – MARCH 1993

Subsequently, I came to study the enlightenment path with various teachers in the US. I was amazed to learn that they use very similar reference points, creation stories, hidden mysteries and paths of initiation that I learned from Credo.

The amazing thing is that all these teachers felt familiar, although I had never heard of any of them nor had I ever met any of them before. Yet when we did meet for the first time, there was always some kind of recognition on a universal level. At last I was meeting my true family – kindred spirits and companions of destiny. The guidance I received within was to let go of my biological family to some extent, because they couldn't understand the new path I was taking and I knew that any attachments there would hold me back and confuse them unnecessarily.

Biblical teachings

In Luke Chapter 12, Jesus the Nazarene, the Christ, says: 'Do you think I came to bring peace on earth? No, I tell you, but division... They will be divided, father against son and son against father, mother against daughter and daughter against mother...' Initially, we may have to take leave from some members of our family. If this happens to you take comfort in this. I remember it helped me to know that my physical family are my family in the physical world, but my true family exists in powerful hidden worlds and in awakened others, true companions of destiny, helping me to face my fears and live my dreams to miraculously turn the lead of personality into spiritual gold.

And just how exactly do we create a miracle?

The twelve conditions of a miracle

'There are only two ways to live your life. One is as though nothing is

a miracle. The other is as though everything is a miracle.'

ALBERT EINSTEIN

I am realistic and I have come to expect miracles, so they happen. Miracles are only right-brain technologies and I am learning to master the right brain. What I have discovered is that where there is greatest love, there are always miracles. Miracles are not contrary to nature, but only contrary to what we know about nature…

In his book, *The Twelve Conditions of a Miracle*, Dr Michael Abrams retranslated portions of the Bible. Working with the original ancient Greek, he discovered layers of information that had not been revealed in contemporary translations. He believes that the author of the original composition embedded a subtext within the subtleties of the Greek language that tells us the techniques for manifesting miracles. It is found in the Gospel according to St Matthew.

The first condition is Emptiness. It involves establishing a condition of stillness, a vacuum. Nature rushes to fill a void. A vacuum is a very special situation. Because it is empty, it possesses the tremendous potential to be filled. Like a magnet, a vacuum exerts a force that pulls things inexorably towards it. The less a vacuum contains, the emptier it is and the more powerful the attractive force it exerts on the surrounding world. This is why learning to practise mindfulness is so important.

The second condition is Alignment. This means getting our own lives and intentions to move in the same direction as the universe. This means swimming with the current to its final destination. We need to evaluate our dream in terms of whether it will harm us or hinder our progress to a state of compassion. Then we must adjust our course – shift our goals so that we are in alignment with the flow of the universe, even or especially if this means swimming against the current of the masses.

The third condition involves Asking. If we know what we really desire, and how to ask for it, the universe will fulfil our request with startling accuracy. Never attempt to ask for anything that is not organically connected to a higher purpose.

The fourth condition involves Maximizing. Expansion of the food that fed the multitude is an expansion of what already exists, not materialization from nothing. The universe is very careful. It hates waste. Those who use its precious energy with appropriate gratitude and care are invariably rewarded. Conversely, if we don't use our gifts, we can expect to lose them.

The fifth condition involves Giving. The act of giving relieves congestion and stimulates the flow and increase of resources. This is why to tithe (give) is so crucially important. Whatever we give freely is returned to us ten fold.

The sixth condition involves Grounding, at a physical and metaphysical level. As in electrical power, if a circuit is not grounded, currents cannot flow through it. The power of the current that flows through us will be directly proportional to the strength of our conviction and our connection to Mother Earth. This is why our daily self-healing practice with Reiki is so important because it helps us to create, empower and maintain our connection to the earth.

The seventh condition involves Seeing or Visualizing. Unless the desired end is clearly felt, visualized and seen, it cannot be reached. Even as 'the worst' transpires in livid detail before our very eyes, it is an important part of our whole purpose as human beings to learn how to see 'the best'. That is one of our greatest and most important tasks as humans.

The eighth condition is Gratitude. When a human being is in a state of true gratitude, the fabric of time and space is favourably altered. Divine intelligence generally won't go too far out of its way to provide for us in a miraculous way if we are negative and complacent about the gifts we have already received.

The ninth condition involves Acting As If. I sometimes call this 'Fake it to Make it!' A person enacting a miracle acts as if the miracle has already occurred. Jesus didn't wait for the bread and fish to multiply – he began to feed the people with what he had. Spirit helps those who help themselves. The universe funnels its energy into the lives of those who take action, those who work, those who make an effort to actually get things accomplished.

The tenth condition involves Engaging the Cycle. Energy flows in a cycle or circuit throughout the universe, from the microscopic to the astronomical plane. Only when a person works with a circularity of flow can miracles occur. What goes around comes around. Every enlightened person in history has tried to tell us that we receive as we give.

The eleventh condition is Receiving. Often we believe that receiving or accepting what the universe gives may be the easiest part, but often it is the most undeveloped aspect of our evolution. It is about being totally open to what is going to happen. Being ready and willing to accept the flow that comes towards us and enjoying it and being totally conscious of it when it comes. Remember, spirit abhors a vacuum. As soon as we prepare an empty container to receive, the universe will automatically begin mobilizing to fill it.

The twelfth condition is Recycling. When all of the people had eaten and were finished, the fragments were not left on the ground, but were gathered and recycled. Throughout our ecological and biological systems, nature maximizes by recycling everything it possibly can.

What happens after the manifestation has crystallized is just as important as what happens before. The flow of energy must never be abandoned once the dream becomes reality. Whatever we dream we can become. Remember the poem from Goethe called Providence: 'Boldness has genius, power and magic in it. Begin it now.'

Along the way, I discovered so many miracles and so much wisdom to accelerate awakening on the Western mystical path – Qabalah was one such discovery.

The Qabalah

The word Qabalah (also spelled Kaballah and Cabala) is from the Hebrew root, *cabal* meaning 'to receive'. Qabalah means 'the reception'. The word refers to the reception of an energy that quickens the mind and enlivens the heart of the one who receives. Qabalah is the teaching of the sacred wisdom of Judaism, which is usually passed on in the oral tradition. It's interesting to note that when Qabalah is spelled with a 'Q' it means 'reception or tradition', yet when it is spelled with a 'K', it means 'confusion'.

The medieval Qabalists were disenchanted with life, seeking to build a bridge from the 'Vale of Tears' to God. They renounced the world with its snares and sought the spiritual, the hidden and the unknown. Only the 'elect' (those who were worthy) could benefit. Commentators say that Qabalah drew upon an eclectic collection of ideas: Jewish ethics, Zoroastrian dualism, Pythagorean numerology, neo-Platonic emanations and medieval asceticism. Yet these concepts can nearly all be found together in Essenism, a form of Judaism, still displaying strong Persian roots, of 2500 years ago.

Today, most Western mystery schools use the teachings of Qabalah for both instruction and for the rituals of initiation for enlightening their pupils. Why do we go to the root of Judaism for contact with Source? New dispensations do not arise out of thin air, but rather emerge from existing ones. Judaism was the matrix for the spiritual culture of the Western world. It was the only monotheistic religion available. And when you recall that Jesus was a Jew, it becomes clear that our Western religious culture does have Judaism as its root. Christianity emerged from Judaism just like Buddhism arose from the matrix of Hinduism.

This short introduction to Qabalah relates to the way the tradition is used by modern students of the mysteries. Although we won't go deeply into the traditional Qabalah of the Rabbis, a small look at its origins will enrich us.

As to the original source of Qabalah, the authorities are unanimous. The angels gave Qabalah to humankind. Before we scoff at this idea, let's look more deeply into the matter. Hebrew mysticism arose from the star worshippers of ancient Chaldea. Then a magical figure, the great priest-king Melchizedek (who was neither born nor died according to Hebrews 7:3) arrived on the scene to teach Abraham, the father of the Hebrew race.

Melchizedek initiated Abraham into the mysteries and gives him the first Eucharistic feast of bread and wine. His influence continues unabated. The Bible even says that Jesus is a priest after the order of Melchizedek (Hebrews 5:4-6).

Many of the leaders of the Hebrew race studied with the adepts of the mystery schools in Egypt, Tyre, Babylon and elsewhere. Many influences flowed into and enriched the esoteric wisdom of Israel. This adding to and expanding of the wisdom teachings continues to this day.

The Tarot and the Tree of Life are the central symbols that embody the mystery teachings of Qabalah. It is upon these that the student of the Western mysteries contemplates and meditates. The 22 major 'arcana' of the Tarot correspond precisely to the 22 paths connecting the ten spheres of the Tree of Life. Together, the 22 major keys and the 10 spheres make up the famous '32 paths of wisdom' of Qabalah.

Qabalah is truly the 'yoga of the West'. Its methods are perfectly suitable to the Western race-type and lifestyle. Eastern methods train the student to become more and more sensitive until a point is reached where the student becomes aware of the subtle divine energies. The Western mystery method is to use ritual and ceremony to intensify the divine energies to the point where we cannot help but perceive them. Then the ritual ceremony is ended and the energy levels return to normal, leaving the student able to return to his busy life and work. The ceremonies include much use of symbolism, colour, movement, spoken words and the chanting of divine and archangelic names. Through the use of such symbols, ceremony and ritual, the divine energies make a profound impression in the subconscious mind of the student and continue to work there, gradually transforming the student and awakening the divine within. Symbols instil beliefs and shape attitudes that underpin social structures. The binding force of culture, by and large, is a web of symbols that enables people to control and make sense out of experience in patterned ways.

In Qabalistic training, like the Essenes, the teacher rarely answers a student's questions directly. Instead, the teacher will tell the student a story that contains a principle of truth. The student must then apply this principle to his circumstances and thereby derive his own answer. The teachings of Qabalah do not so much inform the mind as teach the student how to think. Beyond that, they direct the student where to extend consciousness so as to eventually be able to consciously go far beyond the limitations of thought. One cannot precisely define that consciousness which is beyond thought. For those who have learned to consciously operate in that realm, no explanation is necessary. For those who haven't, none is possible.

About symbols and Qabalah
'Programmers and marketing people know how to get into your subconscious – they spend millions of dollars researching colours, shapes, designs, symbols, that affect your preferences, and they can make you feel warm, trusting, like buying. They can manipulate you.'
RICHARD HATCH

'The best leaders... almost without exception and at every level, are master users of stories and symbols.'
THOMAS J PETERS (MANAGEMENT CONSULTANT, TRAINER)

The method of Qabalah is to give the student a series of related symbols to meditate upon and think about. Gradually, the student begins to learn to 'think' in symbols while awake. The average person is only vaguely aware of doing so in dreams while asleep. The Qabalistic student learns to consciously direct a similar process to dreams, and to do so while awake. Gradually, this process guides the student into direct contact with the root of all being, with Source. It is this direct contact with Source that is the goal of the seekers. Through this process, the successful student of Qabalah learns to consciously move in realms beyond thought and thereby becomes one of those for whom no proof is necessary.

How do you recognize those in whom the 'spirit has been quickened' by contact with Source? In *Sexual Energy and Yoga*, Elisabeth Haich says, 'It is difficult to find them, for in appearance they are no different from other men, and they are recognized and understood only by those who are at the level immediately below their own, or those at similar or higher levels of purity. Others may worship them because they feel their greatness, but they cannot understand them. Some even hate them because they feel their greatness and imperviousness to all temptation, and therefore feel inferior and insignificant beside them. And yet he who seeks God from the depths of his heart finds these men, for "by their fruits ye shall know them..." (Matt. 7:20).'

For those who are ripe for spiritual awakening, being in personal contact with those who are already in contact with Source is infectious. The 'awakened' have a peculiar enthusiasm and vitality that makes them very charismatic. Being in their presence is a truly magical experience. There is a no-nonsense style about them that gets to the root of any matter directly. The energy of their presence is often quite like a breath of fresh air or a splash of cold water in the face. It startles and awakens. However, it will also energize and stir up any immature behavioural patterns in the student. Unresolved problems of character will be magnified, often to the chagrin of the student. Under the impact of the presence of one who has more direct contact with Source, the student is put into a kind of spiritual hot-house and will be forced to spiritually 'grow-up' far more swiftly than otherwise. This is exactly what's happening in my own spiritual community just outside Glastonbury.

Gnosticism

'If you bring forth what is within you, what you bring forth will save you. If you do not bring forth what is within you, what you do not bring forth will destroy you.'

GOSPEL OF THOMAS

From studying the Gnostic Gospels of Nag Hammadi and particularly the above quote, I was led to understand that we all have a divine plan and a divine spark within us, which helps us to achieve this plan. If we do the work necessary to open up to the light and love within, it will transform us and heal our karma. If we resist the unconditional love within our hearts but instead turn to darker emotions, then that negativity will become an anathema to the Christ within (our best self). To put it another way, nearly every person who goes through the near death experience and is able to remember it, finds out that God and the divine hierarchies never judge us. We are our own judges. The Christ within (best self and our own conscience) are our judges. The super-luminals showing us our karmic records radiate pure love. The divine light encompassing our souls has an innate intelligence. It cannot be fooled. There will be a reckoning some day, some lifetime, when the karmic clock runs out. Is this what's happening now, I wonder?

Esoteric Christianity (Gnosis) flourished for four centuries after Christ. The Gnosis has strong roots in the Greek and Egyptian mysteries. It was a powerful mystery teaching that attracted many followers. Seventeen hundred years ago, key elements of our most sacred heritage were taken from the texts that define our history. In AD 325, the Emperor Constantine put together the Council of Nicea. Essentially, he gathered together the historical and religious texts of his time and told the Council that because so many of the texts were redundant, confusing and too mystical to be understood, they were to come up with a condensed version. Twenty-five biblical texts were thus taken out of the references during that time and an additional 20 supporting documents, such as the alchemical book of the Secrets of Enoch, were also removed. The books that were left were rearranged and condensed, and that's what we're working with today – the Bible.

Clearly, it was the decision of the Church to do its very best to eliminate even the memory of mystical Christianity. According to Gregg Braden, we lost sight of the relationship between mankind, thought, feeling and emotion and the cosmos when the sacred texts we relied upon for our understanding were made inaccessible in the 4th century at Nicea. As a result, we became a very logic-based society, but the indigenous traditions preserved those understandings. When the Essenes left the Qumran area to escape persecution, they carried with them copies of entire libraries. Some of them went to Bolivia and Peru, and there are today active Essene monasteries in southern Peru. The Hopi and Navajo traditions also confirm these texts, and others went to the monasteries in the highlands of Tibet for safekeeping for later generations.

Hypatia and the emergence of Tarot

Hypatia, a remarkable young woman and charismatic teacher, became head of the Platonist school at Alexandria in about AD 400. There she lectured on mathematics and philosophy, in particular teaching the philosophy of Neoplatonism. Hypatia based her teachings on those of Plotinus, the founder of Neoplatonism, and Iamblichus, who was a developer of Neoplatonism around AD 300.

Plotinus taught that there is an ultimate reality, which is beyond the reach of thought or language. The object of life was to aim at this ultimate reality, which could never be precisely described. Hypatia came to symbolize learning and science in Alexandria, where she became Chief Librarian of the Libraries of Alexandria. Unfortunately, she threatened the new world order coming into being at that time of the early Christians, who identified her with paganism and labelled her a heretic. Nevertheless, among the pupils whom she taught in Alexandria there were many prominent Christians. One of the most famous is Synesius of Cyrene who was later to become the Bishop of Ptolemais. Many of the letters that Synesius wrote to Hypatia have been preserved and we see someone who was filled with admiration and reverence for Hypatia's learning and scientific abilities. In 412 Cyril (later St Cyril) became patriarch of Alexandria. Three years later, Hypatia was brutally murdered by the Nitrian monks, a fanatical sect of Christians who were supporters of Bishop Cyril. Whatever the precise motivation for the murder, the departure soon afterwards of many scholars and free thinkers marked the beginning of the decline of Alexandria as a major centre of ancient learning.

Most of the wisdom of the ancient world had been gathered together in the great Library of Alexandria. Although there is still controversy as to whether it was the Christians or the Moslems who burned the library, it is said that the burning of the books and manuscripts for six months fuelled the great baths and bakeries of Alexandria. Our spiritual history, our esoteric wisdom, was nearly eliminated. Only in this century have discoveries been made of ancient manuscripts that were hidden in caves or covered by seas since before the Christian purge. In these we find clues and treasures of true spirituality that orthodox Christianity tried so hard to destroy. The Nag Hammadi Scrolls of Egypt and the Dead Sea scrolls are examples of these recently found treasures. Below the cliffs of Nag Hammadi were found gospels of Thomas and Phillip that may predate any of the gospel versions in the Bible.

After the burning of the Library of Alexandria, a group of magi (elders or wise men) from many countries and traditions met near Alexandria in Fez, which is today in the country of Morocco. Since they spoke many different languages, communication between them was at times difficult. To solve this problem, they used the language of symbols.

Many symbols have a pre-existing meaning, independent of conscious understanding. They are to the subconscious mind what words are to the conscious mind. However, unlike words, symbols already exist and their root meaning does not need to be learned by the subconscious. To the subconscious mind, meaning is multi-faceted and global. When trying to understand a symbol with the conscious mind, one finds that its meaning changes with the reference frame. It's rather like the blind men describing an elephant. Each touches a very different part and comes up with a very different definition. Unlike words which each have discrete meanings, symbols imply and cast veils of allusion, taking on different meaning in different contexts. Like dreams, individual symbols are interconnected with others and form a field of knowing, a way of apprehending that which one does not yet comprehend.

Beyond their inherent subconscious meaning, when symbols are used by groups of people for years or even generations to embody a specific teaching, they become imbued with extra meaning. Later students with no personal instruction can, by meditating upon such symbols, retrieve the meaning that was imbued into them. This is indeed a variation on the hidden mind treasures theme in the Buddhist Sky Dancer legend.

As the Christian Church and the Moslems were systematically eliminating all their 'competition', there was a real danger that the wisdom gathered by the adepts for thousands of years of human history could have been lost forever. The magi who met in Fez devised a method to assure that their collective teachings would survive the test of the times. They embodied their wisdom in a series of combinations of symbols. They imbued meaning into the symbols with their shared meditations. This is a good example of the hidden mind treasures from the Buddhist Sky Dancer legends, brought to life. And they devised ways to use this series of pictures for games and for fortune telling. Today these pictures are the major arcana of the Tarot, the root of our modern playing cards, according to Builders of the Adytum (B.O.T.A) a highly respected international non-profit corporation based on the mystical-occult teachings and practices of the Holy Qabalah and Sacred Tarot, founded by Dr Paul Foster Case and extended by Dr Ann Davies. This noble work really resonates with me and feels intuitively familiar. I have long since learned to trust my abdominal brain and such gut feelings.

The very first Tarot key, key zero – the fool – is the joker in our modern decks of cards. Like the fool who represents the life-breath that takes form as all things, the joker is a 'wild card' that can be any other card as defined at the start of a game.

Making a game and a way to tell fortunes insured the popularity of the Tarot, which quickly spread throughout Europe. Some of the symbolism was modified so as to not arouse Church opposition. For example, in popular early Tarot decks, the name of the Hierophant (spiritual teacher, inner teacher) was changed to be 'the Pope'.

Although the Christian Church did try to stamp out all things mystical, the mystical urge exists in all and cannot be eliminated. People will always find a way to make contact with the Source of all being. Some in the Catholic Church found a way to do so through devotion. Very lovely and inspirational literature has been written by Catholic mystics. However, only a certain sort of person is attracted to the life of devotion. Having 'burned the bridges' to God, the Church is bereft of its own esoteric (hidden, secret, sacred, mystic) tradition. What a tragedy it is that the living fire that could have made the Church an instrument for the awakening of Christ consciousness in the world has been almost extinguished by the Church itself. Again, I wish to reiterate that the behaviour of the Church is not bad or wrong, merely 'incomplete.'

Because our Western esoteric tradition was nearly annihilated, many of mystical inclination in the West have attempted to adopt the methods of Eastern traditions. The East is rich with many different paths suitable to the many types of humans. However, unless you are willing to live away from the mainstream of social life and have an advanced guru to supervise your efforts, Eastern methods of spiritual awakening may do more damage than good. Many Westerners have adopted a vegetarian diet, a celibate lifestyle and breathing exercises from Eastern traditions with less than optimal results! Some become so sensitive that they cannot emotionally withstand the hustle and bustle of Western life and may experience nervous breakdowns.

The Essenes

At the time of Jesus, there were three main religious movements in Palestine. The Pharisees and the Sadducees are often spoken of in the Bible. Of the third group, the Essenes, all mention in the Bible has been excised. The mystery schools teach that when Jesus' merit was recognized, he was sent to live in the Essene community where he was trained in the esoteric lore. He is said to have lived there until he was thirty when he visited John the Baptist and began his mission openly. Whether this is exactly true or not is open to question. However, the man who wrote the Lord's Prayer knew his Qabalah. Malkuth (the Kingdom), Hod (the Power), and Netzach (the Glory) form the triangle at the bottom of the tree of life.

The Essenes were a community, a brotherhood-sisterhood that studied all religions and extracted the pure principles from them all. To them, each religion represented a different stage of revelation. They gathered all these principles into a living science. They thus became the guardians of divine teaching. They are said to have lived about 500 years before Christ and were often referred to as the Elect or Chosen Ones by the Jews.

Although they lived very simple lives in villages, there were also Essene monasteries where their initiations took place. Some of them travelled continually, spreading the word and visiting the various Essene villages and monasteries. Thus they maintained good communication throughout their greater community, which extended through many countries. To the Essenes, the soul in a human was asleep, drowsy or awake. For the sleeping, they provided assistance and succour. For example, the Essenes maintained inns where pilgrims could stop, eat, rest or sleep. These inns were located on well-travelled, main roads in a great number of locations.

Well known for the assistance they provided to those in need during difficult times, they were also known for their healing, which they offered to the rich and poor alike. They worked with plant and crystal energies (what we today refer to as 'vibrational remedies') and are said to have been able to heal diseases by chanting over the one who was ill. They were recognized by their white robes, their extreme cleanliness (washing themselves many times a day) and their laying of hands upon each others' heads to reinforce the unity and love between them.

The Essenes worked to awaken the drowsy. Although they kept their inner teachings secret and known to their initiates only, their presence was well known. They made no attempt to remain unnoticed but rather kept themselves in the public eye by the presence of their inns and their assistance to the needy. A large group of them lived just outside the walls of Jerusalem. They were often ridiculed, as is usually the case with those who are misunderstood. However, they were generally respected for their good deeds, their gentleness, their love of peace, their devotion to the poor as well as the rich, and for their excellent abilities as healers. They even had their famous 'Essene Gate' through the wall for entering and exiting Jerusalem. Many educated Jews held the Essenes in high regard as they knew that a great number of the Jewish prophets had been trained in Essene orders.

The Essenes rendered vital training and guidance to the awakened. When you were admitted into their monastery school, the process of awakening had begun. Awakened souls could apply for initiation into the mysteries. These initiations moved the student into the fast lane of spiritual unfoldment. They believed that the spiritual process so begun never stopped and even extended through all future incarnations.

PRACTICES

Personality versus soul behaviour checklist

Below is a checklist to identify spiritual attributes versus personality defects. There is no behaviour that is always wrong. There is always some extreme situation in which extreme behaviour is the best choice. Did Jesus practise compassion or turn the other cheek with the money-changers? No, in his righteous anger, he thrashed them out of the temple and told them in no uncertain terms what he thought of them. Such is the action of a true spiritual warrior. What it really all boils down to is this: are you coming from a place of love or from fear? These two are the basic emotions. All other emotions can be accurately seen as an expression of either love or fear. It can be an expression of love to be very angry, to be dissatisfied with your lot or to rebel against the status quo. It can also be an expression of fear – particularly fear of change. However, there are some general signs that your reactions are more attuned to spiritual attributes and less an expression of your personality defects. Where would you place yourself and your reactions in the following sets of opposites?

Personality Behaviour	Spiritual-Self Behaviour
Fear	Love
Blaming	Taking self-responsibility
Hatred	Love
Anger	Forgiveness, compassion
Resentment	Forgiveness
Hostility	Gentleness
Aggressive	Assertive
Stubborn	Steadfast
Doubt	Trust
Panic	Calm, equanimity
Worry	Trust
Low Self-Esteem	Self-acceptance
Self-worth defined by external objects	Self-worth defined by spiritual values
Greed	Generosity
Dissatisfaction	Contentment, satisfaction with your lot
Denial	Open and self-aware acceptance
False Pride	Humility, true pride
Arrogance	Humility
Jealousy	Detachment, understanding
Violence	Gentleness
Problems	Challenges, lessons
Stumbling Block	Stepping stone, opportunity
I win. You lose	We win
Poor me	Take responsibility
Intimidate	Wield power appropriately
Have sex	Make love
Superficial	Inner value

Bored	Engaged eagerly
Curse	Bless
Rationalize, make excuses.	Tell yourself the honest truth
Scattered	In focus
There's not enough for me (poverty)	There's enough for everyone (abundance)
Go along with (conform)	Follow your own light
Rebel against	Find your own way
Envy	Find joy in the other's success

Goal setting and affirmations – staying positive in a negative world

Today's news on the TV and in the newspapers is BAD news. News 'programmes' and articles are filled with negative information: economies on the verge of collapse, unemployment continuing to rise, family shootings, drug abuse, global climate crisis, war, terrorism, political corruption, religious corruption, corporate corruption, famine and chaos! Ordinary people are working harder than ever with less to show for it. If we listen to the news regularly, we may wonder whether or not the sky is actually falling in.

Best self always knows it is critical to maintain a positive mental outlook, no matter what's going on in the external world. So how do we develop and maintain this attitude? These are some ideas I use personally to stay positive in a negative world. I didn't learn these ideas from priests or shamans, I learned about goal setting and affirmations from high achievers in the corridors of corporate power.

Mission statement

The starting point with all high achievement is a clear sense of purpose. So our Mission Statement becomes 'a personal promise or commitment'; it describes who we are and what we are all about. The first thing I do with all of my students is to have them develop a Mission Statement, then have them commit it to memory and recite it every morning. Why? Napoleon Hill, in his classic book *Think and Grow Rich*, stated, 'Any idea, plan or purpose may be placed in the mind through repetition of thought'. Spiritual teachers use this methodology in the form of mantras and chanting to focus intentionality.

Affirmations

To become a 'legend in our own lifetime,' we must first be a legend in our own minds (and hearts). One way to ensure this is to use affirmations: a repetition of positive statements in the present tense as if they are already a fact. A simple example is to affirm, 'I am powerful, loving and courageous and I always achieve my goals!'

Goals review

There's a famous 20-year study of Harvard graduates that demonstrated the power of goal setting: researchers found that only 3% of a graduating class had clearly written goals. 20 years later they documented that this group of goal-setters had accumulated more wealth and success than the other 97% combined. This is not lost on high achievers, who commit clear goals to writing and review them regularly.

Visualization

One of the important skills taught to professional athletes is to mentally picture specific successful outcomes (i.e. the perfect golf swing) in a meditative state. So if this skill is being taught to millionaire athletes, why would it be any less effective for you? Visualize an award-winning marketing campaign, being congratulated by the CEO. Visualize the spiritual warrior, transcending ego and living Christ consciousness on earth.

Physical exercise

Spiritual warriors understand the importance of staying in shape. Just like professional athletes, the ones who make it to the top know they must keep themselves fit. And a regular and balanced exercise regimen has a multitude of benefits – it reduces stress, clears the mind, builds endurance and contributes to that 'look of a winner.' It makes no difference what form of exercise you choose, just as long as you enjoy it enough to do it 4 to 5 times a week. I'd like to recommend you to read *Making Waves*, an awe-inspiring book written by Roger Lewin, one of the top science writers in the US today. This book tells the story of Dr Irving Dardik's big new scientific theory with regard to exercise and the circadian rhythms and returning to health. Dardik is being hailed as the new Einstein by the American scientific community. (More on this in Chapter 4.)

Positive support group

Unlike magnets, likes attract. So if you choose to be your best self, start hanging out with like-minded others, rather than those locked into the matrix-type consciousness of do/have/consume. One assignment I give my students is to identify successful people on this path, then invite them to lunch to find out what they're doing. Spiritual warriors or adepts are enthusiastic to share their success stories.

It's simple to be our best selves today, but it isn't easy. We have to forget what we have learned in the matrix, dismantle the lies of ego, shadow and persona and wake up. If we can master these techniques, we will enhance our value to ourselves and our world. People who use the ideas I've described here KNOW how to stay positive in a negative world and they know how to create that which they choose to experience and how to accept loss an as opportunity in disguise.

Harness your mind

What do you choose for yourself and your family? In the short term (this year) and over the next five/ten years? Think about it when you're out walking. Talk about it with your family until your mind becomes clear and focused on what you choose. Dare to dream!

Wish list – visualization for manifestation

Write down your wish list. Write it all down. Then choose your top priority 3 to 5 items from the wish list. Write these on a card, or use your computer to create something spectacular. Read this wish list every morning and every evening, today, tomorrow, this week, next week and forever! Find a picture that captures each item on your top-five list. Add the pictures to your Wish List and pin the list in a prominent place at your office, in your bedroom, on the fridge in the kitchen, in the car... Choose places that are very visible and noticed. Show your friends who you know will encourage you and feel enthusiastic about this. Practise containment and camouflage (fox medicine) around sceptics.

Review your day before going to sleep

Review the events of the day before you go to sleep. Identify any situations in which you behaved less than optimally; in which if you could live it over, you would choose to act differently. Then strongly visualize the situation happening again in your mind's eye and act in your chosen better way. This programmes you to act optimally in similar future situations. Then, since your have already resolved the issues of the day, you can use your valuable sleep time for other things than rehashing the stresses of the day.

Essene practices

Remember that the Essenes preached and practised moderation. Avoid making drastic changes or changing any habit too swiftly. Use Essene principles to make small continual changes and gradually purify your life.

Angelic Initiation

Returning to the angel guides we mentioned in the first chapter, you may be ready now for an angelic initiation. Here's a possible outline of one for you to practise – an opening to communicate with spirit and angelic beings.

Clear and clean your space, clean yourself, light a candle and some incense. Put on some relaxing music with no words. Use some Young Living therapeutic-grade pure essential oils – on your hands and feet. Also read more about Young Living Oils in Chapter 4 and discover scientific tests which prove the efficacy of these particular oils.

Make sure you won't be disturbed for at least 30 to 60 minutes.

Intending that you are in a space of great protection, open all your receivers and transmitters, call in your guardian angel and ask to be reconnected to unity consciousness. Imagine a golden white light coming from the heart of Father Sky into your heart and then sending this ray into the heart of Mother Earth. Intend that this light is travelling through your entire endocrine system preparing you to hold greater light and accelerated frequencies of healing – the universal life-force energies. Intend that these two energies – masculine and feminine – are merging and then travelling back up into your heart where they ignite into a threefold flame of divine love, wisdom and power, connecting sky and earth to you, the magical child evolving within.

By intention, send this energy to every cell of your being, every molecule and atom, All That Is, and ask for initiation to Great Mystery so that you may serve all sentient life.

Ask your angels and universal life-force energy guides to continue to protect you and heal you in this way in ever-increasing levels daily and feel the gratitude for this overflowing in your heart... this is how we pay our guides, with loving gratitude. Give gratitude and thanks for the healing and empowerment this is bringing.

Do this daily – two or three times if possible. Notice the magical power of universal life-force energies in your life and see how much better you feel and how much more positive and magical your life becomes.

Working with animal totems

EAGLE: This spirit medicine is for soaring high with spirit above earthly matters to gain greater clarity, perspective and focus. It provides added power to transcend the mundane in order to perceive deeper truths in the heart. Eagle spirit medicine enhances spiritual and creative vision through opening to the divine at the very highest levels.

MOUNTAIN LION: The mountain lion guides us to take courage, to be bolder and braver, and to risk being a living example and walk our talk. The path of the mountain lion is the path of purposeful action. Mountain lion spirit medicine teaches us to be a leader without followers. It provides powerful support for manifesting dreams and visions. Self-confidence is greatly enhanced when working with this powerful totem.

Reiki Symbol 3

 Symbol No 3 – Hon Sha Ze Sho Nen (Karmic Absolution), pronounced 'Hon Sha Say Show Nen', is the third of the four original Reiki symbols given to Dr Usui. One of the literal translations for this symbol is 'May the Buddha in me reach out to enlighten and bless the Buddha in you'. It's related to forgiveness and clearing karma carried deep within the soul through many lifetimes. It's a symbol which when worked with regularly encourages us to align; to be of service to others and to our world.

With the third symbol, we are able to connect with the Soul or Essence of another person, place, object, situation or being. The use of this symbol enables profound healing as we remove barriers and limitations, moving from separation to Oneness.

Again, incorporate this with the Cho Ku Rei and Sei Hei Kei mantras into your daily Violet Flame Mindfulness Meditation. The results will be profound.

CHAPTER 4

TRANSFORMATION

'The greatest of all lessons is to know your Self,
for when a man knows himself he knows God.'
CLEMENT OF ALEXANDRIA, ONE OF THE GREATEST
TRUE GNOSTIC CHRISTIANS

OVERVIEW

One of my Tibetan esoteric teachers explained to me that the soul is neither spirit nor matter but is the 'relation' between them; the soul is the mediator between the duality of spirit and physical matter; it is the middle principle, the link between God and form. This really resonates with me...

Gnostics believed that in order to know God, we needed to know ourselves. This book is about the map that teaches us to know ourselves. Today most of us have forgotten who we really are, but the Gnostics clearly knew. To describe their teachings, the Gnostics used the simple symbol of the circle. The circumference of the circle symbolized the physical body or matter, which the ancients referred to as 'physis' and they called this our 'outer self'. The radius of the circle, the line from the circumference to the dot in the centre of the circle, symbolized our 'soul', sometimes also referred to as the 'psyche'. They referred to the soul or psyche as our 'inner self'. Gnostics believed that the soul was a higher level of our true identity than the physical body. Finally, the dot in the centre of the circle symbolized our true essence – what I call best self. The ancients called our essential identity 'pneuma', which means spirit.

'A Map to God' upholds the great Gnostic belief that the quest for self-knowledge is identical with the quest to know God. I believe this is how it is because when we do the work to discover best self (spirit), we discover that this is in fact God. This became clear to me when I read John Bunyan's words:

'Although I have been through all that I have, I do not regret the many hardships I met, because it was they who brought me to the place I wished to reach. Now all I have is this sword and I give it to whomever wishes to continue his pilgrimage. I carry with me the marks and scars of battles – they are the witnesses of what I suffered and the rewards of what I conquered. These are the beloved marks and scars that will open the gates of Paradise to me. There was a time when I used to listen to tales of bravery. There was a time when I lived only because I needed to live. But now I live because I am a warrior and because I wish one day to be in the company of Him for whom I have fought so hard.'

When we reconnect to spirit, earth becomes like heaven and we become Godlike – conscious creators of our chosen experience. Gnostics believed that there is only one universal consciousness (God), which expresses itself through each one of us. Of course we forget we are God when we become too identified with the body and get lost in doing, having and consuming. The Gnostics called this the 'hylic' state of consciousness, where we are alive but dead. The initiation we undergo to exit this lowly state is baptism with water, according to the Gnostics. When we begin to awaken to the fact that we are much more than matter, thus begins the journey back to wholeness (travelling to the dot in the centre of the circle via the line, which is the radius of the circle). When we are dismantling the lie of ego but not yet our essential best self, this is what Gnostics referred to as the psychic state of consciousness. The type of initiation relevant to this stage according to the Gnostics is called Crucifixion. When we merge with soul, we begin to reflect Christ-like qualities until we are completely Christ consciousness and have merged with the dot in the centre of the circle. This initiation is called Resurrection. I trust you are now beginning to understand how this all fits into the map of the alchemists I am sharing with you here?

First of all we are 'hylic' and utterly dead to spiritual things. Then we become psychic, identifying with our psyche. Eventually, I was guided to understand that soul is another name for the Christ aspect, or Christ consciousness. Matter I came to understand is the vehicle for the manifestation of soul on this plane of existence, and soul is the vehicle on a higher plane for the manifestation of spirit. Through the use of matter the soul unfolds and finds its climax in the soul of man. This map guides us to consider how we use 'matter' – for ego or with mindfulness for the greatest good. It teaches us how to know our best (God-) selves in every word, deed, thought and action.

Polishing our mirror

A tarnished mirror will shine like a jewel when polished. A mind clouded by the illusions of the innate darkness of life is like a tarnished mirror, but when polished, it is sure to become like a clear mirror, reflecting the essential nature of phenomena and the true aspect of reality.

By the time we reach Level 4 of the alchemical path we have come to realize that if we use matter to serve lower self and ego desires, this doesn't bring true happiness or everlasting peace. It doesn't work for us and it doesn't work for our world. The results of using matter to serve lower self (ego) are toxic lifestyles, thoughts, feelings, emotions and a toxic environment, which mirrors our own toxic inner state. The only solution to healing all this toxicity within ourselves and within our world, is to become best self, true and whole (holy) Christ consciousness, and learn how to access and use Christed energies and higher alchemical power to return to love and balance. According to Buddhist principles, our environment is said to be a mirror of our life. So everything that happens to us, the toxic state of our environment, the way people react to us, is a reflection of something in ourselves. If someone is abusive, then they behave like that due to something in us that prompted them to behave like that – it could be a judgement of that behaviour in ourselves (unforgiveness) or fear of or denial of that behaviour in ourselves. We are therefore encouraged to polish ourselves everyday, through improving ourselves. This process is called spiritual evolution (conquering ego and attachment), which allows for spiritual involution (reconnection to best self). I learned from Buddhist teachings that if the minds of living beings are impure, their land is also impure, but if their minds are pure, so is their land. There are not two lands, pure or impure in themselves. The difference lies solely in the good or evil of our minds. It is the same with a Buddha and an ordinary being. When deluded, one is called an ordinary being, but when enlightened, one is called a Buddha.

At Alchemical Level 4 we commit to merge matter with soul and begin the journey of merging soul with spirit. We undertake the Gnostic transformation from hylic to psychic to pneuma states of consciousness. We go back to the dot in the centre of the circle. We let go of all that we identified in Alchemical Level 3 that no longer serves the best self emerging (soul) and soul's merging back into spirit. Our new Christ consciousness focus is on bringing together all the best aspects of self that we decided to keep in Level 3 and ditching everything and everyone else. This is how we build the new Christ identity within self. Then through the art of mindfulness we live this in every word, thought, deed and action.

I believe every person born into this existence needs to be taught everything from this map from an early age. Then, in the old system that is failing, when we replace a corrupt politician or a dishonest corporate director with another person, the replacement person will have been trained to resist the temptations that corrupted the first man. This is how we will create a new system that works. And surely this is the simplest way to create world peace and the return to environmental harmony and balance?

For success in Level 4 we need to learn to self-nurture, balance and develop right relationship to food, exercise, sleep, play, work and spiritual practices. We need to organize our lives and get rid of old junk – people, places and things. We need to identify and stop all energy-stealing patterns. We need to learn, via attunement to and working with Reiki, how to draw energy from Source rather than from other people. We need to make sure other people no longer drain our energy. We will learn how to take action because we choose to, and how to do our very best in all that we do, realizing also – with tolerance and patience – that our best changes.

In the last three levels, we resolved the stress between the conscious and subconscious. In this level, these two have an inner marriage – the conjunctio. We begin to experience the opening of our heart as we reconnect to soul and experience Christ consciousness. Working with Christ consciousness we begin to find the answers to our life questions. We are reborn as the hero – best self. The author Ayn Rand really taught me about being a hero when she said:

'In the name of the best within you, do not sacrifice this world to those who are its worst. In the name of the values that keep you alive, do not let your vision of man be distorted by the ugly, the cowardly, the mindless in those who have never achieved his title. Do not lose your knowledge that man's proper estate is an upright posture, an intransigent mind and a step that travels unlimited roads. Do not let your fire go out, spark by irreplaceable spark, in the hopeless swamps of the approximate, the not-quite, the not-yet, the not-at-all. Do not let the **hero** in your soul perish, in lonely frustration for the life you deserved, but have never been able to reach. Check your road and the nature of your battle. The world you desired can be won, it exists, it is real, it is possible, it's yours.'

As the hero, we give our lives to something bigger than ourselves. We become a servant leader by first of all learning to truly lead self well. Thus begins the training to lead others wisely. We feel, perhaps for the first time, real altruistic love that truly wishes the best for the other and our world. It feels as if we have made it. And we have made it, but only to the half-way mark – Christ consciousness. Matter has merged with soul and much energy will be expended to integrate the higher energies of this new better self now emerging. Simultaneously another journey within this journey is now beginning. This is the real journey of 'developing' spiritual integrity where soul begins to merge with spirit.

The life trials, tests and initiations of Level 4 have been designed so that disciples of the map come to know, or are learning to know, that they are not this or that particular personality illusion, but all of life itself. We are not merely the physical body or its emotional nature; nor the mind or that which the mind knows. We begin to realize at this level that knowledge must be transcended by unconditional love and selfless service. Higher love is the only love best self is capable of and we only become capable of higher love when we have disciplined ourselves to think and feel only unconditional love. Then we truly know who we are (and are not) and can practise moderation. When we can live in this higher state in moment-to-moment conscious awareness, we know we have merged with soul. Then, later, comes the awful 'moment in time' when we discover that we are much more even than the soul...

Co-dependency versus sacred relationship

One of the most important balances is that of gender. For me, relationships with men were like falling into the black pit. Songs and films programme us to believe we are incomplete without a man or a woman. In the film Jerry McGuire, Tom Cruise declares when he gets the woman, 'You complete me'. This is co-dependency, perpetuating the lie that we are less than whole without a partner.

What I learned about relationships from a spiritual perspective is that we need to complete ourselves and become whole before we can even contemplate a successful intimate relationship with another. If we haven't done this self-awareness work, identifying and clearing all our wounds and balancing our own male and female aspects within, the type of partner we attract is only filling something missing within ourselves. Amazingly enough, this psychological clearing and balancing of our inner masculine and feminine energies is also vital to becoming spiritually powerful.

Incomplete people are like half circles. They are searching for someone who will be the other half of their circle. When they get together, they make a kind of whole circle. However, they are dependent upon the other for their sense of wholeness. Should one move away, both feel a terrible tear in their being. They are being ripped out of their dependent wholeness into being only half again.

In ideal relationship, each person finds and joins with their inner partner first. They both are complete circles. When they enter into partnership, they do so by choice and are not dependent upon one another. Nor are they then independent. They are something new and more evolved than either alone. They are interdependent. They each find that together they are capable of endeavours that neither one alone could master. When we reconnect our inner male and female and balance the two, spirit can merge and we become whole. In real terms, only then are we truly ready for sacred relationship with another.

Authentic sacred relationship, and all that this entails, is not for everyone I realize. This type of relationship is based on radical truth and open honest sharing, both with the self and the partner. We share openly about our ego, shadow, persona defects – all our petty and jealous thoughts, all our fears as well as our hopes and dreams. Everything is brought out into the open for each partner to see. Sacred relationship doesn't work if both partners fail to be absolutely impeccably honest with each other. Without this radical type of honesty, sacred alchemical relationship cannot occur.

We have all noticed that relationships seem to have a honeymoon period, but after a while the incredible excitement we experienced at the beginning of the relationship starts to disappear. People get into ruts and so do relationships. It requires continual awareness, determination and hard work to sustain and maintain a relationship that is conscious and alive. So many relationships fail because we aren't willing or are unable to put in the required effort to make things work. Tom Kenyon and Judi Sion describe this brilliantly in their book *The Magdalen Manuscript* (Orb Books).

'...a kind of psychological and emotional lethargy sets in and both partners succumb to the dulling effects of unconsciousness. This type of unconsciousness is a death knell to psychological awareness and insight:

and although it is rarely mentioned, this type of unconsciousness has a negative effect on ones spiritual life as well.'

In the alchemy of relationship, the form that needs to be transformed is quite simply the form of the interactions that habitually take place between the two partners. According to Kenyon and Sion, the necessary ingredients for this to occur successfully are: 'something to be transformed (the habitual patterns of the interaction) and the container (the safety both partners feel in the relationship) and energy to drive the alchemical reaction'.

No doubt we are all aware of the intense 'heat' created between two people when their neuroses mix. Yet if both partners choose to be totally open and radically honest with themselves and each other (no projecting, blaming and denying), this heat can produce the transformation a relationship needs to move to a new, higher level of intimacy and understanding. Unfortunately, in the matrix, most people would rather end the relationship and run away and continue to run away for an entire lifetime. What do we usually do when relationships become psychologically too hot to handle? What do we all usually do when we are faced with something we'd rather not feel? In the matrix, we have been trained to find all sorts of ways of avoiding ourselves and our stuff – with all the 'isms' (alcoholism, workaholism; the list goes on and on).

In sacred relationship, however, these emotional hot spots are in fact a blessing. They are a call to be present and real, an opportunity for each partner to share their truth with each other, regardless of how frightening or embarrassing this may be.

And the relationship is quickened by an enlivening element – truth.

Psychological honesty creates psychological insights and this leads to new awareness and transformation. This is how we perpetuate sacred alchemical relationship. On the outside it might look as if all hell has been let loose, and it has as all kinds of dross gets brought to the surface to heal. Actually, this chaos is a sign that we are doing this correctly. What makes sacred relationship sacred is that it's truly a holy way of being, involving unconditional love, truth, understanding and forgiveness. Holy means to make whole and when we create true wholeness in relationship we are engaged in a holy way of being.

Kenyon and Sion go on to share that, 'In this crucible of mutual safety, honesty and appreciation, it is possible to forge a new kind of self. This new self is psychologically more honest, more aware and freer than its counterpart before entering the foundry of relationship. And like the phoenix that arises from its own ashes, this self has wings. It can fly places that it could only ever imagine before.'

As I have said, sacred relationship is not yet for the masses, but for those who are courageous enough to be this intimate with themselves and their partner, it's the key to a vast treasure trove where sacred power is greatly amplified. It's not for the faint-hearted or the unawakened and I for one could settle for nothing less.

From separation to unity consciousness

Another key relationship is that between ourselves and the planet. I discovered how important it is to feel oneness with all life. I learned from the Zulus that my real father energy comes from the sky. My real mother is the feminine energy of the earth. I discovered that my biological earth parents are just teachers I chose before birth to come and learn from. I learned that everyone and everything is part of me. The Zulu language like the language of the Hopi Indians has no words for 'that rock' or 'that tree or river over there'. Their language recognizes the 'oneness' and reflects this by saying 'that rock which is part of me' and 'that tree or river which is part of me'. When our mother language is so formulated that outer things are a part of us, we are less likely to destroy something. It's all so simple and it works. How tragic is it that we sophisticated, technologically advanced Westerners have forgotten the power of the word?

I was shown how to open up to the sky and earth energies and re-claim my spirit by re-establishing this simple spiritual connection. Then everything became much easier on the path. Whilst the energy I had was limited to only the physical, mental or emotional realms, I was weak and vulnerable. The moment I learned to remember and re-connect to spiritual power from above and below, sky and earth, then at will, I could invoke or recall the energies I felt in that hotel room in Japan with my friend, the athlete. I knew I was covered and guided every step of the way.

We never see birds flying around the sky and then suddenly dropping to the ground in fear because they are uncertain where their next worms will come from or worrying about how many twigs they need for a new nest! They know they are covered and so too are we. The universe is a friendly place. Abundance flows freely to those who can remember how to connect to this flow. First I had to do the work on myself to allow the flow through me. I had to ensure I felt worthy to receive, could receive and could transmit on all levels. Then all I had to do to receive was ask.

To recap, in Alchemical Level 1, we didn't know we didn't know and we were lost in the matrix... I call this unconscious incompetence. We were just living the lie we had been programmed to obey – just like almost everyone else around us. We thought the purpose of our lives was to obtain external symbols of power – money, career, status and possessions. We aimed to have a family and security, insurances and a pension fund. Yet, eventually, living this way became meaningless, most likely we felt empty. We compensated for this lack of purpose by consuming more and keeping ourselves diverted with all kinds of external stimuli – do/have/consume. We had lived our lives as we had been conditioned to do so. We made everything as safe and secure as we could for both self and family. We avoided thoughts about death as much as possible and acted as if we were going to live forever.

Then at Alchemical Level 2 some loss or great disaster came along and burst our bubble. Perhaps someone close to us died or maybe we lost our health, our job, our career. This was our wake up call to something better – to embrace best self and the bigger picture.

If we failed to respond or stay awake, such disasters increased in intensity and frequency until our defences were broken down. If we surrendered we realized this was opportunity disguised as loss, that we could be healed and made whole, but if we resisted this would be hell... Separation is the theme of this level. In the intensity of this alchemical spotlight it became impossible to deny our feelings any more. We were confronted with all the things we had been hiding from ourselves. We saw all the good, the bad and the ugly. For many this is a bitter brew indeed to cope with, to see the un-censored version of our life story. Yet if we could persevere, this would become breakthrough instead of breakdown.

At Alchemical Level 3 we started to build foundations for our new best self. In Level 4, we move out of the darkness and our light begins to increase. Our ego is humbled and there is clarity of mind. Now it's the time to sort through and organize all that we have seen. The feminine within, our subconscious mind, has shown us truth. She is with us in this renaissance period, to assist with this process of rebirth. We identify our assets, talents and virtues versus our liabilities, failures and vices. We consider all we have done and NOT done and learn our lessons from this. We stop denying our failures and face them bravely, admit them honestly, make amends where possible, make a commitment, a promise, to do better and move on and move up. Now it's time to throw out the junk and reassemble the good stuff. Now it's time to create the new us, gathered from all the good parts we have sorted out. This new self will be a blend of emotional resilience and mental clarity. As we become a whole person with a thinking heart and a feeling mind, the synchronicities in our lives increase. We are guided to the people we need to meet and the places in which we need to be. Our hearts open up and we follow our passion and find our bliss.

When we can learn how to follow our bliss, pathways will open up to us where previously there were none. As we shine our light, others with similar qualities are attracted to this higher energy. Our capacity for compassion grows to the point that the heart embraces the whole world.

Rediscovering the hero within
It feels like we have made it. We are the hero. We have dedicated our lives to something bigger than personality pursuits. We teach and others drink in

our words with wonder and joy. We heal and others are freed from their afflictions. However, we are walking a fine line here. There is a subtle danger that we could become too inflated with ourselves and this will re-activate ego again. We need to remain humble and above all truly grateful for all the wonderful gifts in this new life. We commit to actually live the dream, now we are more prepared. We strengthen our dialogue with the inner female, the unconscious mind and learn how to listen to the direction arising from within. We start to compare feelings with purest rational thoughts. When we are living in harmony, these two should harmonize and agree. Our instinct and intuitions will gel with our thinking. Our feelings will be in sync with our thoughts. When the right and left hemispheres of the brain merge as one and alchemically balance, which is what begins to occur at Alchemical Level 4, we will experience:

Increased left and right brain coherence

Heightened self-awareness

Increased vitality and joie de vivre

Elimination of dysfunctional feelings, thoughts and behaviour

Dissolution of depression and stress

Enhanced mental clarity and focus

Deepening spiritual practice

Raised overall vibration

Quickened progress to enlightenment

Visualizing our best self and best life

In the first three levels, we ate 'humble pie'. We reviewed the errors of our matrix-type life and gathered all the good parts – the traits and virtues we chose to retain. Now it is time to do something with them.

We begin to visualize our best selves, perfect in every way, embodying all our best traits and virtues in a wonderful way. We commit to getting our lives organized. We strive to rid ourselves of all that is out of harmony with best self. We throw out the old junk, organize and arrange the items we choose to keep so that they are ready to use when needed. We assemble the chosen parts into the new and wonderful best self.

Having recognized, honoured and made amends to align with our emerging super-conscious state, our conscious mind (the inner male) and the unconscious mind (the inner female) are able at long last to reunite. This new unified self recognizes the special talents of both the conscious and unconscious minds and chooses to consult both in order to make decisions together. Our intuition is now amplified and becomes permanent. The synchronicities flow more powerfully and increase in frequency. We follow them and our experiences are far richer as a result. We have reconnected to what the Chinese call the 'Tao'.

Now we move deeply into the heart and radiate love to all. We come out of the closet and shine our newfound light. Some paths call this Christ consciousness. We teach. We heal. We are a light unto the world. We are our best selves – this is a process, a journey and we become ever more perfect.

Remember that all gifts are from Source and that the wonderful energy that flows through us is from Source and not personality or ego. It is the clear connection with Source and the inner harmony with our subconscious that generates our capacity to be a hero. Realizing this and remaining humble, we will remain in the Tao.

We have faced our fears and now it's possible to live our dreams. We have reconnected to Source. This powerful light shines out of every pore and we choose to live aligned with our spirit's purpose.

Organizing and assembling the best self

In the last level, we went through a pretty thorough self-searching. If we did our work well, we have a good idea of both our highs and our lows – our virtues and our vices. And, during the last level, we separated from the parts of self and our creation, with which we no longer wished to be associated. There may be more to do here. Be scrupulously thorough. We need to say goodbye once and for all to all the fair-weather acquaintances who prevent us from being our new selves. This separation from the matrix-type consciousness and people still programmed by it is vital. Working with the Universal Law of Detachment is of paramount importance at Level 4. In fact this is the lesson of Level 4 and information on this essential spiritual law is given in the next section of the book.

WISDOM

Honour the best self – create a new vision of health

To live the vision of our new best self, we will require strong minds, bodies, spirits and emotions. We need to make sure that our lifestyle and diet support this new growth.

Cleanse and detox

Did you know that nowadays we experience more toxins in just one day than our grandparents experienced in a whole lifetime?

We clean our homes, our cars and our clothes regularly but we don't do the same for our bodies and just as a waste pipe needs regular cleaning, our bodies are made of a series of tubes that also need regular cleaning. Detox, short for detoxification, is the removal of potentially toxic substances from the body. Although detox is primarily thought of as a form of drug rehabilitation, used to treat alcoholism or other drug addiction, the term also refers to diets, herbs and other methods of removing environmental and dietary toxins from the body.

If it's true that we are what we eat, we are in dire danger of becoming something compact, micro-waveable, doused in chemicals and encased in cellophane. Despite your best intentions, have your eating habits declined perhaps without noticing it? Are you relying more and more on take-away meals, convenience foods and cafeteria chow of uncertain parentage? Are you feeling 'off' — not as energetic in your workouts, more fatigue than usual and battling a weird weight gain that all the usual tricks just can't budge? What to do?

The general idea, supported by many mainstream as well as alternative health-care providers is simple:

- Our bodies, specifically our livers, work overtime to rid themselves of the toxins (or at least unnecessary substances) we put through them daily, including pesticides and growth hormones in our food, alcohol, tobacco, caffeine and hard-to-digest substances like dairy products.

- Eating only organic produce and limiting the amount of chemicals we put into the body allows the liver and body to 'cleanse' themselves of the impurities we ingest by habit.

- By cooking all our meals from the freshest, most nutritious ingredients, we revive our bodies and also help eliminate the cravings for things we all know are bad, like overly refined white flour and white sugar.

- And eating well for a month, plus gently cleansing your system with natural herbs, is easy and painless – right?

Any bad habits around food or lack of exercise must go. Habits are just that – habitual. If we don't actively change them, they remain the same. Habits are wonderful. Thank God for habits. Once we have learned something, we don't have to consciously concentrate upon it anymore. Our mind is freed for other activities. However, if we have some habits that we wish to change, it will require discipline and continual effort to delete the old patterning and make the new behaviour habitual. I read somewhere it takes 21 days to integrate a new habit and to supersede an old habit with a more optimal way of behaving.

We need to develop routines that help us to stay awake and aware. We need to be alert to recognize pitfalls, which may distract us from the path of the soul. The path of the soul requires radical truth, both with ourselves and with others. We need not be hurtful towards others, but on the path we do need to, at times, speak truths that others would not utter.

Why do most people resist waking up? It's because generally we lack organization and discipline in our lives. We lack organization in our personal lives and lack meaningful group organizations around us. The only experience of organization most of us have is our family – and the dysfunctional behaviour of our family has in most cases been the cause of our own imbalance and dysfunction. So we need to create new support groups, new families of light.

Establishing community – consciousness as a new norm

'Intense control dramas of all kinds, whether they are violent or just perverse and strange addictions, come from environments where life is so abusive, dysfunctional and constrictive, and the level of fear is so great, that they spawn this same rage and anger or perversion over and over, generation after generation.

The individuals who are born into these situations choose to do so on purpose, with clarity... because they were sure they had enough strength to break out, to end the cycle, to heal the family system in which they would be born. They were confident that they could awaken and work through the resentment and anger at finding themselves in these deprived circumstances, and see it all as a preparation for a mission... usually one of helping others out of similar situations...

JAMES REDFIELD, THE TENTH INSIGHT

In the beginning, when we set out on the path to self-improvement, we may attract all kinds of disapproval from those around us – anything from ridicule from friends to withdrawal of emotional, moral and financial support from family and friends – as many a woeful tale reveals when told by those who risked it all to have a life of greater meaning and fulfilment.

What causes family members and certain friends to become resistant, resentful and disapproving when we make conscious our choice to be the best we can be? Why do they, who claim they like us – even love us – turn a deaf ear to our yearnings and sometimes go so far as to toss emotional obstacles in our way that are sure to thwart our achievement? Do they really intend for us to be unhappy?

Except for those who irrefutably DO intend to block our way, most of our friends and family don't really intend for us to be unhappy and would likely be shocked if they were accused of such intention. Yet, it's undeniable that some behave as if a real threat of abandonment exists if we succeed in our endeavours. Our success might even trigger a painful reminder of where they themselves have fallen short of their dreams and have lost the courage to strive to be their best; perhaps because they, too, were thwarted and discouraged in some way by family and friends, and eventually withdrew their enthusiasm and gave up on any possibility of realizing their spiritual dreams.

Even though we may come to understand the reasons for their behaviour, such displays of disapproval are enough to discourage even the very strong among us... so much so that we may delay in our striving for a better life and put our plans and goals on hold, hoping for a better opportunity in the future, which may or may not come.

And so some of us may forget what we came here to do on planet earth... and may never remember again for an entire lifetime. But what price do we pay when we forgo our hopes and wishes to appease the wishes and needs of another? This is after all co-dependency – where instead of craving a drug or a drink, we crave love and attention from another person. This is a major addiction on the planet today.

Are we really being more noble and loving when we remain within the confines of someone else's shattered hopes because we don't wish to hurt their feelings or don't want to risk being ostracized and possibly having to walk our path alone for a little while? Are we really being better people by stifling our yearnings... or are we only appearing 'better' in the eyes of those who want us to stay the same?

Living in spiritual community

In her book *Emergence*, renowned author/teacher, Barbara Marx Hubbard, talks of several stages to spiritual maturity. She says it's extremely rare to find people who have advanced beyond infancy and childhood yet! Only the rare few make it to the next stage, which is 'youth'. She states that this is because so few people have been able to surrender their egos, find their higher life purpose, create even a small community of kindred souls and begin their true work in the world. She goes on, however, to say that now it is time to do exactly this. We all need safe arenas to test and experience our ideas and to stabilize our emerging spiritual consciousness with others doing the same thing.

We all need a support system because we are basically group-oriented – and the survival of the individual depends upon the help and co-operation of the rest of the 'village', which in ancient times was often populated by relatives.

When we first begin to break away from the original 'tribe', because we choose to venture beyond the boundaries of the old beliefs and old ways of doing things, a very real fear is often experienced; a trembling deep down in the subconscious as we remember that we cannot survive without the support of the other village members.

Yet break away we must and break away we do because the urge to evolve becomes far greater than the need to conform, fit in and remain the same, which is stagnation. There will come a time in everyone's life where it becomes far more painful not to grow – lest we wither much too soon before we blossom. We strike out on our own and eventually, we find a new 'tribe' and a new 'village' of like-minded souls who becomes our new family... a 'spiritual family' so to speak. This is the dream I am creating at Studio Psalm Philosophie, my Holistic Spa in Wells, and at my Retreat Centre, where I live in spiritual community. Until we find our new 'tribe', our new 'community' and 'village', we often find ourselves alone. And so, the act of walking away from the old is a very powerful act of courage... just as courageous as any warrior who faces his challengers.

It takes great courage to live in spiritual community. To the faint-hearted, authentic spiritual community is a terrible place. It is the place where our limitations and our egoism are revealed to us. When we begin to live full-time with others, we discover our poverty and our weakness, our inability to get on with people, our mental and emotional blocks – our seemingly insatiable desires, our frustrations and jealousies, our hatred and our wish to destroy. However, when we identify this ego behaviour we can dis-identify from it. We are not our behaviour. We can change our behaviour and this is the quest of the spiritual hero.

Antoine de Saint Exupery said, 'Perfection is achieved, not when there is nothing more to add, but when there is nothing left to take away'. Living in group we learn how to transcend our own ego behaviour. As we evolve to perfection, we can then lovingly, gently or sometimes sternly confront the other so that they can keep taking away that which no longer serves the new self emerging. It's fast-track spiritual enlightenment and I highly recommend it. In our community we have found our spiritual 'kin' and companions of destiny. We always find those who – just like us – took the risk of walking a different path. And then we know that it was all well worth the courage it took to walk alone for a while. When we are ready to live in spiritual community, it's vitally important that we are totally committed to mastering energy-stealing patterns, denials, projection and blaming. We need to be mindful to only drawing energy from Source. I explain how in the PRACTICES section of this chapter.

The road to change and healing oneself – whether it's building better physical health, improving ones behaviour, or creating a happier and more fulfilling life – can start out being lonely and challenging. Choosing the 'high road' so to speak, is never a popular choice… at first. I have released many dear friends, lovers and even a much-loved husband who all baulked at the steepness of the way I have chosen. This apparent loss of those I love so very much has been a real test... yet the road less travelled, the path of the soul, the way of love, strength and balance, is the only way for me nowadays.

Essenes on communal life

Living in spiritual community is not only an opportunity to heal both the dysfunctional family and social systems we have inherited, but to also consciously create new healthy forms based in love and co-operation that will not only sustain life on this planet but will also support a thriving experience for all. Releasing fear of lack that promotes greed and the need to survive at the expense of others and their well-being is an important step. When we co-operate and share our resources with one another there is plenty for all. This is what community is all about.

From research of the Dead Sea Scrolls, I found the following mention of the Essenes and their relationship to wealth, community and sharing.

'They despise riches and their communal life is admirable. In vain one would search among them for one man with a greater fortune than another. Indeed, it is a law that those who enter the community shall surrender their property to the community; so neither the humiliations of poverty nor the pride of wealth is to be seen anywhere among them. Since their possessions are mingled, there exists for them all, as for brothers and sisters, one single property.' (Jewish War, 2.122)

'They neither buy nor sell anything among themselves; each man gives what he has to whoever needs it and received in return whatever he himself requires. And they can even receive freely from whomsoever they like without giving anything in exchange." (Jewish War, 2.127; see Jewish Antiquities 18.20)

Star Trek Voyager episode

A couple of years ago, I heard about a *Star Trek Voyager* episode that brilliantly demonstrated the powerful potential of engaging co-operation with each other including different races and even different species of intelligent life. If only we had eyes to see and ears to really hear plus, of course, a heart strong and courageous enough to live the change we wish to see in the world...

The story begins when Voyager is accidentally pulled into a Void, where it turns out other lost ships were struggling to survive. When Voyager first arrived they were instantly attacked by one of the other ships and 90% of their food and supplies were stolen. Voyager's crew soon discovered the other ships already in the Void survived by stealing supplies from each other and whenever possible stealing from new unsuspecting ships the moment they stumbled into the Void.

When Voyager's crew discovered they did not have enough power to leave the Void on their own Captain Janeway asked the other ships to form an alliance where each ship would pool their resources and technologies with the other ships in the alliance and thus they would all find a way out of the Void together. It was difficult to convince the other ships this was a good idea, but eventually several ships did join the alliance, shared their resources and technology, and made it possible for all the ships that were working co-operatively to leave the Void together. Those who refused to join the alliance due to their entrenched patterns of fear and lack were left in the Void to continue as they had before.

This story demonstrates the power of co-operation and working in community to achieve what otherwise might seem impossible. Some of the ships had been in the Void for years, barely surviving by competing for the limited supplies and resources that might wander in through other lost ships. Living from competition had created separation, distrust, hatred and loss of resources that could have benefited everyone if they had chosen to live in co-operation with one another. The ships that chose to co-operate and share resources ultimately changed their lives, moving their existence from the experience of lack in the Void into an expansive and abundant world. Co-operation unifies and strengthens the greater whole, moving our experience from struggle to survival, into a whole new more abundant world of possibilities.

The Hawaiians' Ohana

The Hawaiians call humanity the 'Ohana' – the family that breathes together. I felt strongly drawn and guided to embody and create this simplicity and sharing. In the last three years since I settled back in England, close to magical Glastonbury, England's holiest land, I have created a family that lives together and works together, sharing and healing each other with Reiki and by gently, lovingly alerting one another to their energy-stealing patterns.

By the time we have reached Alchemical Level 4 we are consciously competent – knowing we know but still having to think about it. Sometimes we may have glimpses of unconscious competence, a taster of what's coming in the higher levels yet to be mastered. It requires conscious effort to awaken and remain awake. This kind of continual effort requires motivation. We have to wish to change like a drowning man wishes for air or we will not likely continue with the new behaviour long enough to make it the new habit. We need a vision of the desired state to guide us. And this vision needs to be intensely attractive. The vision of the new best self developed at this level is just what we need to motivate us to make the needed changes. To succeed, we will need motivation, discipline, determination and commitment.

We need to learn to feed ourselves well by choosing the highest quality locally produced organic living foods. We do this because we love ourselves now and wish to nurture ourselves – best self deserves the best.

Planetary influences help us to wake up

An astrologer advised me that in recent times the transits of Saturn and Chiron through the Cancer Capricorn domain have provided opportunities for shamanic healing and a complete redefinition of the current competitively based system. The challenge is: are we ready, willing and able to wake up and heal the old faulty, failing systems and embrace new systems based in co-operation, recognizing everyone has a right and a responsibility to thrive together?

This is challenging because the current programming is based in a competitive world suggesting there are limits to what is available. So this kind of change requires tremendous trust and a willing leap of faith to revolutionize the ways we participate with reality. When we open to trust that all our needs are met from an ever-renewing, ever-regenerating, ever-flowing vast and abundant divine Source that originates within each of us and provides all we need to fully live and express our divine purpose, then we can truly operate from this experience, creating an entirely new paradigm of peace and plenty shared and for everyone. And by the way, this is how our community lives at the Manor House!

Open the heart and shine the light

One characteristic experience of this level is a great increase of spontaneous joy. We recognize that all our experiences have been not only necessary but also perfect – the good, the bad and the ugly. We see that they were all necessary preparations for our awakening. We can look back at our whole life and honestly say, 'It was worth it. It made me who I am and that is someone wonderful.' When we can honestly say, 'It was worth it,' we become free from the repercussions of old karma. This falls away like a heavy stone from the heart. Bliss ensues...

Another sign that we are on the right track on this level is an increase in the frequency of experiences of synchronicity. We know, feel and experience that we are guided every step of the way. Through this inner guidance, the spiritual alchemist now comes to know what to do to achieve lasting enlightenment. This stage is referred to in alchemy as the 'lesser stone'. At the completion of this stage, the individual, personal work of transformation is complete. However, there is much more work to be accomplished before the 'greater stone' is complete. Be sure to follow the synchronicities. This is our guidance system at work, leading us home on our path to greater wholeness.

We find that we are in love with this new best self, with all others and with all of life. It is an intoxicating state of bliss that brings a smile to the face and a song to the heart. We open up and let the light shine upon all we encounter. We have merged and are becoming one with the light.

How to proceed: discover our dharma – follow our passion and find our bliss

'The Universal Law of Dharma is that everyone has a purpose in life... a unique or special talent to give to others. And when we blend this

unique talent with service to others, we experience the ecstasy and exultation of our own spirit, which is the ultimate goal of all goals.'

DEEPAK CHOPRA

The ethos and ideology behind my synthesis of teachings is about achievement. However, it's never about achievement in the material sense of the word. For the last decade or so now I have steered a course to embody peace of mind, living mastery and enlightenment... I do know that if I had continued to focus on society's norms (do/have/consume), I am certain I would have died unfulfilled and dissatisfied. I see so many people die not knowing why they have lived, finding it all so pointless. This is hell on earth. I have created heaven on earth for myself now. This book is aimed to show people how to find the key to create the miracle of true heaven on earth for themselves. For me, this has been about shedding the skins of my former personality-self values and attitudes of compete, judge, attack and fear. I have replaced these learned behaviours with noble spiritual principles, remembered AND learned, which I live by – love, co-operate, share, discriminate, be!

Myth of the king in his small kingdom

Once upon a time a king lived in a very small kingdom. Rather than making his subjects pay taxes to him, he made everyone bring him a gift daily. The story goes on to say that the spinner gifted him wool; the weaver offered him some cloth; the farmer gave him a piece of fresh fruit. Everyone came with an offering daily without fail. During each visit the king would wisely use this time to chat to his subjects to find out what was going on in the kingdom.

Daily, as each new gift was received by the king, he would express his gratitude for the gift and then throw it over his shoulder into the treasure room behind him.

One day, the king was hungry and bit into the pear gifted to him by the farmer. To his surprise his bite encountered something very hard and he almost broke a tooth. He looked inside the fruit and was astonished to discover a precious jewel, a very large ruby. Then he wondered about all the other fruit the farmer had given him and if this contained gems too. He went into his treasure room to investigate.

It was a chaotic mess containing all kinds of cloth, paintings, statues, carvings and, of course, fermenting, rotting old fruits. The stench was terrible and many of the gifts were ruined because of the rotting fruits. The king tore open the old fruits and found emeralds, sapphires and diamonds. It would seem that, on inspection, each piece of fruit indeed contained a gem of precious worth!

Interpretation:

We all tend to throw the gifts of the day (our experiences) into our memory (the unconscious) without paying much attention to them. We create a huge stockpile of energy and information – undigested – that might have given us new fuel to transform if we had digested it properly in the first instance. Despite the chaotic mess, it's so worth the time and effort to re-examine and re-evaluate the experiences of our past as we may find something of immense value…

The universal law of detachment

In detachment from outcomes, people, places and things we find a gift, the wisdom of uncertainty, not knowing and not needing to know. The wisdom of uncertainty gives us another gift, the freedom from our past, from all that was and is known, the bondage of our past conditioning. When we find the courage, humility and willingness to open up to the unknown, a place where all potentialities exist, we surrender ourselves to the one heart-mind – the Tao. We need to learn to commit ourselves to detached involvement, with no attachment to outcomes, specific or forced solutions. Thus we are vulnerable, uncertain, yet if we can trust the wisdom of uncertainty this leads to liberation. We are the open vessel to and through which an infinite number of solutions, choices and outcomes will occur. We need to practise this with our own vision of our new best self and in the assembling and living of that vision.

It doesn't matter whether the ideas that flow into us are material, emotional, physical or spiritual in nature, but what is essential is that we learn to dedicate our time actioning strategies to accomplish these aims. Doing this daily we will find joy, abundance and total well-being. We will find ultimate joy. However, it's vital we know our life's purpose. It's even more vital we then commit to take action consistently to create and manifest this in our lives. The great masters call this 'dharma', which is only in fact the Sanskrit word for 'life purpose'. Dharma is about going beyond ego, practising no distraction to find higher or best self. Spend some time in silence and focus only on your unique talents. This will lead to a state of bliss. Commit to serving others. In every situation, ask yourself, how can I assist and show more love to the other.

From dharma comes inner peace, harmony and true lasting contentment. Dharma is based upon the ancient wisdom teachings that every one of us has a heroic mission when we incarnate on this planet. We have all been granted a unique range of talents, gifts and skills that will readily allow us to realize this life work. The key is how to discover what these are and what the bigger picture is on earth. This is what this book, my workshops, retreats and events are about! My dharma is to help others discover their path, unique talents and gifts that bring true and lasting joy.

Usually, on the path of the soul, we are required to take a blind, empty-handed leap of faith into the void with a guarantee of nothing... I have done this time and again. Having separated from, for example, an inappropriate job, we are now ready to find a job that provides for us to better express and live more in harmony with best self. When choosing, consider carefully what would be most deeply fulfilling. As children, what did we always wish to be? Can we somehow be that now? What would it take? Is this in harmony with who we are now becoming? We may have responsibilities to support a family. However, consider the responsibility to honour best self first. When we honour self, follow our passion, find our bliss, we also find abundance and our best destiny. This will work out best for everyone... so get to work exploring and creating this state.

Most importantly, be in passion and joy. Doing what we are passionate and joyful about automatically attracts abundance into our experience. It also increases the frequency of synchronicities. Following these signs and signals will help us achieve our goals more rapidly.

Before beginning any new activity, consider carefully if it serves the new best self and the new identity. Before making a decision and acting, consciously recognize the 'choice point'. Consciously consider what will be brought into being as a result of that activity. If this is in harmony with the new self, go for it! Make a commitment and follow up on it. Conscious, awake and aware, our new life will take form, step-by-step.

In this level, we do a lot of questioning and reorienting. And now we do begin to find the answers to our questions. The quest has begun in earnest. There is still much travelling along our chosen path before us, yet if we have done our foundation work at this level well, we know the direction in which we are headed.

Spiritual principle: decreeing – the power of the word

'Words have no legs, yet they walk.'

MALI PROVERB (BAMBARA PEOPLE)

At Alchemical Level 4 we emerge from our previous introspection and speak our truth into reality; we learn to decree. Making new choices with strong feeling is characteristic of Level 4 when the ego (choice) blends with the subconscious (strong feelings). Speaking these deeply felt choices aloud with conviction is decreeing.

And God said, 'Let there be light', and there was light. The universe is spoken into existence. God didn't say, 'I am moving towards, possibly after attending another angel workshop, one day gradually being able to maybe perhaps try to make light, because I should, ought to – must...' Why do we speak like this and dis-empower ourselves with words?

Conscious language

'Whatever words we utter should be chosen with care for people will hear them and be influenced by them for good or ill.'

BUDDHA

Robert Tennyson Stevens, creator of 'Conscious Languaging' says, 'Every word we speak is a prayer coming into reality.' He teaches very good ways of 'reframing' seemingly negative states of experience so that we see the good within them and move towards that good.

Stevens says that when we make a choice to move towards something positive, the next natural progression of feeling is to experience states of fear. Incidentally, he recommends a couple of drops of Young Living Oils 'Wintergreen' rubbed onto the base of the neck to help combat fear. He goes onto say that it's natural that when we make a choice (ego) with strong feeling (subconscious), memories from our past will arise; memories that are opposed to the new choice.

This theme is often seen in mythology. When the hero is motivated to change the status quo, he shows new courage and goes into the forest to save the damsel (subconscious, spirit) in distress. Just before he reaches her, a sleeping dragon (ego fear, old habits, memories) awakens, breathes fire in his direction, and blocks his path. He must successfully battle with the dragon if he is to save the maiden and set her free.

Similarly, when we make a new positive choice and desire it greatly, all the 'reasons why not' arise in us. All the times in the past when we did not succeed, all the training from our parents and authority figures that taught us that such a thing is not possible, all these fears arise and tell us to leave things as they are and not to even try to make changes.

This is a good and natural step of the process. In order to make deep changes, we need to confront and vanquish all the 'why nots' within us. Confronting and conquering fear is a natural stage towards developing a deeper state of courage, self-assurance and faith. These fears need to be met with courage and love. The energy they embody needs to be freed from the old forms and reinvested into new feelings and new beliefs.

Love is the key here. When we project love into our fears, and practise gratitude for our prior experiences, they melt and the energy they embody is freed for projection into new forms of our choice. Then all the negative images and emotional states that have previously blocked our advancement may be transformed into positives:

Anger -	Forgiveness and loving action
Fear -	Courage
Sadness, grief -	Joy
Hurtfulness -	Caring
Stress -	Challenge
I can't -	This is something new, but I know I can
Stumbling block -	Stepping stone

As we awaken in consciousness, many of our old memories and the associated beliefs will need to be transformed. As memories arise, welcome them. Love them, learn from the insights gained. These memories contain great energy, reconnect to this energy and prepare to project it into the new desired image, emotion and belief.

Having done this preliminary work, now the energy is freed up to make decreeing possible. The fears need to be neutralized and transformed before decreeing can function. Otherwise, making a positive statement aloud will call up images of fear and these fear-based projections will tend to manifest instead of the desired decree state.

Decree a thing thus, and it shall be established unto us
There is an important yet subtle aspect to consider before we attempt to decree. To decree is never about forcing our personal ego desires upon the universe. This is what so many people in ego do and in a sense this is black magic. Stevens taught me that every desire contains a 'gift of God' – something that can come true for the good of all. Yet how do we find the

gifts of God within our personal desires?

When we become aware of a personal desire, we need to first purify it of separateness and identify it with its universal aspect. In old religious language, we need to become aware of how our personal desire accurately reflects some aspect of the Divine Will. This means that we need to find out how the fulfilment of our personal desire is an aspect of the direction that evolution is moving.

In an old alchemical treatise, Thomas Vaughn exhorts: 'When Venus first comes to us, she is dressed in dirty rags. It is up to us to cloth her in glorious raiment.' Venus represents the desire nature. When we first become aware of a desire, it is usually clothed in separateness (fear). Ego wants to have, do or be something for itself – selfishness. Best self always comes from love and wishes something for the greatest good of the whole – selflessness.

Inner/outer world transformation

Is it truly possible for one person reconnected to spirit to make a difference to global environmental challenges and world transformation?

In solving a problem I have found that it is always more powerful to move beyond the ego lens of perception and go within to sense the expanded spiritual perspective. Regardless of what is happening in our lives *vis-a-vis* challenging events and situations, if we are centred and therefore more energetically balanced, we will always deal with our 'stuff' more effectively and create the best possible outcome for the greatest good. This is also why a daily Reiki self-healing practice is so vitally important because nothing balances us quite so fast-track nor quite so effectively. For those who have not attended my energy mastery workshops and are not attuned or initiated to Reiki, you will find under PRACTICES a simple ancient alchemical practice, an Earth Alchemy Unity Consciousness Meditation, which returns us to love and restores balance immediately.

I learned that the ancient alchemical practice of establishing unity consciousness allows an individual to elevate him/herself in consciousness in an incredibly fast-track yet simple way. The effect is that consciousness is raised high above the mundane levels and therefore way above the consciousness where we are experiencing the challenge. When we soar high above our issues, in the way that a shaman works invoking Eagle spirit medicine, we are taught how to soar above the mundane world and see a higher perspective. So too we can begin to see new opportunities and relationships that were invisible or inaccessible before. This is how the alchemising of consciousness can be used to have very immediate and practical benefits. In addition, as individuals become more resourceful and creative in their responses to the chaos of change around them, society itself is elevated, and collectively we will be able to work through challenges that at first seemed irresolvable.

There is a third aspect to this energetic balancing, however, and that is regarding Mother Earth herself, as a conscious, living being. By circulating Reiki (universal life-force healing energy) into the earth as part of an alchemical unity consciousness meditation, we help to bring balance to the planet itself. The intention of the Earth Alchemy Unity Consciousness Meditation is to assist us to move through unconsciously learned self-limiting states of fear, separation, dualistic thinking and resistance to change, and to access a platform for higher understanding about personal and collective enlightenment. The process of growth called enlightenment requires that something be dissolved, like the seed when it begins to grow, which pushes through the old husk that has been protecting it. This is the process that many levels of our culture are going through.

The old head in the sand approach to dealing with the world, with life, with economics and with environmental chaos has failed. Many institutions blindly clinging to these old patterns are floundering, refusing to embrace new ways. The end result of all this is truly chaotic, because the new way of being collectively in relationship to life is in the process of forming, but it has not yet formed fully, whilst the old ways are dying but are not yet dead! As the pressures for death and rebirth, evolution and transformation grow, we will see an increase in tension and stress on all levels within and without. Externally, we are already seeing an increase in stress within the tectonic plates, the continents themselves; stress within the ecosystem, the biology of earth and global climate crisis; stress within the institutions of our society as they struggle to deal with the massive changes that are and will be occurring; and finally stress individually as we try to cope with the changes that seem to be ever increasing. Take a look at my personal 'symptoms of transformation' list in Chapter 5. In a very real sense, the earth is quite capable of recovering from the damage that has been done whilst we have lived out of harmony with spirit, but in the process of purifying herself many species are beginning to disappear completely – will the human species be one of these? Know this, many eminent scientists feel that mankind, if it carries on living out of harmony with spirit, might pollute itself into extinction. It is not clear at this time what the outcome will be. This is very much in our hands individually and collectively.

From a universal perspective, circulating alchemical energies through our own inner energy pathways, the nadis, and out into the energy pathways of the earth via the ley lines (earth meridians), may help to awaken individuals, by assisting us collectively to break through denials and recognize the dire truth of our situation. Accordingly, this Earth Alchemy Healing Mediation, while directed to the earth, is actually directed towards everyone and everything riding on her back. If we collectively awaken to the sacredness of life and remember daily, in moment-to-moment conscious awareness, our connection to everyone and everything, and our duty to protect this, then we can avert the prophecies of gloom and doom and catastrophe. The Mayan and Hopi prophecies say that if we are unable to elevate ourselves in consciousness, the earth will simply shake us off. This happened before during the Flood...

Regardless of the prophecies, if we elevate ourselves to attain unity consciousness and alchemical transformation within, we will reach heightened states of awareness and be opened to new ways of being not readily accessible to others. This is where I believe we will access or be privy to magical, alchemical solutions to world peace – politically, religiously, environmentally, and in terms of personal health and wellbeing.

The 'Udjat' or Eye of Horus symbol is a potent Egyptian symbol found on temple walls, inside pyramids, in their art, and it was often used as a talisman or amulet to protect the living and the dead; it was sometimes found in mummified wrappings. The mythical story about the Eye of Horus is fascinating and was inspirational to this particular meditative practice and initiation. The Eye of Horus symbol is believed to have powerful healing and protective powers, even some say, the ability to raise the dead. Horus it is said lost this eye during a terrible battle with his evil, jealous Uncle Seth, who had killed Osiris, his brother, the father of Horus. Seth tore the eye of Horus into pieces. Thoth, another Egyptian Godman, healed and regenerated the eye returning it to wholeness and new life. When Thoth gave this eye back to Horus, he gave it to his dead father, Osiris, who was restored to life.

Most often the Eye of Horus symbol was depicted as being the right eye, sometimes called the 'Eye of Ra'. This eye was connected to the sun, above and below, and symbolized solar energies – the divine masculine principle – according to ancient hermetics. It was representative of masculine qualities such as transmitting, rationality, logic and the scientific mind. The left eye of Horus symbolized lunar energies – the divine feminine principle – and was connected to the moon representing qualities of intuition, mysticism and the receptive magical mind.

Alchemical iconography often pictures the sun and the moon merged, which is the experience to be gained from the energy initiation this meditation creates within. I wonder if Einstein knew about this? Perhaps this sacred alchemical union of sun and moon energies is what he hinted at when he said, 'The rational mind is a faithful servant. The intuitive mind is a divine gift. We have created a society that worships the servant and has forgotten the gift.' When you practise the powerful Earth Alchemy Unity Consciousness Meditation, consider it as an initiation to receive an ancient gift – the merging of our inner sun and moon.

Honouring Intuitive Guidance

Throughout history intuition has proven a major source of inspiration leading to innovation. In *Awakening Intuition*, author Frances E. Vaughan explains this process: 'Time after time it appears that major human achievements involve intuitive leaps of imagination. It is the intuitive, pattern-reception faculties associated with the right hemisphere of the brain that break through existing formulations of the truth and expand the body of knowledge. The stabilization of intuitive insights and their usefulness to humanity are subsequently determined by careful, logical examination and validation, but the original vision or insight is intuitive.'

Carl Jung described intuition as 'one of the four ways human beings process the world', placing intuition as 'the function by which one can see around corners'. Albert Einstein is also remembered to have said, 'There is only the way of intuition,' considering it the most important aspect of his talent, crediting intuition as 'the free invention of the imagination'.

If we take a look at world-famous author Dan Brown's work, *The Da Vinci Code* and *Angels and Demons*, in particular, we'll note that the storylines which have so effectively gripped millions of readers, focus around battles between science and religion, the masculine, and introduce the defender of the feminine, the hero, the Priory of Sion. There doesn't appear to be a conclusion in the battle of opposites from each side of the Hermetic teachings, science and church-type religion versus spirituality. I therefore believe that if we, each of us, can unify these energies and connections within and without, we'll heal the illusion of duality and separation from within. Surely this is the alchemical solution the ancients have hinted at for generations... as we unite opposites within, our external world will reflect this love and harmony. I believe this may have been what Christ was hinting at in the *Gnostic Gospel of Thomas*, part of the Nag Hammadi Scrolls, when he said: 'When you make the two one, and when you make the inside like the outside and the outside like the inside and the above like the below and when you make the male and the female one and the same... then you will enter the Kingdom of God.' Perhaps the unified light that this meditation creates is what was referred to in the *Chandogya Upanishad*, which states, 'There is a Light that shines beyond all things on earth, beyond us all, beyond the heavens, beyond the highest, the very highest heavens. This is the Light that shines in our heart.'

So let's learn how to use this light as earth enters ever more rapid times of transformation; let's use this light to transform the ever-increasing levels of chaos we are discovering all around us and within us. Let's rest assured knowing that these chaotic states are a necessity in the transition from one level of energy and consciousness to another. This chaos is showing up in our lives individually, collectively and globally. It causes great imbalance, tension, pain and suffering within if we deny or resist it. Today, more people are dying of stress-related diseases than ever before. How we deal with these states of chaos, stress and tension has a tremendous impact on our ability to move through them gracefully or NOT. My guidance is to offer a very simple alchemical process to create balance in our own subtle energies thereby assisting us to be centred and self-empowered in these times of chaotic transition.

In addition, I am presenting now a means for us all to work universally using the same high alchemical process. From an alchemical standpoint, higher states of consciousness and awareness are attained when the solar and lunar channels within our subtle energy bodies are balanced. It is a question of balancing the active (male) and receptive (female) aspects of self. By accomplishing this task individually we purify the subtle pathways within our own body and bring our consciousness to a more balanced place. By doing the alchemical meditation regularly we can empower and strengthen ourselves to deal with the various levels of chaos around us and eventually heal this chaos within and without.

Christ unity consciousness

In verse 113 of the Nag Hamadi Library, Jesus is asked about the end of the world as we know it:

'His disciples said to him, "When will the Kingdom come?" Jesus said, "It will not come by waiting for it. It will not be a matter of saying 'here it is' or 'there it is'. Rather, the Kingdom of the Father is spread out upon the earth, and men do not see it."'

When Master Jesus walked the earth plane, great crowds would come just to be within his touch. The mass consciousness of thousands of people fed into and reinforced the Christ consciousness. With so much power being emitted from his hands how could he not but heal? Master Jesus made the claim that 'Whatsoever I do, so can you.' All are part of spirit, and the level of clarity we reach is the measure by which we may contribute to the healing of the world.

What makes us human? Is it the ability to walk on two feet and think? Is it the complexity of emotion that permeates our lives like an ocean fog? Who are we really? Even when we define ourselves as a soul, what are we talking about? Is it some mysterious connection with an 'inner self' that few human beings have access to while others simply live their lives in robotic imitation or denial?

Teilhard de Chardin said, and has been quoted extensively since, 'We are not human beings having a spiritual experience, but spiritual beings having a human experience'. Most of us have had peak experiences in our lives where we can identify with this 'spiritual being', but few of us feel able to sustain this awareness. Meanwhile, all kinds of dogmas, rituals and religions have grown up around this awareness of our inner self, which have unfortunately done more to clutter than to illuminate the truth, leading to a painful disconnection from our inner being, with each other and with all life on Mother Earth. This is a view shared by Indian guru and teacher, Sri Kalki.

Sri Kalki

Sri Kalki, or Bhagavan, as many of his disciples call him, is known as the 'Mukti Avatar', a Divine Incarnation whose specialization is to impart enlightenment. His presence and his mission reflected to my good friends, Grace Sears and Kiara Windrider, the highest gifts Mother India has to offer humanity. They told me that having met him and experienced who he is, they feel that they can now rest in complete trust that humanity is going to make it, no matter how fragmented, meaningless and chaotic our existence has been.

Kalki spoke to my two friends of the dilemma most people experience if they are serious about enlightenment. No matter how hard we may try to get there, we still have concepts and expectations about what enlightenment must look like. There is always an effort to get from the state of non-enlightenment to a state of enlightenment, which creates and furthers the very duality we are trying to dissolve. Even when we let go of the effort, we are still 'conditioned' by the deep, unconscious programming within our minds that keeps us separate from external reality, separated from directly experiencing the world without the running commentary of our thoughts. We cannot through effort alone empty out our minds any more than a bucket can empty out an ocean. Enlightenment happens through intentionality, hard work, focus, dedication and by grace in the recognition that it is our natural pre-conditioned state.

Like me Kalki teaches that it does not require centuries of effort, and that anyone could indeed get enlightened, just like Buddha or Jesus. Kalki teaches that not only is enlightenment easily attainable, but it is our natural state. We were originally created with a different programme implanted in our DNA, and every child was born with the ability to directly experience the world as a unified field of consciousness. We have mutated from that state due to various distortions in our collective conditioning, yet the original programming still remains within our DNA. Just like a computer cannot change its own programming from within a programme, we cannot change our mental programming from within our minds alone... It must either come through divine grace, which is difficult for many people because of their restrictive concepts about God, or it can be transferred by someone who knows how. This is how attunement to

Reiki works.

Furthermore, revolutionary new research in 'wave-genetics' reveals DNA can be activated, non-invasively, by radio and light waves keyed to human language frequencies. Studies by cell biologists further demonstrate that the genetic code can be stimulated through human consciousness – specifically, the unity consciousness associated with unconditional love – to heal not only the mind and spirit but the body as well. Benefits of DNA activation, I have learned, can range from allergy relief and increased energy to better relationships and even renewed life purpose. Since DNA regulates all physical, mental, emotional and spiritual aspects of our being, the possibilities are endless!

Kalki, like me, insists that enlightenment is a neurobiological process and he sees his own role as being merely a 'technician'. Through a certain kind of 'divine surgery', and with adequate preparation, the neurobiology and the DNA of a seeker can be changed so as to naturally become enlightened, and then all teachings and guidance naturally flow from within. According to Kalki, divine energy is transferred into the neo-cortex of the brain, which reorganizes the entire framework of consciousness. It has its own intelligence, and interfaces with the deepest longings and blueprint of each individual soul to create a new command centre that bypasses the lower mind (ego). When I first heard about this, I felt truth resonating within me very deeply. I began to understand that this is what had happened to me when I had my near death experience with Archangel Michael.

In genuine enlightenment, the awakening of the true self within and the permanent dissolution of conflict and suffering occurs. The entire framework of past conditioning disappears, as do expectations of the future. Since suffering is caused by addictions, attachments, cravings and aversions based on past conditioning, when this conditioning disappears, suffering disappears as well.

This is often accompanied by states of cosmic consciousness, journeys to celestial realms, profound perceptual changes, sharpening of the senses, various 'siddhis' (spiritual gifts) and profound ecstasy. The physical body becomes illumined with an inner light, and the sense of a separate, continuous identity dissolves. The questioner vanishes along with the questions. The mind becomes a hollow reed through which all creation can flow. Thoughts can still flow through the mind, but do not emanate from the mind. And this is exactly what happened to me. How great to get this confirmation of my own experience from a living avatar.

PRACTICES

Earth alchemy meditation

To do this alchemical meditation, sit comfortably or lie down and focus all your awareness about an inch inwards – between the eyes, behind the bridge of the nose. This area in the brain is where the pituitary and hypothalamus glands are situated. The pituitary is the 'seat' of the endocrine system. It regulates the entire endocrine system and is the key to unlock higher states of consciousness. The hypothalamus is the brain's information-relaying centre.

Just off the physical body, between the eyes, in what mystics call the etheric body, there is an energy vortex or chakra, called the Third Eye or Ajna Centre. On the right side of the Third Eye is a small sun, and on the left side of the Ajna is a small moon. The hermetic alchemists of ancient Egypt coined a phrase, 'As above, so below. As within, so without'. This means that each level of creation is mirrored in the next level above and below.

Modern day alchemist, Tom Kenyon, explained this concept well in a newsletter I received after attending a conference he gave in Glastonbury a couple of years ago. I'll attempt to paraphrase what he said:

'If we look at the atom, the electrons move about the nucleus in elliptical or spherical orbits, just as at the level of the solar system, the planets move around the sun in a similar fashion. Within the human energy system, the solar energies of the sun on the right side of the third eye centre (brow chakra) extend up into the centre of the head in the area of the pineal gland, and down the spine to the root chakra at the base of the spine. This comprises the solar circuit.

On the left side of the third eye centre (brow chakra) the lunar circuit runs up to the centre of the head in the area of the pineal gland, as does the solar circuit. It then runs down the left side of the spine to the base of the spine, into the root chakra to form the lunar circuit.

The sun emits a golden coloured ray or energy that can be perceived as having almost liquid-like qualities. The moon emits a silvery coloured ray or energy that can be perceived as almost liquid. When the gold and silver rays combine the result is a powerful White Gold ray or energy, which at an alchemical level represents the distillation of the balance between the solar and lunar, the masculine and feminine circuits.'

So it is that the two become one...

According to ancient hermetic teachings, White Gold has many alchemical properties, including an ability to purify our meridians, the subtle pathways within the body, called nadis by the yogis and yoginis. This White Gold ray or energy has an immediate beneficial and balancing effect upon consciousness – within and without, above and below. By itself it has immense abilities to refine consciousness and awareness, and this process can be used on its own or in a preparation for even deeper more advanced alchemical practices and meditation, for it greatly facilitates heightened states of awareness.

To do the meditation, sit or lie down, as already indicated. I use the following verse from Shantideva, *A guide to the Bodhisattva's Way of Life*, to really inspire myself beforehand.

'May I be the doctor and the medicine and may I be the nurse for all sick beings in the world until everyone is healed. May a rain of food and drink descend to clear away the pain of thirst and hunger and during the aeon of famine may I myself change into food and drink (light). May I become an inexhaustible treasure for those who are poor and destitute and may I turn into all things they could need and may these be placed close beside them.'

Suitably inspired with this strong intentionality held-in focus, close the eyes and access breathing patterns that are very comfortable and relaxing, and begin to relax into each exhale. It's definitely helpful to play music that is relaxing and which assists us to go within. I'd recommend Tom Kenyon's *Wave Form*, which helps the brain adjust to the alpha brainwave state or even deeper states of relaxation.

Before you start this alchemical practice, remember what Einstein said, that imagination is more important than knowledge! Know that your imagination has within it the power to create and manifest whatever you choose. Choose wisely. Thus advised... call in all your spirit guides to protect and empower you.

Imagine a hollow tube exiting the top of the head, the crown chakra, moving upwards into the sky. This tube is about the size of the circle you create when you connect the thumb to your middle finger. Will and intend that this is connecting to Father Sky energies.

Next, imagine these Father Sky energies coming down the tube into the crown, moving down the spine through the brow and throat chakras into the heart chakra... Feel the warmth, feel the deep healing and relaxation.

Now, imagine the other end of this hollow tube exiting through the perineum, in the root chakra at the base of the spine and connecting to Mother Earth energies, which are female and cool. Imagine these alchemical Mother Earth energies coming back up the spine into the heart and mixing with the Father Sky energies to balance male and female within, above and below...

Imagine these powerful, balancing, alchemical healing energies now permeating every cell, every atom, subatomic particle, every molecule, everything that you are, physically, mentally, emotionally and spiritually. In your imagination, command these energies to ease, soothe and relax you; balance, heal and empower you on all levels, through all times, space and dimensions.

Take about five to ten minutes to really feel this healing taking place, all the time affirming, 'I am unity consciousness.' Feel the divine Father Sky energies and Divine Mother Earth energies combining within your heart, nurturing the divine Christ-self within.

Deeply relaxed, in a deep meditative state, now begin to breathe in, simultaneously imagining a golden solar ray flowing out of the inner sun to the right hand side of the Third Eye travelling up into the centre of the head into the pineal gland. Breathe out, allowing this golden ray to circulate through the entire brain centre and move downwards along the spine to the root chakra at the base of the spine.

Next, breathing in, work with a silver lunar ray flowing out of your inner moon, to the left hand side of the Third Eye. Imagine this travelling up into the centre of the head into the pineal gland. Exhaling, command the silver ray to circulate through the entire brain centre, moving downwards along the spine into the root chakra at the base of the spine.

On the third in-breath, simultaneously imagine both gold and silver rays from your inner sun and moon flowing along together upwards into the pineal gland where they meet and are transformed into White Gold Christ light.

On the exhale, as before, imagine – will – intend that the alchemical White Gold Christed rays are circulating through the entire brain centre, downwards along the spine into the root chakra at the base of the spine.

I would suggest repeating this at least twelve more times in order to experience the alchemical effects of the White Gold. This would take maybe 20 to 30 minutes, and it generates immensely positive, feel-good benefits.

Finally, go within deeply and ask for permission from the guides to send this healing alchemical ray into the earth and imagine it healing whatever needs to be healed for the greatest good of the whole.

Practising this on a regular basis will greatly enhance your ability to deal with and overcome chaos, through the balancing effects of the Christed consciousness you are becoming. You will also find your general intelligence and creativity increasing as well as your subtle intuitive abilities. All of these effects occur as a simple result of activating and balancing the internal solar and lunar circuits. My guidance is that this simple inner initiation to the White Gold ray within and shared without, will energetically create the foundation and prepare the way to 'enter the Kingdom'. Again, quoting from the Gnostic *Gospel of Thomas*, Christ says when you love one another and stop doing what you hate you will be worthy of this. I say – do these two things and this process daily and you will enter the higher levels of consciousness previously only known to the great sages, avatars and bodhisattva's.

Discovering dharma - our life's purpose

As you evolve spiritually, mentally and emotionally, your ability to know your dharma, your true life purpose will increase. Start practising this exercise every year or even twice yearly if you really wish to accelerate your growth.

Make a list of all the things you have ever wished to do, have, be or experience in your life. Give yourself several days to keep adding to the list. When you cannot think of anything further to add, go back to the list and pick the ten most important things you desire – ask your guides and angels to help you prioritize.

Next, work out what each desire would mean to you or to others and what would be the desired outcomes for self and others.

Read through all the answers and work out what kind of person would desire such experiences or things. Make a mission statement about this person... and with luck you will begin to see your life purpose forming before your very eyes. Your higher desires will create the direction you need to be heading in. Knowing your life purpose will make it easier for you to set goals and achieve them.

Establish the targets you choose to achieve. Be strategic – make action plans in terms of how you see yourself achieving your goals and approximately within what time frame. Then practise detachment. Let go. If you ever find yourself 'thinking' about how this could all come about... stop – let go and just trust.

Practices for the physical body to cope with 'enlightenment stress'

With all the cellular changes we undergo related to enlightenment, we are sometimes going to feel rather disoriented, as though we are walking between two worlds. We may feel exhaustion, because we are literally changing cells and becoming new beings. Like a new baby, we may need lots of rest.

Mental confusion and not being able to concentrate on routine tasks may happen as we are being programmed for something larger. Aches and pains throughout the body for which there is no specific cause are common 'for living avatars in training'.

Many people feel as though they are going nuts. If we go to an orthodox medical practice, most likely we will be given anti-depressants, because the orthodox medical model is unable to define what is wrong. It is difficult for the medical profession because they are not used to dealing with symptoms of what I call 'enlightenment stress'.

Because the chakras are related to our endocrine system, women will go through hormonal changes. We may be crying without knowing why because crying releases hormones. However, these hormones help us to heal and transform. Many women are going through menopause earlier because of enlightenment – we are all accelerating to reconnect to best self. Men may be very frustrated with symptoms of exhaustion when they are normally used to being very active. They may feel stronger connection to their inner female and find this emotionally confusing. My PSA Life Mastery, Map to God and Integrating Transformation workshops have all the answers to balance the physical, mental, emotional and spiritual.

Let's examine how I would treat someone who is going through these changes…

I approach it from the viewpoint of working with individual beings instead of treating a disease. 'Doctor' in Latin means educator. The only effective service we can perform as a true healer is to empower individuals with the necessary tools and reassure them that what is happening is real, and that they can heal and be free of the 'negative' symptoms while healing. The real key is that each person takes responsibility and does their own work.

Essentially, I work with all kinds of energy medicines, but especially MS-REM, my own form of super-Reiki. Also, I use homeopathy to work on the energetic body, Young Living therapeutic-grade pure essential oils, vitamins, herbs and flower remedies to cleanse and detox. There's more detail on the symptoms and remedies in the appendix. Psychological recapitulation is also key. Ultimately, the therapy package depends entirely on individual needs.

Much of what I am guided to do has been accessed from those whom I refer to as wise elders – ancestors – incarnate and disincarnate, who trod the path long before me. I see my work as a bridge from one level of experience to another.

There is an old Chinese saying, 'May you live in interesting times'. Some people believe this is a curse. I believe every challenge, however, gives us a gift. Without doubt there is a great deal of anxiety and fear being felt because of global climate crisis, earth changes and changes in collective consciousness. This, too, I refer to as 'enlightenment stress'. It does exist even though many people might not be conscious of it yet. However, when we choose enlightenment, the changes to our physiological makeup accelerate and there are many temporary physical symptoms that are occurring in our bodies as a consequence of this.

Other useful enlightenment stress antidotes

Go with the flow, don't fight it. If you feel tired and exhausted, rest and get plenty of sleep.

Postive affirmations like 'This too shall pass!' work.

Be sure to drink lots of water, for you are detoxifying and dehydrating more quickly than usual.

Taking valerian relieves emotional tension and stress.

Fenugreek relieves stress on the lymphatic system and helps detoxification.

To relieve muscle spasm, take valerian. And try mud baths or a long, hot soak in a bath to which is added a cup of Epsom salts. Do this daily.

Remember, even if we are having heart palpitations or breathing difficulties, it is the heart chakra or the throat chakra that is unblocking and that the symptoms are temporary. We aren't dying physically, we are simply dying to an old behaviour pattern or aspect of self that no longer works – it's transformation! If it's impossible to source a particular oil or some valerian immediately, try this… simply say the name in your head and thus invoke the substance when you need relief. All healing energies are transmitted via the sound of the name and are just as effective said in the mind or aloud, as in physically taking them. Try it and see.

In self-healing and balancing sessions, ask the angelic or Reiki guides to help relieve any pain. They are just waiting to be asked! Most symptoms seem to last a couple of weeks, then clear up. Some symptoms may recur from time to time, and if we can learn how to work with the power of decrees, this can also greatly assist us.

Decreeing

'Decree a thing thus, and it shall be established unto you.'

The most powerful decrees begin with the words, 'I am'. Discover what best self desires through you and decree the desired state as an expression of your true identity. Speak with authority, imbue your words with great feeling and thus (in harmony with, identified with and united with Source) become the author of your own life.

When you become aware of any situation, any condition that appears to express less than the ideal, immediately decree with deep feeling the desired state and thus call it forth. Or, as Jean Luke Piccard from Star Trek says, 'Make it so!'

'Fake it to make it' is something I learned to work with… Imagine, will, intend… pretend that the desired state is already here. What do you see, now that 'I am powerful, loving and courageous'? How do you feel, now that 'I am powerful, loving and courageous'? How is your life different, now that 'I am powerful, loving and courageous'? How is the whole world different, now that 'I am powerful, loving and courageous'? Visualize these qualities – get into the desired state emotionally. Visualize, think and feel – how does this improve me, my world, my relationships? Intend and manifest your desires in the physical reality, where you focus attention, energy is magnified. Remember, this does work but you have to work on it!

Identify, list and stop energy-stealing patterns

Observe our culture within its proper historical context. The first half of the past millennium was spent under the thumb of the Church and in the second half we became obsessed with material comfort and possessions. Now at the start of the 21st century, we have exhausted that preoccupation. Some of us who are more highly evolved are ready to discover life's ultimate purpose of truth and reality.

Start to get acquainted with the subtle energy that infuses all things. With daily practise you can learn to see the aura around any living being and to project your own energy around it to give it strength. The practice of Reiki fast-tracks this process greatly.

An unconscious competition for energy underlies all conflicts. By dominating or manipulating others (even through attempts to rescue them), we get the extra energy that we think we need. Yes, it can feel good to be in control of others. However, both parties are damaged in the exchange and in the resulting energy conflict.

The key to overcoming conflict in the world is the mystical experience. This is available to everyone. To nurture the mystical and build your energy, allow yourself to be filled with a sense of love. When the pupil is ready an appropriate teacher will appear. Make sure this teacher is pure and has dealt with his/her own dramas. In other words, find someone who walks their talk and can teach you all the high-level protection techniques you will need.

Childhood traumas block our ability to fully experience the mystical.

All humans, because of their upbringing, tend towards one of the four control dramas that Redfield explains in *The Celestine Prophecy*. Sometimes we are chameleons, ricocheting from one role to another, depending upon who we are trying to control or who is trying to control us.

Intimidators steal energy from others by threatening them.

Interrogators steal energy by questioning and judging.

Aloofs attract attention or energy by playing remote or mysterious.

Victims ('Poor Me') make us feel guilty and responsible for their pain and failures.

Work out the control dramas of your family members. Then consider how these prompted you to create your own control drama. Armed with this awareness, notice how you utilized your own control drama in situations of your past and how it appears in your present behaviour. Know that you did the best you knew how. Use this information to empower yourself to make changes and eliminate your energy-stealing patterns.

Review the memories in which you experienced trauma. Know that others were acting from their energy-stealing patterns and doing the best they then knew how. Forgive yourself and forgive them. Let go of the past. Resolve the old traumas. Then you can focus on your essential question, which is how to make of your life a higher-level synthesis of the lives of your parents.

Once cleared of traumas, you can build energy through Reiki, 24/7 mindfulness, contemplation and meditation. As you then focus on your basic life question, you will start riding a steady stream of intuitions, dreams and synchronistic coincidences. These will all ultimately guide you in the direction of your own evolution and transformation.

You can't do this alone. Begin to practise the new interpersonal ethic in community. Instead of stealing energy, give energy to others through giving them your full attention. As you really listen to what they are saying, you are uplifting them. Talk to the people who make spontaneous eye contact with you. Avoid co-dependent (energy-stealing) relationships. Be there for people. As you notice their energy-stealing patterns, call attention to them in a non-controlling, loving way. Instead of just filling the air with words, wait until spirit (instead of ego) moves you to speak.

Working with animal totems

FOX: This spirit medicine is about protection through camouflage and containment. As well as being a powerful protection totem, fox enables us to develop confidence, focus and clarity of thought. It assists us to make important decisions. It enables us to feel strong enough to know when it is safe to show others who we are. Fox spirit medicine reveals to us how to exercise the powers of greater discrimination and discernment in our lives.

HORSE: Horse is power! This is a great tonic for the heart and kidney, for both yin and yang energies. It shows us how to develop stamina, endurance, strength, power and speed in our life process. Also, horse spirit medicine is a highly supportive energy to see us through busy periods in our lives where immense change is occurring.

Unity consciousness manifesting technique
Reiki Symbol 1

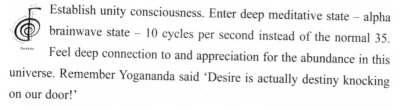 Establish unity consciousness. Enter deep meditative state – alpha brainwave state – 10 cycles per second instead of the normal 35. Feel deep connection to and appreciation for the abundance in this universe. Remember Yogananda said 'Desire is actually destiny knocking on our door!'

1. Visualize your wish with you in it.
2. Place the earth behind it (and you).
3. Bring a golden grid over the picture, diagonal or spiral, running from sky to earth.
4. Draw the Cho-Ku-Rei over the whole picture.
5. Hold the image for as long as you can, then let go.
6. Be careful what you ask for. You might get it!

CHAPTER 5

INTO THE FUTURE
SOUL MERGING WITH SPIRIT

'Do not think that the resurrection is an illusion. It is no illusion, but it is truth. It is more suitable to say then, that the world is an illusion.'
THE EPISTLE TO RHEGINOS FROM THE NAG HAMMADI, GNOSTIC TEXT

OVERVIEW

The above quote has always stuck in my mind. When I saw the film, *The Matrix* I couldn't help but wonder if the people who wrote the film had read this quote or knew about the Gnostic teachings. One quote in particular from the film might suggest such a connection.

'You're here because you know something. What you know you can't explain – but you feel it. You've felt it your entire life; that there's something wrong with the world; you don't know what it is, but it's there, like a splinter in your mind, driving you mad. It is this feeling that has brought you to me. Do you know what I'm talking about?'

'The Matrix?' Neo asks.'

Gnosticism is an ancient set of secret beliefs centred around a 'knowing' that the adept can learn how to transcend the illusion, see through the veils and experience Grace or God directly in their everyday lives. The Gnostic adept can truly create heaven on earth. The Gnostics taught that we can reach a higher understanding and experience the divine through leading an exemplary life. Having reached a perfected state, the few, it was believed, would then receive eternal life on another plane of existence. This is also what the Theosophical Society teachings of Helena

Blavatsky suggest.

The word Gnostic comes from the Greek 'Gnosis' meaning higher knowledge. Why and how did these teachings get lost, until now? Well, wherever orthodoxy existed, the keepers of these sacred wisdoms and hidden mysteries have been declared heretics, subsequently tortured and put to death.

In *The Da Vinci Code*, the sacred chapel at Rosslyn is said to be full of Gnostic (pagan) imagery and symbols. When John Hunt at O Books was editing this book, by synchronicity, he was also working on a book about Rosslyn Chapel in Scotland. He very excitedly remarked to me that 'A Map to God' is unveiling the same mysteries as the stones in Rosslyn Chapel. The Rosslyn archivist, Robert Brydon, has in fact described the chapel as 'an allegorical book in stone'.

A visit to Rosslyn Chapel is deeply spiritually uplifting. Rosslyn is like no other church in that it has no obviously traditional church imagery – no Madonna, no Jesus and no apostles. Yet per square foot this surely must be the most richly and elaborately decorated place of worship in the British Isles. There is an exotic blend of Judaic esoteric carvings, Masonic symbols, traces of Christianity *and* Islam. Everywhere pagan iconography abounds with the face of the Green Man and other elemental forces in strong evidence. In a truly pagan framework, there are masses of fruits, herbs, leaves, spices, flowers and vines, together with dragons, trees and serpents...

Incidentally, the serpent energy or Kundalini, as it's known, is one of the most important secrets of Gnosticism...

The secret of eternal youth

'You have the energy of the sun in you, but you keep knotting it up at the base of your spine.'

RUMI

The Kundalini is the spiritual fire, the dynamic creative power that resides within every one of us – curled at the base of the spine rather like a coiled snake. It's a sacred, mysterious, energy channel that starts at the base of our spines in the root chakra and travels upwards to the top of the head into the crown chakra. Contained within the Kundalini is unlimited creative potential, energies which spiral upwards through the nervous system via nerve endings attached to the spine. It is said that divine wisdom and enlightenment is achieved when the Kundalini is fully awakened and streaming unimpeded up the spine, illuminating the brain, pouring out through the crown chakra to merge with Source. My Kundalini has been fully awakened for many years now... I have learned everything we need to know and do to raise the Kundalini safely and effectively. I do these simple exercises daily. This would certainly explain how I just know things without knowing how. It's truly the only logical explanation for the 180 degrees turnaround I have been able to make from 'crack cocaine to Christ'.

In an 'enlightened' person the Kundalini is fully raised and active in a functional, balanced way – running freely from the base of the spine to the top of the head. An enlightened being knows how to control the profound power of the Kundalini and is fully conscious of the entire mind/body/ spirit complex. They have normally opened this sacred channel gradually as a result of powerful spiritual disciplines... perhaps yoga, meditation and prayer. However, I believe that attunement to, and working with, Reiki is one of the most fast-track and safest methods, coupled with psychological recapitulation. This is what's worked for me.

In most people, however, the Kundalini remains dormant, suppressed and tightly coiled at the base of the spine, particularly for those whose self-limiting, ego-based thoughts and beliefs prevent them from experiencing greater joy and true creativity. Such suppression of our life-force and our emotions (energy in motion) also prevents us from knowing best self or expressing our true natures. Fear, lack of self-love, low self-esteem, lack of confidence, doubt, oppression and giving our power away to others, are some of the attitudes and forces that prevent the Kundalini from being activated. Christ warned us about the seven deadly sins... all of these negative states would block the Kundalini. This is why it's so vitally important to do the psychological recapitulation work or we are going nowhere.

Sometimes we can blow open our Kundalini through abuse of drugs, malnutrition or extreme stress. Then we encounter spiritual emergency, possibly high anxiety states, delusions of grandeur: Messiah complex, insanity and sometimes even death has occurred if the Kundalini is opened before we have done the correct foundation work to prepare for this. Once activated safely, however, the Kundalini life-force energy begins to travel up the spine in a spiral-like fashion – igniting, opening and purifying the chakra energy vortices along the way – until it reaches the brain where it illuminates, transmutes and transforms. In all honesty the raising of the Kundalini is the only way to come to know best self. We don't get this through reading a book or attending a workshop, we have to live the spiritual principles, which produce this state and enlightenment. This is exactly what I teach to the spiritual community at my home just outside Glastonbury in the UK. The reason I chose to return to live close to Glastonbury, the place of my birth, is that alchemists are always drawn to live on or near to the most influential earth dragon points, to benefit from the higher life-force emanating from these profoundly powerful energy vortices.

Natural activation of the Kundalini is also assisted through changing our beliefs, purifying our diet, changing our lifestyle to a more spiritually focused state. This is what I mean when I talk about reconnecting to best self. Attunements such as the ones I have been sharing in this book, which originated in ancient Tibet, also safely awaken the movement of Kundalini. Developing and deepening our creativity is a potent activator as well. Ultimately nothing is as powerful as receiving training and guidance from an experienced Kundalini teacher.

The Kundalini is expressed in art forms as two serpents intertwining with one another around a central, magical staff as they both spiral up towards the top or crown where outstretched wings symbolize enlightenment, divine love, power, mastery and wisdom. When our

Kundalini is fully risen and functions in a balanced way, this allows us to receive wisdoms and divine insights; to create and manifest in accordance with our supreme nature (best self) and live in an enlightened, higher state of consciousness and awareness. This is how we come to experience heaven on earth...

When we are truly open to our full creative powers and express more of our best self, living our best destiny, spirit streams come forth to ignite the 'power of the sun' that lies dormant within all of us.

When we awaken to and know how to be empowered by more of the Truth that is within us... then the world around us becomes transformed too.

Recent mysterious planetary aspects influencing Kundalini

Certain extraordinary astrological aspects have been intensely affecting our Kundalini energy for some time now. However, such planetary influences are, I have learned, especially relevant to a certain age group – people between the ages of 50 and 68. All those of us with Pluto in Leo – the 50 to 68 age group – are being gifted a chance to ignite the Kundalini energy like never before. All those 50 and under are also blessed these days because there is so much previously hidden or secret wisdom freely available so they can train to awaken Kundalini with expert guidance. As for children being born in the last twenty years or so, these fabulous 'Indigo/Crystal Children' are being born partially or, in some cases, with their Kundalini totally awakened. With the right help, their journey is a magical one – without understanding and help, however, it can be a nightmare. So many kids these days are being diagnosed with Attention Deficit Disorder (ADD), whereas in actual fact there is nothing wrong with these children other than they are extremely advanced energetically, very awake and aware. We need to help these children to understand their evolved consciousness and energy structure, and my workshops do exactly that. Also, the Young Living remedy, 'Peace and Calming', which is a powerful blend of therapeutic-grade pure essential oils, helps to calm these magical children so they can cope with the lower frequencies on earth.

Transformation and rebirth

Pluto – legendary god of the Underworld and Master of Death and Rebirth – tends to inspire havoc and chaos for the purpose of breaking down the old to breakthrough to the new. This can be intense, dramatic, radical and dark. It's also a luminous, cathartic and liberating experience. It is the force that carries life through its metamorphosis.

It can be summed up in one word: transformation.

Accordingly, right now, there is a mass potential for powerful spiritual awakening and transformation during the next five or six years especially. Some people call this collective initiation 'ascension'. Those who have already awakened to best selves, who are living in harmony with their true spiritual nature will be magnetizing even more opportunities to themselves, to rise to an even greater level of spiritual awareness.

These influences have been particularly disruptive recently because Saturn, often the bringer of challenging phases into our lives, is currently transiting into and across the field of the Pluto in Leo aspect. This will accelerate and amplify this already intense aspect. The higher-view offers that Saturn brings opportunity for enlightenment and positive change specifically through adversity and hardship.

This is what purification is all about: the death of something in our lives or personalities that is not in our best interest... and the beginning or rebirth to best self, best destiny. Some people resist it because this phase can present a trying time in their lives. However, those who manage to embrace the challenge will always come out the other end in much better shape than they went in: so much lighter, more awake, more aware, more free, more magical and powerful.

About spiritual integrity

'Integrity is one of several paths. It distinguishes itself from the others because it is the right path, and the only one upon which you will never get lost.'

M H McKee

The alchemical journey has many names – enlightenment, supra-mental descent, nirvana, samahdi, transformation and some call it ascension.

Ascension – the supreme transformation, is an event in which an individual shifts and transforms from a dense physical body to a light body of higher vibrational frequency. To summarize what we have learned so far, ascension is achieved by balancing and then raising the Kundalini. I have already explained that in order to raise the Kundalini, we first need to balance all the chakras, move up through the various initiatory tests, clear energetic and/or karmic blocks and unite the inner male and female energies. The transcending of the ego is so vitally important because denials cause blocks to the sacred Kundalini – life-force energy.

Due to earth's entry into what some scientists call the Photon Belt – a band of light out in space – our planet is ascending in frequency of vibration. Therefore, everyone and everything is ascending. We are all of us presently moving into a higher frequency of energy in which the cells, molecules, atoms of our body are vibrating at a faster level. Love vibrates at a very high frequency. Fear vibrates at a very low frequency.

What we experience when we undergo initiation or attunement to universal life-force energy (Reiki, chi, ki, orgone, élan vitale, prana) is a quickening of frequency. With Reiki the empowerment is fast-tracked whereas with meditation the enlightenment is much more gradual and subtle. Originally prayer and meditation were just trainings to prepare students to be able to communicate with and listen to higher self, whereas initiation is entrance into the inner sanctum: giving birth to the magical alchemical child – Level 4 – and becoming and being God/Goddess in carnate – Level 7.

The truth is, we already have everything we need within us to fulfil our own personal ascension. However, in rediscovering what this is, there are some very real advantages to using the same simple processes, such as those presented by this book and during my workshops. I work with processes, rituals and techniques researched from all the great lineages of spiritual teachings – traditional and some less traditional.

Using these processes in groups we create a mass collective consciousness thought-form that will benefit ALL humanity and the entire planet earth. When thousands of people work with the same processes for ascension, they visualize and energize the Light and the Love in exactly the same way through unified intentionality. Through this unified effort, the light energies are greatly empowered and will manifest much more quickly. Christ said, 'Wherever two or more are gathered in my name, I am present'. If everyone is creating a different image by working alone with individual methods, their collective individual efforts, though valuable, will be fragmented and scattered. Consequently, their individual efforts will not be nearly as powerful and effective. This is why the ceremonial order and ritual of Reiki or any divine process is so important!

The information collected for all of my workshops and this book has been sourced from the adept or mystery schools of all the major religions and cultures: Sufism, Gnosticism, Qabalah, Hinduism, Shintoism, Buddhism, Shamanism to name but a few, in order to assist us during this critical time of transformation... ascension.

The processes and techniques are much more than creative visualizations. They are divine consecrations. These consecrations are designed to prepare us in our physical bodies to be powerful and effective 'Instruments of Universal Creation' and will assist each of us to reach our highest potential during these wondrous times of great shifts in consciousness and transformation.

The message in this book is about truly understanding this trans-formation and how to achieve greater levels of wholeness, integration, synthesis and assimilation. Let's make corporeal the promise of 'Heaven on Earth' and 'oneness'. Let's emerge from ego and truly embrace the spiritual ideal – true essential and best self. It's vitally important to remember that spiritual alchemy may begin with knowledge, but knowledge not lived and mastered is just so much mental baggage. This book shows everyone 'how to' understand and live the ideal. The work of awakening spiritual integrity truly fulfils Socrates' injunction to 'know thyself'. When we know who we are, we will discover the true purpose of our lives. Then our actions will reflect our higher purpose and make this world a better place.

About the mystery of ascension

I'd like to share some direct inner guidance given to me concerning multiple realities. As the planet ascends, third dimensional grids of consciousness containing morphogenetic energy fields, based on matrix-type, limited ego beliefs, are now collapsing. These are transforming to make way for new more positive and powerful grids of consciousness with higher vibratory rates of frequency pertaining to sound, light, and colour. Something is being crucified and something is resurrecting in its place... something much better.

Imbalanced emotions linked to the old lower, third-dimensional grid frequencies – fear, anger, jealousy, shame, grief, guilt, hatred, etc. – will ultimately no longer be part of our conscious reality. This is achieved by identifying our old negative ego, energy-stealing patterns, which lower our vibration, cause disease and trap us into lower levels of vibration. It serves our ascension process to let go of all the negative ego emotions previously mentioned. To do so, we need to know ourselves and practise moderation. We need to practise mindfulness, living consciously in 'moment-to-moment' awareness and to consistently replace negative thoughts, feelings and emotions with states of unconditional love, forgiveness and compassion.

Integrating transformation

Everything is vibration. The higher vibrations are transforming the lower vibrations. Changes of vibration affect most things in our lives: eating, drinking, sleeping, love relationships, friendships, health – indeed all of consciousness.

The great Indian freedom-fighter, yogi and avatar, Sri Aurobindo, knew this. He spoke about a new force that is beginning to move through human affairs. The Divine that we are in our true essence is beginning to move towards the fractured divinity of our embodied form. He referred to this as the 'supramental descent'. It is a unifying force that is beginning to permeate our collective human drama, reverse our distorted identification with physical form, and awaken our true potential within the fields of matter. It is a new evolutionary force that is here to create a new species of humanity as different from humans today as we are from the apes. It is a Divine force that is re-splicing the very basis of our DNA so that we can fully express our Infinite Universal Self within transformed bodies of light capable of multi-dimensional access.

What we refer to as 'enlightenment' is the first step in this journey, he explains. It is a neuro-physiological process whereby the mind is linked with the heart which, yoked together, link with the dimensions of soul. It is only the first step, however. As our DNA begins to respond to these linkages, the physical body begins to mutate and transform. The cells begin to absorb nourishment directly from the cosmos, the mind allows increasing access to higher dimensions, and the soul finds fuller expression in the body of purified matter. Eventually the body becomes a clear, perfect reflection for the intent of spirit, and soul can incarnate fully within the body. Some call this process of spirit into matter 'ascension'. (Perhaps a more appropriate term would be 'descension'!)

Working with Reiki daily has precipitated this transformation for me. Conquering ego, shadow and persona has removed the energetic blocks to experiencing true higher, best self reconnection. My Kundalini has risen, is fully awakened, balanced and functional. Although I live in the same world as before, it's a world that's been transformed for me by enlightened perceptions connected to this higher consciousness state.

The quickening

For the masses of humanity, however, conscious awareness of the ascension process is still to come. It may not be till certain shifts take place in the energetic balance of earth that we become fully capable of living as limitless spiritual beings in human bodies. As we come closer to the end of linear time as reflected in the Mayan calendar (2012), the energetic balance on earth will go through a profound shift. Until then, we can begin with contemplating our true potential. Let's awaken from all the illusions of who we are not. Let's dream who we can become. Once we recognize who we are not, our souls can work more directly to illumine our bodies and minds. Although the mass enlightenment and ascension of humanity may not happen until later, each of us can begin our individual journey here and now. And that's exactly what this book is about…

Exactly *how* does one person embracing and being best self make a difference to the whole world in the midst of global climate crisis?

As we encourage ourselves to be consciously aware of and take self-responsibility for all the crises that exist on so many levels, personal and planetary – toxic thoughts; feelings and emotions; food, air and water; the near collapse of the ecosystem; geological planetary changes that are just beginning; the drastic weather changes that are taking place which threaten food supplies; and the breakdown of people, systems, societies and institutions – we can be forgiven for feeling somewhat anxious or overwhelmed.

The intention of this book is to assist people to move through unconsciously learned self-limiting states of fear and resistance, to change and to create a context for higher understanding about ascension. The process of growth called ascension requires that something be dissolved, like the aforementioned seed when it begins to grow, pushes through the old husk that has been protecting it. This is the process which many levels of our culture are going through. Transformation can be stressful and this is no exception. Here are some typical symptoms of transformation which, as mentioned, I have come to refer to as 'enlightenment stress' connected to this collective ascension process:

A creeping sense of discomfort with our familiar environment, which may manifest as feelings that we are no longer content with our jobs, friendships, family or partners.

The inability to identify why we are filled with despair, depression, fatigue and exhaustion.

Loneliness, often accompanied by anxiety, that our isolation and 'feeling that we don't fit in' will never end.

A penetrating awareness that something in our lives is changing and that, although the future is uncertain, we definitely cannot continue or go back to live in the old way.

A deepening enthusiasm to explore what we really need out of life as opposed to what we have been programmed to think we want.

Needing increasingly to be with like-minded others who share, reflect and validate these new desires.

Allergies and increased sensitivity to certain foods, fabrics, environmental toxins, medications.

A burning desire and curiosity about areas related to self-development, through choice or necessity.

An emerging sense of a new best self, new goals, behaviour and lifestyle.

A feeling of spiritual liberation – freedom from bondage to the former ego-based way of being and thinking – breaking through to spirit.

A need for time alone to re-charge and to commune with nature.

A need to break free from fundamental organized religions – the realization that institutional religion is incomplete and no longer enough.

Unbearable boredom and no enthusiasm for the do/have/consume lifestyle that once brought us satisfaction and contentment.

A disease that cannot be successfully cured by conventional medical procedures.

'The truth shall make you free.'

JOHN 8:3

Book 2 'Developing Spiritual Integrity' – preparation for the final stages

The reason this book stops at Alchemical Level 4 – the stage of Christed consciousness – and proceeds no further on the map is that the final three stages, as perhaps one may have already imagined, are incredibly challenging and demanding. This final part of the journey makes *The Da Vinci Code*, *Harry Potter* and Indiana Jones-type adventures look dull and easy by comparison!

At Alchemical Level 5 a truly fierce refining process begins where higher life-force energies become available to us. We feel as if we are falling apart or being torn apart by forces beyond our comprehension. Actually, this is exactly what's happening; we are beginning to disintegrate physically, mentally, emotionally and spiritually to make room for the more highly refined energies of ultimate best self – soul is merging now with spirit. We are completing the journey of ego reconnecting to soul and beginning the journey of soul reconnecting to spirit. It's a similar process but the way becomes more difficult and we get tested like almost never before, over and over until we fully embrace this natural process to disintegrate so we can integrate more light. This is likened to the shedding of old skins in order to allow even higher energies or aspects of best self to be integrated. The success and accomplishments of the last level – Christ consciousness or reconnection to soul – pale into insignificance almost, as we are confronted with our worst personal shadow aspects and the worst shadow challenges of the entire collective consciousness. As more light comes in, more shadow is exposed and needs to be purified and cleared. It all 'sounds' so simple and it is simple, but far from easy. We feel as if we are dying and of course we are dying, dying to find God.

The beginning of the alchemical process to reconnect to spirit – all that is – is truly overwhelming, dark and frightening. The places we are asked to go are almost where angels fear to tread... a good reason that the higher path, the final three levels of the map are discussed in a separate book. This higher path is all at once fascinating and terrifying, yet totally compelling.

It's not for the newcomer or beginner and definitely NOT for the faint-hearted. If the drowsy or newly awakened were to know about the final tests of the higher levels too soon, there is a real danger that they'd be forever discouraged from the path. This is surely the most valid reason for discussing Levels 5, 6 and 7 in the next book.

At Alchemical Level 5 consumed by darkness, it feels like the light has deserted us and gone out. We may wish to give up and many do because they feel so world-weary. I remember a phrase from Star Trek that sums it up perfectly – 'the higher the fewer'. It's a terribly frightening experience to feel as if all that was gained so far has been lost or perhaps wasn't ever true.

In *Developing Spiritual Integrity*, the final three levels of the map will be outlined, showing us that we are never alone in this higher refining 'polishing our diamond' process. Like never before, there comes a growing sense that everything we do is for all of humanity. We lose all interest in attaining personal ego goals and feel focused only on the bigger picture. This is a major choice point, where it becomes terrifyingly too apparent that the collective shadow can only be transcended via each one of us being willing to personally deal with and transcend this evil within self.

Oh what a glorious battle ensues! We come face to face with our dharma and the realization that no matter what it takes to transcend our own karma and that of the collective, this was always to be our life work. If we wish to continue higher up the path, we accept this. Resistance is futile and whatever we resist persists holding us back. If we are ready to go higher, all the way, these realizations animate and inspire us to see this through. Re-animated we release the echoes of outworn 'victim consciousness' beliefs and deal with each issue as it arises – with wisdom and with spiritual integrity. It's tough, it's terrible and it takes sheer guts, determination, detachment, love, courage, faith, hope and patience to never give up and never surrender ever again to the lower path of ego.

As Jimmy Carter once said, 'We should live our lives as though Christ was coming this afternoon.'

When I was introduced to the higher initiations of the last three levels, I began to experience all kinds of loss, rejection, abandonment and betrayal from those nearest and dearest to me, my teacher, my husband, all sorts of 'friends' – even my best friend. I lost my job, my health and my home. I experienced all kinds of blocks to succeeding and all kinds of loss, pain and suffering. The challenges were dark, devastating and fierce. It took everything I had to remain true to the higher path and hold strong to my beliefs. I continued step by step, little by little, each day. I learned to keep everything in the day – sometimes repeating over and over to myself 'this too shall pass!' I was soothed, I made it through and I have never looked back. This map helped me to keep the faith and to keep on keeping on… a favourite saying of mine.

The map of the alchemical levels, however, is not really about reaching a destination – enlightenment. You see there's always work to do, more to unfold and I live in a perpetual state of excitement and joy, welcoming the challenge, the incredible mystery that reconnection to spirit and ultimate best self is.

So where do we go next?

Entering Alchemical Level 6, we learn to create yet only motivated by how our creativity will be for and help the greatest good of the whole. We will still experience times when we feel the illusion of separation from spirit, yet we will always know that our guardian angel is merely focused elsewhere and that with the slightest flutter of wings will return to aid us. Most likely we'll experience the dangers of self-inflation or delusions of grandeur. At times we may feel as if we are ahead of all others and feel tempted to look down on them as un-evolved and stupid. Be compassionate and never judge the darkness or it will claim us too! At this level, the last vestiges of personal identity are gradually blotted out by periodic inner experiences of the One – the true highest best self. Personal awareness is purged by a growing awareness of the One – the Absolute – All That Is.

At Alchemical Level 7, the final stage, our best self is fully present all of the time. Our full reconnection with spirit is manifested in the earth physical and we feel and sometimes see (and others can see) a golden glow about us. We are the ones we have been waiting for. We are the one who is all this and we are filled with ultimate confidence, power, wisdom, compassion and love. Because what we wish and desire is what the One self wishes and desires for the greatest good, all our actions have great success. If the time is right and the vision is perfect, instant manifestation is possible. Even when engaged in interactions with others less aware, we never forget the best self and our best destiny. Most who attain this state remain here only to serve others and the greatest good. Thus we learn how to live spiritual integrity.

Summary

As stated earlier, earth is quite capable of recovering from the damage that has been done whilst we have lived out of harmony with spirit, but in the process of purifying herself many species are harmed and might even disappear...

I would urge everyone to go and see the film, *An Inconvenient Truth'*, the new film on global climate crisis made by ex-Vice President of the US, The Honorable, Mr Al Gore. We see the Arctic and Antarctic ice caps melting. We see Greenland oozing into the sea. We see the atmosphere polluted with greenhouse gases that block heat from escaping. We see photos from space of what the ice caps looked like once and what they look like now and, in animation, we see how high the oceans might rise. Shanghai and Calcutta swamped. Much of Florida, too. The water takes a chunk of New York. The fuss about what to do with Ground Zero is no longer relevant because according to scientists, it will be under water.

An Inconvenient Truth is a cinematic version of the lecture that Gore has given free of charge for years warning of the dangers of global warming. Davis Guggenheim, the director of the film, opened it up a bit. For instance, he added some shots of Gore mulling the fate of the earth as he is driven here or there in some city, sometimes talking about personal matters such as the death of his beloved older sister from lung cancer and the close call his son had after being hit by a car. These are all traumas that Gore had mentioned in his presidential campaign and that to the uninitiated may have seemed cloying at the time. Here they seem altogether entirely authentic and appropriate.

The case Gore makes is worthy of sleepless nights: our earth is in extremis – something has to give… Actually, we have to give. A quote by Martin Luther King, Jr, that gave me hope to continue comes to mind, 'We must accept finite disappointment, but never lose infinite hope'. Ego fears but best self hopes, and always for the best. So it is with all of our relationships in ego and this is why we need to reconnect to best self, so that magically, coming from true unconditional love, we can give something back – healing! It's not just that polar bears are drowning because they cannot reach receding ice flows or that 'The Snows of Kilimanjaro' will exist someday only as a Hemingway short story – we can all live with that. It's rather that Hurricane Katrina is not past but prologue. In the future, people will not yearn for the winters of yesteryear but for the summers. Katrina produced several hundred thousand evacuees. The flooding of Calcutta would produce many millions. We are in for an awful time. So, it's not just humans who go through a dark night of the soul – it happens to planets too, albeit because of humans lost and unconscious in all that doing, having and consuming... I see this as a test of our spiritual valour to rediscover the ability to consider two opposing ideas at the same time, whilst remaining fearless and functional. We need to be able to see that whilst things may *seem* hopeless on the surface, deep within, our determination will create something magical and different.

As long as people can be led to hope and focus on the solutions rather than the problems, it may be that Gore will do more good for his country and the world with this film than Bush ever did by beating him in 2000. Well that's one thing we know for sure! When he was robbed of the presidency, Gore said something very profound: 'In situations like this, all we can do is our best.' Are we ready, willing and able to do our best now?

In his own way, Gore has raised his sights to save the world and in my own way so, too, have I. Will we accept his message, identify with the issues that need to change and then ever hopeful *BECOME* the change we wish to see in our world. I truly *know* that hope not only provides us with a sense of destination, but also gives us the energy to get started. Here's a quote to inspire hope that has proved true for me over and over: 'And let us not be weary in well doing: for in due season we shall reap, if we faint not.' Galatians, 6:9.

From the global perspective, circulating universal life-force healing energies through self and through our own energy pathways down through all the pathways of the earth may help to awaken other individuals and heal the planet; it may help us collectively to recognize what the bleep is going on. So in this regard, this book, while directed at enlightening self, is ultimately directed at healing planet earth through our reconnection to and living in harmony with spirit. If we collectively awaken to the sacredness of life and our duty to protect it, then we can avert the prophecies of gloom, doom and disasters. The Mayan and Hopi prophecies say that if we are unable to rise to the occasion, the earth will simply shake us from herself, and our history and culture will pass into oblivion like so many before us… remember the Flood?

Regardless of the prophecies, if we achieve reconnection to best self (alchemy) and can live in spiritual integrity (purity), we will attain heightened states of consciousness and awareness, which create transformation for our world and ourselves. As we transform and integrate higher and still higher aspects of best self, something magical happens: our words, thoughts and feelings carry great power – the power of healing miracles. Ultimately, higher awareness opens us to new mysterious ways of being that will become obvious and available to us that may not be readily available or apparent to the sleeping masses. Let's all remember something truly pertinent here that Albert Einstein once said:

'The fairest thing we can experience is the mysterious.

It is the fundamental emotion, which stands at the cradle of true science.
He who knows it not and can no longer wonder,
No longer feel amazement, is as good as dead.'

It seems to me that a dense fog is lifting in the light of the morning sun. I feel so strongly the whispers of the angels, and the multitude of light beings who are guiding our journey into the dawning new higher consciousness. I have been courageous enough to walk between the worlds. I am a way-shower, here to remind people of something blatantly obvious that CS Lewis once said, 'A man can no more diminish God's glory by refusing to worship him than a lunatic can put out the sun by scribbling 'darkness' on the walls of his cell'.

I have spent many years studying ancient cycles and systems of time. I have been looking at celestial phenomena through the eyes of visionaries, great sages, mathematicians, geologists, astrophysicists, prophets and mystics. I have spent much time in quietness and meditation, listening to the voices that speak from the vacuum within the silence.

I am feeling that what comes next, the time of great mystery we are entering will be qualitatively different from anything we have experienced yet. I am not speaking of gloom and doom, wars and horrors, although we undoubtedly will see more of this if America is allowed to continue to pursue its terrorist fantasies that, by the way, ensure global domination. I am not speaking of freak weather patterns and earth changes, although this may come into our experience as well. What I am feeling is literally a thinning of the veils between dimensional realities, and the splitting of time-lines.

Again to quote Einstein, 'Few are those who see with their own eyes and feel with their own hearts.' He also said, 'Two things inspire me to awe – the starry heavens above and the moral universe within.' These quotes gave me the courage and inspired me to speak my inconvenient truth in this book…

For those who have eyes to see and ears to hear... There is over-whelming evidence from a multitude of sources, spiritual teachers, avatars, sages, prophets, visionaries and scientists that there is something very big going on right now. Many people are suggesting that we are moving from third-dimensional time to fourth-dimensional time. Time is no longer simply experienced in linear fashion.

Multiple time-lines are beginning to appear, based on the power of our choices.

These time-lines began to split (I believe about 1992). Many of us are experiencing this split as the sense of a widening gulf between our personal reality and global mass consciousness, or consensual reality. There is a sense of disorientation in regard to world events, a feeling of walking between worlds and mass symptoms of 'enlightenment stress'. Many of us are engaged, not so much in resisting or attempting to make sense of an old paradigm in its final dance of death, but in visioning the new world rising from the ashes of the old. It's important to remember in these times of great shift that where we focus our attention, energy is magnified – so we need to focus on solutions. I remember the advice of Robin Morgan, editor of the Sunday Times magazine to my great friend Hazel Courteney. He said, 'I don't want stories about problems, Hazel. Just bring me solutions!' On some level he must have known that our thoughts create our reality and where we focus our attention, energy is magnified.

As we travel deeper into fourth dimensional time and consciousness, as we raise the Kundalini, the same events will be experienced very differently in different time-lines or perceptions of consciousness. Naturally, there could be potentially an infinite number of time-lines, but there are three primary ones, corresponding with different dimensional realities, that stand out for me. Here's a scenario for how this could manifest:

The third dimensional time-line will continue to be fuelled by the consciousness of duality, grinding its way in fulfilment of karmic laws to environmental catastrophe, political insanity and social chaos.

We will experience major earth changes during the coming years, in response to celestial events and energies, to the mass thought-forms of those who choose this reality, and to the changing magnetic fields of the earth. The density of this earth will be too heavy to withstand the high-vibrational incoming energies. All the major doom and gloom prophecies we hear about have relevance to this time-line, and this time-line only.

A fourth dimensional time-line will gradually emerge through the collective visions of those whose Souls have called them to build a new world. A parallel reality and a parallel earth is being formed, whose destiny will be governed by the laws of Grace. Its vibrational frequency will be such that the pro-evolutionary energies currently pouring through the earth's auric fields will lift her, and those who choose to move with her, into a quantum leap of awakened spiritual consciousness. As dimensional veils thin further, we will experience a reunion with all the guides, teachers and helper spirits that inhabit the invisible worlds. There could still be an experience of earth changes and chaos, but not nearly as intense, and any negativity will be transmuted quickly. The prophecies of heaven on earth have relevance to this time-line.

A fifth dimensional time-line is also being created. This time-line, governed by the laws of mastery, is about using the incoming evolutionary energies to activate full soul and spiritual reunion. We will use the incoming cosmic energies to fully transfigure our individual and planetary bodies into bodies of light, preparing the way for the fourth dimensional earth to follow in good time. The prophecies of planetary ascension have relevance to this time-line.

The process is being influenced by certain favourable planetary influences according to astrologers and according to mystics, carefully guided by a multitude of light beings from across the galaxies. Beginning with the events of 911 and its aftermath, and corresponding to the ending of the prophetic time-line represented in the Great Pyramid a few days later on September 17, a planetary initiation has begun.

The time-lines are separating gradually, almost imperceptibly, in a process that will gain momentum over the next few months and years. What time-line we wish to follow is entirely up to us, individually and collectively.

As long as we remained in third dimensional time, 'reality' was something that was imposed on us from the outside. It was fixed in duality, and our options in responding to this fixed reality were somewhat limited. The forces of 'darkness' *seemed* to dominate in this reality. Many of us felt powerless or victimized in the face of social oppression, environmental collapse, or political madness. Strangers in a strange land, we felt it was not very acceptable or safe to stand in the power of our light.

As we begin to step into fourth dimensional time, this changes. Reality is no longer something external to us, but is created from a unified space within and then externalized. It is the quality of our thoughts and feelings, the strength of our Soul, and the power of our dreams and commitments, that increasingly creates and shapes the world around us.

If we are no longer locked into a single version of reality, we no longer need to struggle with opposing versions of reality!

We discover the enormous power of our choices, and more than ever before, we become co-creators of our planet's future. We choose where, what, and how we choose to be, and if an external reality no longer fits, we simply step out of it and create a different shared reality with those who resonate to a similar time-line.

More light than we can ever comprehend in all the universes is guiding our journey. When we encounter doubt, darkness and dread, as we inevitably will in these times to come, let us remember who we are, and what we wish to create.

The time-lines will still run together for a while, and we may during this time be tempted to fall into despair in response to world events and earth changes. I say to you all, 'Look to your own soul during these times. Feel what is real for you. Understand what is not real. And know that your choices are powerful!' This is why it is so vitally important to be the master of all of who we are and are not. It is imperative that we learn to control (master) every word, thought, feeling and action; stay mindful to align to the highest time-line, the spiritual level of consciousness.

A new earth is being birthed in the powerful alchemical cauldron of our deepest desires, hopes, longings, dreams and visions. We are called to become the midwives of this incredible new paradigm. These are truly the times we were born for. Let's learn how to once more walk in truth, love, and beauty! This is the path of love, strength and balance... the road less travelled. I feel this quote is rather apt:

> 'The Foundation of Wisdom is the selfless awe of God.
> Sceptics deny that this is so, and the ignorant ignore the discipline
> That leads to it, but you need not be among them.'
> Proverbs 1:7

Conversations with God

In order to best understand the remarkable life and death experiences that I share in this book, let's refer to the best-seller by Neale Donald Walsch, *Conversations with God* (Hodder & Stoughton USA).

Like me, Walsch was experiencing an all-time low point in his life. At that time, he decided to write a letter to God, venting his frustrations. Like me, what he did not expect was 'contact' or a response. As he finished his letter, he was moved to continue writing and out came extraordinary answers to his questions. Similarly, in the vicelike grip of a $1,000 per day cocaine habit, I pushed myself past what I thought was the point of no return. Following an incredibly massive overdose, as I felt all life-energy leaving my body and I knew I was dead, instead of the nothingness that I expected in death, I found myself before some kind of super-luminal Life Review Board. At that point, in actual fact, my life only really began to be lived. I was privy to a truth that was almost too much to bear, one world is ending and another world is beginning... I was shown revelations that would come to pass especially with relevance to new time-lines determined by levels of consciousness gained.

Suppose we could ask God the most puzzling questions about existence, questions about love, faith, life and death, good and evil. Just suppose God provided clear understandable answers. It happened to Neale Donald Walsch. It happened to me. It could happen to anyone. In short, following a fatal drug overdose, I had my first conversation with a divine ambassador, the Archangel Michael. I was lovingly given a chance to view the major events of my life and helped to find deeper meaning and higher purpose to all I had suffered. Then I was persuaded to come back and share the insights I had been shown, plus many more that I have gathered on my own journey of enlightenment and awakening spiritual integrity since then. Since that time in 1992, I have been consistently and lovingly guided by angels and master guides. They have directed me to write this book – to assemble this simple yet challenging plan to lead others into their own unique path of spiritual integrity.

In different ways, Walsch and I both found the same answers to our questions. These answers reveal the universal truths underlying all mystical and religious traditions. These answers changed my life. Read and lived, they will change the lives of many others. Those who read this book and perform the practices will come to view others as part of a unified whole, as part of themselves. The basic truth that Walsch and I found is that we are not separate, one from another. We are all leaves on the same tree! When we recognize this and live the truth that we are all one great being, it becomes impossible to practise anything less than harmlessness towards all others. When we forget this, however, we create chaos and destruction. Isn't it obvious? If I know from experience that everyone else is part of the greater me, and I love myself, then how could I wish to hurt or take advantage of any other? The personal experience of this truth is, I believe, the key to resolving issues of conflict and establishing a working peace on all levels from the interpersonal to the international arenas.

As the earth enters a more rapid period of transformation, and this is inevitable now, we will find ever-increasing levels of chaos and trauma. For the uninitiated, these chaotic states are a necessary experience in the transition from one level of experience and consciousness to the next – sleeping to drowsy to awakened states. This chaos is showing up in our lives individually, collectively and globally. In the physics of this universe, there is no other way to transition. Yet remember this and be reassured, that 'out of chaos comes order'.

Whatever way in which we deal with these states of chaos has a tremendous impact on our ability to move through them with poise, grace and ease or otherwise. My teachers and guides have given me all the simple wisdoms shared in this book to allow us to balance our own subtle energies thereby assisting us to self-heal, create balance and empowerment in these chaotic times of often traumatic transformation. Like Sky Dancer, the Reiki lineage of masters also gifted us with 'mind treasures'. They gave us secret symbols imbued with the consciousness of all the information we will ever need to become reconnected to spirit. All we have to do is show up daily and use the symbols and processes to self-heal and evolve.

In addition, I am presenting now a means for all to work a broad spectrum right across the board using the same alchemical processes. From an alchemical standpoint, higher states of consciousness and awareness are attained when our inner male and female energy pathways/channels within the etheric body are balanced. Thus we equalize the active and receptive aspects of self. By accomplishing this task individually we purify the subtle pathways within our own bodies and centre our consciousness, returning always to love and balance. By doing this alchemical work regularly we can reinforce our commitment to higher beliefs, empower ourselves and be ready, willing, able and equipped to cope with all the various levels of chaos in our lives.

In the next book, we discover that the ultimate goal of the map is the reunion with our divine essence and the alchemical transformation of the very substance of our base (physical) being back into its true spiritual essence, which is light. The alchemists of ancient Egypt and Medieval Europe and the yogis and yoginis of India and Tibet spent their lives in pursuit of this sacred destination. The Egyptians even believed that through this practice, it was possible for a human being to realize their immortal body of light and become a star in the heavens. I know it's possible to become this spiritual best self because I have been shown that this is so. I was also shown that the more people who can achieve this and work miracles in their daily lives on earth, the more this will help heal our environment and avert global climate crisis. To quote Einstein again, he said that, 'True religion is real living; living with all one's soul, with all one's goodness and righteousness.' So, what are we waiting for? Well, nothing actually, because we are the ones we have been waiting for!

The magical rainbow body of light

In Tibetan lore, there are many stories of the manifestation of what is referred to as a 'luminous rainbow body' by highly developed adepts and practitioners. As a result of their devotion and disciplined practice, they are able to totally purify themselves and transmute their karma, becoming more light (spirit and less dark) physical matter. Such masters can transform their physical bodies into radiant energy, and vanish like a rainbow in the sky. I actually witnessed this in a group of advanced students I was working with in Mt Shasta, where the whole group disappeared for several minutes as a result of the high energies we were working with. The only person who didn't disappear was my assistant, Savannah, who had been told to turn over the tape and was thus on some level blocking the higher energies, whilst she focused on being present to turn over the tape! Now that's what I call devotion.

Throughout European lore there are legends from the alchemical tradition that tell us of men and women who have also achieved this extraordinary transformation that was once the ultimate goal for all human beings. In the Christian tradition, the magical transmutation of Christ into a shining body of glory, I believe may very well be a manifestation of this very same process.

Visual evidence of this extraordinary achievement can be seen in the religious art of various cultures all over the world. Beings with haloes, flying on golden wings of light, resting within shining spheres or depicted upright in a glowing aura of light, the images of Gods, Goddesses, Saints, Boddhisattvas, Kachinas and Star people offer us symbolic visions of the fully illuminated being. The final three levels of the map show us how to get there!

In the next book, I outline these final three stages of the map; those of fermentation, distillation and coagulation. They show us that we are not alone in this higher refining 'polishing our diamond' process. We become aware that we are doing something not only for ourselves but for all of humanity. We choose some aspect of the collective shadow to work to transcend. This was always our destiny, our dharma and our karma to work through in this lifetime. It animates and inspires us to see this through. Reanimated we release outworn 'victim consciousness' beliefs and deal with each issue as it arises – with wisdom and with spiritual integrity.

At Alchemical Level 5 we need to go beyond understanding ego and dismantling the masks of persona. Here we find the courage to face our shadow. In alchemy this is called 'putrefaction-fermentation' and is about wholeness and authenticity, for while the unacceptable parts of us remain judged, suppressed and denied in the darkness of our unconscious mind, we remain victims to these unconscious forces and our true creative power is blocked.

At Level 6, we continue to polish our diamond as we learn to surrender to and fully accept our best self and best destiny. This is called 'distillation' in alchemy: here we need to purify our essence so we know who we are at a best- self level and what our higher purpose is. (This is greatly assisted by the exercise suggested in Chapter 4.)

At Alchemical Level 7, finally we choose to be who we are, God = Man – Ego. This is called 'coagulation' in alchemy and here we live a constant celebration of our undeniable interrelatedness to all life. We never worry because we have faith in, and have become one with, the Great Mystery.

A Map to God takes us through the alchemical journey of turning the lead of personality into spiritual gold. True spiritual integrity is achieved ultimately by changing our programmed beliefs about all kinds of negative states, especially including depression. We can create a new personal definition of depression that this is something good. Depression is a spiritual emergency and it's also a golden opportunity for personal growth disguised as loss – loss of joy. This is how we overcome depression and the terrible effect it has on our lives.

There is a simple yet powerful ancient wisdom, which guides us to learn how to embrace our enemy. Depression is perceived as an enemy in the matrix. If we can detach from this matrix belief and learn to welcome depression, this imbalanced state embraced becomes our teacher and ultimately our friend. Ego battles against this special relationship because the purpose of ego is to protect us. However, if we are prepared to look long and hard and deep enough, we will achieve a level in our evolution where we no longer need to hide, deny and suppress truth. As we give ourselves permission to shine and reconnect to our best self, we can open our hearts and minds to whatever life gives us because our perceptions are different. Life here on earth is best perceived as 'Earth School'. This is where we learn about being human, in all its aspects – the good, the bad and the ugly. Eventually we will truly grasp the meaninglessness of the do/have/consume matrix-type of consciousness and this ultimately leads us to search for higher meaning, reconnection to best self and best destiny.

A vital aspect of learning to be human is having and expressing feelings – this means all kinds of feelings, including anger, hatred, envy, jealousy, fear, guilt, shame, pain and sorrow. When we deny or suppress our feelings this causes depression. Depression is ultimately understood to be an effective tool to alert us that we are resisting our feelings. Depression occurs when we deny our feeling nature. At Alchemical Level 1 depression may hold us in hibernation until we awaken to the fullness of our best self and best potential destiny. What I have discovered is that the most profound richness within me was accessed from teachings learned from my darkest experiences. Depression can take us to this darkness. Welcome it and understand it. If we view depression as a gift and learn how to conquer denial and work through its lessons, we may experience true lasting joy and authentic spiritual integrity, which includes everything in balance – dark and light. Finally we come to understand and know that it is this joy from wholeness that opens our hearts and reconnects us with our best selves.

If we can learn from the teachings of the Hopi Indians, this holds many key secrets for the path of awakening spiritual integrity. The Hopi medicine men and women are consummate shamans. Their knowledge of the inner world is as profound as our scientific knowledge of the outer world. Their teachings hold important keys to world peace. Their prophecies hold vital insights into the challenges of our modern world. They reveal the urgent need for each of us to make the choice between the path of ego (comfort, profit and greed) and the path of the soul (love, strength and balance).

Similarly we need to remember to open ourselves up to and respect the Reiki path and all that this means. Attunement to and daily self-healing with Reiki purifies and detoxifies the physical body by assisting to release energy blocks and accelerates the body's own natural healing mechanisms. Mentally and emotionally, Reiki helps dissolve old entrenched, rigid mindsets and negative attitudes. It's magical and mystical and it works! Simply put, we learn how to tap into our own natural, yet subtle, energy fields to recreate balance and empowerment. Working with Reiki helps us look good and feel marvellous!

Reiki as a treatment greatly enhances mental and emotional well-being, empowers personal vision, creativity, abundance and most especially physical performance. Working with Reiki daily saved my life, and helped to strengthen my connection to the unseen worlds of spirit. I have given and taught my own special evolved type of MS-REM super-Reiki energy mastery to heads of multi-billion dollar corporations, royalty, commissioners of police, MPs, bankers, doctors, lawyers, children, babies and old people. The results of using this advanced type of Reiki have been truly remarkable. I have seen miracle healings beyond belief. At aged 78, having witnessed so many miracles, my Mother asked if she could learn Reiki too.

She did – anyone can and the benefits are just too incredible for words.

The big picture

The Celestine Prophecy and insights popularized by the psychologist James Redfield have provided me with many vital missing keys to the puzzle of understanding the big picture of what we are all doing here on earth. It was from this source that I learned the importance of observing and following up on synchronicities, the seeming coincidences that guide the spiritual awakening of us all. I also learned how to conquer control dramas, by recognizing popular energy-stealing patterns. When we stop stealing energy from others and plug into Source energy direct in our daily Reiki self-healing practice, we access another level of reality, where truly heaven is experienced on earth.

Do come to my workshops, attune to Reiki and find out how to create this bliss for yourself. Unfortunately, I cannot speak for the integrity, power or purity of all Reiki masters. In the same way that I cannot praise or recommend all master chefs – just because they have a similar training, it doesn't always follow that they can make the same incredible dish. So it is with Reiki masters – so choose wisely.

The Celestine vision

When James Redfield wrote the books, *The Celestine Prophecy* and *The Tenth Insight*, he gave voice and form to the awakening spiritual consciousness of our time. Redfield has studied the history of the human race specializing his focus on our psychological and spiritual evolution. He used his personal experience and his intuition to envision the unfolding spiritual awareness which so many people today are apprehending but so few, as yet, are comprehending. How did he do this? As Albert Einstein said, 'There is no logical way to the discovery of elemental laws. There is only the way of intuition, which is helped by a feeling for the order lying behind the appearance'. Without doubt, Redfield has a good feeling for the order lying behind the appearance. And he has the scientific mind needed to render his insights available to others.

Redfield has formulated the blind groping of a spiritually hungry people into an understandable system of knowledge. He convincingly demonstrates that human history has not been a chance process, but is somehow guided by mysterious coincidences toward our spiritual awakening. And like me, he has provided us with practices to actualize our spiritual potential, step by step. This gives us a practical plan concerning how to live our new spiritual awareness, both individually and socially.

Ego and energy-stealing patterns

Redfield's amazing work focuses us on the struggle for power, when we have cut ourselves off from the greater source of this energy and so feel weak and insecure. Then to gain energy we tend to manipulate or force others to give us attention and thus energy. When we successfully dominate others in this way, we feel more powerful, but they are left weakened and often fight back. Competition for scarce, pre-digested human energy is the cause of all conflict between people. Insecurity and violence ends when we experience an inner connection with the divine energy within, a connection described by mystics of all traditions. A sense of lightness and buoyancy, together with the constant sensation of love are measures of this connection. If these positive signs are present, the connection is real and if not, the connection is false and only pretended. Remember in ego, pain is the measure of our disconnection.

Redfield shares with us that the more we stay connected to Source, the more we are acutely aware of those times when we lose connection, usually when we are under stress. In these times we can see our own particular way of stealing energy from others. Once our manipulations are brought to conscious awareness, our connection becomes more constant and consistent. Then we can discover our own growth path in life and our spiritual mission in terms of how we can contribute to world transformation.

According to Redfield, watching for and working with the seeming coincidences, the synchronicities in our lives, is the next step. Synchronicities become more enhanced when we are connected to Source energies direct. We can all learn how to increase the frequency of guiding coincidences by uplifting every person that comes into our lives. Care must be taken not to lose our inner connection in romantic relationships – co-dependency. Uplifting others, I have learned, is especially effective in groups, where each member can feel the energy of all the others. By learning how to see and feel the beauty in every face, we lift others into their best self and increase the chances of hearing a synchronistic message.

Redfield shares with us that as we all evolve towards the best completion of our spiritual missions, the technological means of survival will be fully automated as humans focus instead on spiritual integrity and growth. Such growth will move us into higher energy states, ultimately transforming our bodies into spiritual form (light) and uniting this dimension of existence with heaven, ending the cycle of birth, death and reincarnation.

In his second book, *The Tenth Insight* Redfield suggests, and I agree, that throughout history human beings have been unconsciously struggling to implement this lived spirituality and heaven on earth. Each of us comes here on assignment, as we pull this understanding into conscious awareness, we can remember a fuller birth vision of what we wished to accomplish with our lives. Furthermore, we can then remember a common world vision or unified dream of how we will all work together to create a new spiritual culture. My wish is that we can all learn how to hold this vision through practising mindfulness, working with intention and attention everyday. I also wish that the way-showers and teachers who can heal the illusion of separation and show us all how to be in spiritual integrity be recognized and amply rewarded for sharing their expertise.

The next age

'Humanity is entering the most crucial phase of its existence. The com-

ing decade shall witness the most unprecedented and undreamt of changes in the course of its long evolution. There is nothing much humanity can do about it other than to understand the changes that are overpowering it. Towards the end, humanity will enter a new age – the Golden Age!'

AVATAR SRI KALKI

Is this really happening? Yes! Without doubt, yes. We are entering an age, whether we call it the Aquarian Age or the Golden Age or Satya Yuga or the Fifth World, where the veils between the spiritual and material worlds are actually beginning to dissolve. As I have suggested, Kalki agrees that there once was a time when we were born enlightened, and lived in the constant awareness of the unity of all things. In the course of time, for reasons that philosophers and theologians can argue endlessly about and don't really matter anymore, we chose to create a dense veil between various aspects of ourselves. These veils are held in the morphogenetic fields of humanity as subconscious programmes of separation, forgetfulness, limitation, illusion, fear, and so on. Our genes mutated to align with these fields, and we invented suffering, which is basically another word for soul fragmentation. We have identified with the veils and defined ourselves through them, yet WE ARE NOT THE VEILS!

Underneath all this, the original programme of love, beauty, and oneness, a morphogenetic field of consciousness, which we can refer to as 'enlightenment' or 'Christ consciousness' still exists within our genes, awaiting a timing key emanating from our own souls to wake up and experience the vast beautiful presence of who we really are. This timing key is based on a number of factors, including the completion of certain time cycles and our encounter with a vast energy field that we are currently beginning to experience in our journey through galactic space. These keys are being activated now. We will be changed in the twinkling of an eye, says the Book of Revelation, when the last trumpet sounds.

Well, the last trumpet has sounded, and the fact that in the UK alone two years ago people spent in excess of £700 million on spiritual books and workshops in that one year, surely reflects the deep human thirst to breakthrough the illusion, to unplug from the matrix, to reconnect with a higher divine blueprint – best self? Many are finding that to conquer ego and reconnect with best self is to activate the timing key within our DNA.

Incidentally, I am not saying that this is the only way to get enlightened. I have little interest in telling people what they should do. My consciousness has evolved well beyond the confines of any religion. I see myself as a humble way-shower for all humanity, and my sole mission is to facilitate enlightenment for anyone who is genuinely searching and is willing to put in the work. Enlightenment happens not through dogma, beliefs or rituals, but through a transmission of energy, a divine operation within the brain, when the soul is ready and the time is right. Enlightenment, simply defined, is shifting our centre of personal identity from conditioned mind to unveiled soul.

There are so many who ask, how do I know if I am enlightened? Well, let me see now – how do we know we have been run over by a London bus? We just know. Those who are enlightened will say that it is unmistakable. If we are enlightened, we won't need to ask this question, and if we're asking this question, we're not. It is not a mental or emotional process but a biological event. The moment of enlightenment is when the new bio-circuits get fully turned on, and the Kundalini moves all the way through the physical body to meet up with the cosmic energy. Many of you may have had past experiences of energy surging through the body, but there comes a time when the Kundalini moves through like a freight train to make the final irreversible shift. New pathways get created. The old pathways based on the lower, ego-conditioned mind stop functioning. A link between heaven and earth is created in the neo-cortex of the brain, and the DNA itself is transformed. Our sense of self changes radically, and nothing is the same anymore. Suffering ends, because all suffering is a figment of our conditioned minds and fear-based fantasies.

A variety of phenomena may accompany this state. Many people experience states of incredible bliss and cosmic consciousness. Subtle senses open up. Often, full memories of past lifetimes and the akashic records return, and healing and shamanic gifts awaken. I have heard personal stories of miraculous healings, bi-location, even of people being raised from the dead. Well it happened to me!

Can I emphasize that enlightenment is only the beginning of the spiritual path. Imagine a million Christs running around the planet. What kind of world could we create? It is starting to happen. There are over a thousand who are now fully enlightened in India alone. I have met many, and it is an extraordinary thing. The more who become enlightened, the easier it is for everybody else to achieve this state.

As we move deeper into the Golden Age, many people are beginning to spontaneously experience enlightenment all over the world. It is our natural state, after all – our divine inheritance. The important thing is to connect with our own souls and know that this is possible. I truly know that the wisdoms and practices in this book work to create this. They have worked for me, and to varying degrees, for hundreds of students I have worked with in the last ten years.

The world is filled with empty religious dogma that has done some good but also much harm, and people – nations – have justified all sorts of atrocities and abominations in the name of God. This is insanity.

How did this insanity come about? Einstein gave us a hint when he said, 'Reading, after a certain age, diverts the mind too much from its creative pursuits. Any man who reads too much and uses his own brain too little falls into lazy habits of thinking'. I may be able to shed a little more light on this…

There is a fascinating story in Plato's *Phaedrus* wherein Thamus, King of Thebes, takes issue with Hermes-Thoth about the gift of writing to mankind. Thamus feared that writing (recording information) would hinder memory in that we would no longer use our great and natural capacity of remembering. The king felt that this would precipitate poor memory and laziness and alienate us from the inner world, which links us to God and to nature.

Thoth said: 'Here O king, is a branch of learning that will make the people of Egypt wiser and improve their memories; my discovery provides a recipe for memory and wisdom.' But the King answered and said 'O man full of arts, to one it is given to create the thing of art and to another to judge the measure of harm and of profit they have for those who shall employ them. And so it is to you, by reason of your tender regard for writing that is your offspring, have declared the very opposite of its true effect. If men learn this, it will plant forgetfulness in their souls. They will cease to exercise memory because they rely on that which is written, calling things to remembrance no longer from within themselves, but by means of external marks. What you have discovered is a recipe not for memory but for reminder. And it is no true wisdom you offer your disciples, but only its semblance, for by telling them many things without teaching them you will make them seem to know much, while the most part they know nothing and as men filled not with wisdom, but with the conceit of wisdom, they will be a burden to their fellows.'

It would seem that Thamus was also concerned that writing, if it fell into the wrong hands, could be misused to manipulate the masses for selfish or evil purposes. Surely we all witness this daily in our advertisements and not-so-innocent 24 hours-a-day MTV popsongs? Globally, surely we witnessed this in Hitler's Third Reich where symbols and mantras were used to control a nation?

Another form of insanity occurs when the male (science and tech-nology) energy loses touch with the nurturing presence of the female, Mother Nature. It is always the feminine energy that brings balance, peace and beauty to the male. The male energy principle symbolizes different qualities such as the power of the material world and the resources accumulated from the four corners of the globe. In dysfunction, the male becomes greedy, unaware and uncaring of his environment, blind to the foolishness of his egocentric behaviour and becomes a dangerously unbalanced misrepresentation of humanity. The Emperor's New Clothes is a great example of this. The Emperor appears naked representing material consciousness. He is without clothes because he has lost touch with reality, courtesy of two unscrupulous designers on the make and exploiting the Emperor's limitless wealth (representing ego). A child, with a pure heart is the only being with enough wisdom to expose the Emperor's naked state. This child represents the unconditional part of the soul that reveres truth and order in accordance with nature...

When the male is in balance with the female, there is a potential for grounding such divine wisdom, love and power, which reconnects us to spirituality of the highest order. This can only be achieved when the polar opposites work in harmony and co-operation. We each of us contain polarities of male and female and when we can learn how to cherish and honour both these polarities, we will discover our divinity and our higher purpose or reason for being here. Except for a few, this has not happened for several thousand years. Yet in early Asiatic civilizations, kingship depended on the choice of queen. Marriage with the mundane earthly representation of the Goddess in the form of a queen was essential to the position of kingship. This was the original meaning of 'holy matrimony'. Conjuction at Level 4 on the map is the inner marriage of the receptive female energy with the ordered male energy to produce law based on wisdom and love.

Like the hidden mind treasures of Sky Dancer, the termas, the Reiki symbols I have given in this book have been imbued with intentions – divine magic, from ancient and current-day living masters, great sages, prophets and visionaries of all time. Believe... and use these gifts wisely to return to a state of balance, harmony and empowerment.

One last word...

In the final analysis, authentic spiritual integrity has nothing to do with dogma, knowledge and intellect. We all need to get out of our heads and take the longest spiritual journey there is – 13 inches – out of the head to the heart... Remember the Hopi prophecy and the stickmen drawings on the path of ego – their heads didn't join to the rest of their bodies! This is reminiscent of the image on the back of the dollar bill incidentally, where the capstone doesn't join onto the body of the pyramid. When we reconnect to our hearts all the knowledge of the wisdom of the ancients is made available – we become lions instead of sheep. Remember and practise what the Buddha said: 'Do not believe in anything simply because you have heard it. Do not believe in anything simply because it is spoken and rumoured by many. Do not believe in anything simply because it is found written in your religious books. Do not believe in anything merely on the authority of your teachers and elders. Do not believe in traditions because they have been handed down for many generations. But after observation and analysis, when you find that anything agrees with reason and is conducive to the good and benefit of one and all, then accept it and live up to it.'

We are each on a journey of truth, and truth can only come in the soft whispers of a discerning yet open heart connected to mind. Spirit whispers and ego shouts. Once we have experienced the reality of who we essentially, truly are – best self – no matter how this happens or where or when, then and only then our best lives can truly commence. Within best self every one of us holds the key to end all pain and suffering. When we commit to unplug from the matrix, to begin to truly live our best lives – this is the beginning of Grace, divine power, wisdom, freedom and love.

However, we must remember the old saying that the road to Heaven is through Hell. Jesus must have been referring to this when he said in the *Gospel of Thomas*, 'Whosoever finds the interpretation of these sayings will not experience death.' And Jesus said, 'Let him who seeks continue seeking until he finds. When he finds, he will become troubled. When he becomes troubled, he will be astonished and he will rule over the all.'

To be born into the material world and to become forgetful in ego is to experience pain and suffering, yet these conditions serve to wake us up and sometimes this very pain and suffering is the most common bond that unites us all, in wars, for instance. By learning the lessons of each challenging experience, we begin to understand the vast scope of existence, thus we become the heroes we truly are and need to be. I could only begin to truly understand life in all its totality when I accessed the hero within myself and found the courage to embrace some really staggering revelations about our world and our creation story. I'll be continuing to share in the next book how we have been conditioned to live our lives based on what we believe about our world, our capabilities and our limits. With very few exceptions these beliefs have come from what science, history, religion, and what our political and religious leaders tell us. What if all that knowledge is faulty and incomplete? What if it's wrong? What if we have been deliberately lied to in order to conceal the truth about our birthright? Plato said, 'Access to power must be confined to men who are not in love with it'. Lily Tomlin once said, and I salute her, 'The trouble with being in the rat race is that, even if you win, you're still a rat.' Who wants to be a rat?

The Bible teaches that we are gods, John 10:34, 'Jesus answered them, Is it not written in your law, I said, Ye are gods?' A life span of 120+ years, total well-being through reconnection with all that is, instantaneous healing and manifestation, free energy… this is all attainable and new discoveries in science confirm this today. We are already moving way beyond 'the wellness revolution' to the 'totality of all beingness' revolution. We can accelerate this growth by recognizing initiatory choice points then, using 'Hope' to fuel our choices, we can take heroic action. Focus on solutions and focus on hope. Our hopes, dreams and aspirations are entirely valid. Our wildest imaginings are there to take us sky high, if we'd only give our permission. There is definitely no better medicine than hope, no motivation so powerful, no tonic so influential as the expectation of something better tomorrow. Hope creates bliss and passion for what is possible.

Are we willing to acknowledge that in a universe where we are all connected and patterns of behaviour are learned through copying, and then repeated over and over, the power of our choices assumes great importance, taking on powerful new meaning? Will we be doomed to repeating over and over, less than optimal outcomes that we have created in the past, or will we become heroes and create something different? Have we had enough of disease, global climate crisis, corporate and political lies and corruption, war and misusing technology? Do we choose something different now?

I'll be sharing stunning new archaeological discoveries about our past, in the next book, which will help to guide us in our choices for our future. When we know who we are and where we have come from, we can know where we are going. Above all – always be hopeful. When it becomes very dark, remember the stars come out!

In the next book, as we begin to work with the last three Alchemical Levels, powerful divine influences are magnified within the aura. These energies begin to gestate to unlock universal truths encoded within the very fabric of our DNA. I have come to know that my DNA is a life-code that can be expanded, evolved and upgraded through intention, attention, practising mindfulness, recognizing and responding fearlessly to choice points. Moreover, I have come to know that invisible helpers assist us to make conscious soul memories and information stored in our DNA. My inner guidance is that initiation is the chosen method to elevate consciousness on this planet. Higher consciousness helps us to be able to access the power to upgrade our DNA blueprint, access mastery and achieve a coherent energy field. In a coherent energy state, we can heal, create and manifest instantly. Prayer is talking to God. Meditation is listening to God. Initiation I believe creates the spiritualization of matter, becoming and being God.

Remember God = Man – Ego. Do the psychological recapitulation, always allowing a childlike wonder and innocence to lead the way! Surrender to the higher universal flow. Be mindful and determined to find and nurture all the wisdom of the ancients within. Accept the blessings. Know we are Gods, know we are ready, willing and able to embody the co-creative power that heals lives and transforms worlds – that we begin saving the world by saving one person at a time. And...

Summon the courage for the rites of passage, the initiations that lie ahead.

APPENDIX

YOUNG LIVING OILS

Dr Gary Young, founder of the Young Living Oils, began his quest for knowledge of self-healing after surviving a near fatal accident that left him paralysed and confined to a wheelchair. Unwilling to accept that fate, he began searching for natural ways to heal his body. This led him to the discovery of essential oils. He became very excited when he learned of their high oxygenating molecules and ability to deliver nutrients to the cell nucleus for maximum assimilation. This inspired him to formulate YL herbal food supplements and other products with essential oils, and it set him on a path I follow today. The oils are so pure they can be used on the skin undiluted in many cases and most of them can be taken internally diluted in water.

To ensure that they use the finest quality oils for their products, Young Living is organically cultivating thousands of acres of crops for the distillation of essential oils. It is the only company in the world that is growing plants from seed organically, harvesting the plants, distilling and formulating the oil, packaging and marketing the products, as well as educating people about their use and application. Their ongoing university research is validating the benefits of essential oils and aromatherapy. Research at Manchester University has proved that Young Living Theives Oil destroys the hospital superbug MRSA.

Ingredients: Clove (*Syzygium aromaticum*) is one of the most anti-microbial and antiseptic of all essential oils. It is antifungal, antiviral and anti-infectious. Lemon (*Citrus limon*) has antiseptic-like properties and contains compounds that amplify immunity. It promotes circulation, leukocyte formation and lymphatic function. Cinnamon Bark (*Cinnamomum verum*) is one of the most powerful antiseptics known. It is strongly antibacterial, antiviral and antifungal. Eucalyptus (*Eucalyptus radiata*) is anti-infectious, antibacterial, antiviral and anti-inflammatory.

Rosemary (*Rosmarinus officinalis CT cineol*) is antiseptic and anti-microbial. It is high in cineol, a key ingredient in antiseptic drugs.

I really strongly recommend these oils and all of Dr Young's leading edge work. For the past five years, Dr Young has been working in Ecuador, because the constitution of that country upholds and promotes research into and the use of ancient naturopathic ways of healing. Dr Young has been working with the Medical Association of Ecuador, and a top USA Gold Medal surgeon, where they have been performing operations without anaesthetics, painkillers, antibiotics or anti-inflammatory medications – using therapeutic-grade essential oils instead. I personally saw them remove cancerous tumours in the lymph and brain tumours in this way. Statistics show a minimum of 30% improvement in recovery rate, no fatalities and no side effects. Could this be the way of the future? I certainly see a bright future for pure high-grade therapeutic essential oils...

One of the factors that determine the purity of an oil is its chemical constituents. These constituents can be affected by a vast number of variables, including: the part(s) of the plant from which the oil was produced, soil condition, fertilizer (organic or chemical), geographical region, climate, altitude, harvesting methods and distillation processes. For example, common thyme (*Thymus vulgaris*) produces several different chemotypes (biochemically unique variants within one species) depending on the conditions of its growth, climate and altitude. One chemotype of thyme will yield an essential oil with high levels of thymol, depending on the time of year it is distilled. The later it is distilled in the growing season (ie. mid-summer or autumn), the more thymol the oil will contain. Proper cultivation assures that more specific chemotypes like *Thymus vulgaris* will maintain a good strain of thymol, whereas with wildcrafting, the plant may also produce linalol and eugenol thyme on the same mountainside. An example of this was shown in studies at the University of Ege botany department in Izmir, Turkey where it was found that among *Oreganum compactum* plants within a 100 square foot radius, one plant would be very high in carvacrol and another would be high in another compound. Wildcrafting plants cannot guarantee the same chemotype even on the same hillside.

The key to producing a pure high-grade therapeutic essential oil is to preserve as many of the delicate aromatic compounds within the essential oil as possible. Fragile aromatic chemicals are easily destroyed by high temperature and pressure, as well as by contact with chemically reactive metals such as copper or aluminium. This is why all therapeutic essential oils should be distilled in stainless steel cooking chambers at low pressure and low temperature. The plant material should also be free of herbicides and other agri-chemicals. These can react with the essential oil during distillation to produce toxic compounds. Because many pesticides are oil-soluble, they can also mix into the essential oil.

As we begin to understand the power of essential oils in the realm of personal, holistic healthcare, we will appreciate the necessity for obtaining the purest essential oils possible. No matter how costly pure essential oils may be, there can be no substitutes because, after all, our health is priceless.

Although chemists have successfully recreated the main constituents and fragrances of some essential oils in the laboratory, these synthetic oils lack therapeutic benefits and may even carry risks. Why? Because essential oils contain hundreds of different chemical compounds, in combination, which lend important therapeutic properties to the oil. Also, many essential oils contain molecules and isomers that are impossible to manufacture in the laboratory. Anyone venturing into the world of therapy using essential oils must use the purest quality oils available. Inferior quality or adulterated oils most likely will not produce therapeutic results and could possibly be toxic. In Europe, a set of standards has been established that outlines the chemical profile and principal constituents that a quality essential oil should have. Known as AFNOR (Association French Normalization Organization Regulation) and ISO (International Standards Organization) standards, these guidelines help buyers differentiate between a therapeutic-grade essential oil and a lower grade oil with a similar chemical makeup and fragrance. All of the therapeutic effects of essential oils described in this book are based on oils that have been graded according to AFNOR standards.

Remedies for "enlightenment stress"

The following is a list of classic symptoms of 'enlightenment stress' and some powerful Young Living Oil remedies, which really worked for me and now work for hundreds of my students:

Flu-like symptoms (such as high temperatures, sweating, aching bones and joints, which are not responding to antibiotics) – Use Thieves or Young Living Single Oils: Idaho tansy, lemon, blue cypress, mountain savory, oregano, eucalyptus radiata, myrtle, peppermint. RAINDROP Oils Massage Technique, 1 to 2 times weekly – highly recommended.

Migraine headaches (severe pain that is not relieved with pain-killers) – Placebo-controlled double-blind crossover studies at the Christian-Albrechts University in Kiel, Germany, found that essential oils were just as effective in blocking pain from tension-type headaches as acetominophen (i.e. Tylenol). Use Young Living Single Oils: helichrysum, rosemary. Young Living Blends: Aroma Life, M-Grain and Clarity.

Breathing difficulties – Use Young Living Single Oils: rosemary, eucalyptus radiata, ravensara, thyme, wintergreen/birch, spruce, pine, oregano, helichrysum, tea tree, spearmint, myrtle, Idaho balsam fir.

Blurred vision – Use Young Living Single Oils: Idaho tansy, helichrysum, lavender, peppermint.

Confusion – Use Young Living Single Oils: frankincense, lemon, sandalwood, geranium, lavender, angelica, orange, grapefruit, ylang ylang. Young Living Blends: Valor, Motivation, Passion, Hope, Joy, Brain Power, Present Time, Envision, Sacred Mountain, Harmony, Highest Potential.

Diarrhoea – Use Young Living Single Oils: rosemary, ginger, basil, peppermint.

Depression – Use Young Living Single Oils: frankincense, lemon, sandalwood, geranium, lavender, angelica, orange, grapefruit, ylang ylang. Young Living Blends: Valor, Motivation, Passion, Hope, Joy, Brain Power, Present Time, Envision, Sacred Mountain, Harmony, Highest Potential.

Fear – Use Young Living Single Oils: bergamot, clary sage, Roman chamomile, cypress, geranium, juniper, marjoram, myrrh, spruce, orange, sandalwood, rose, ylang ylang. Young Living Blends: Valor, Present Time, Hope, White Angelica, Trauma Life, Gratitude, Highest Potential.

Ringing in the ears – Use helichrysum, juniper, geranium, peppermint, lavender, basil.

Heart palpitations (fibrillation) – This is a specific form of heart arrhythmia that occurs when the upper heart chambers contract at a rate of over 300 pulsations per minute. The lower chambers cannot keep this pace, so efficiency is reduced and not enough blood is pumped. Palpitations, a feeling that the heart is beating irregularly, more strongly, or more rapidly than normal, are the most common symptoms. Use Young Living Single Oils: goldenrod, ylang ylang, marjoram, valerian, lavender, rosemary, Idaho tansy. Young Living Blends: Aroma Life, Peace & Calming, Joy.

Feeling the whole body vibrate (even when in a relaxed state) – Use Roman chamomile.

Muscle spasms – Use Young Living Single Oils: clove, German chamomile, helichrysum, wintergreen/birch, cypress, lavender, geranium, peppermint, vetiver, valerian. Young Living Blends: Aroma Siez, Aroma Life, Pan-Away, Peace & Calming, Ortho Sport, Ortho Ease.
Muscle weakness – Use Young Living Single Oils: ravensara, Douglas fir, lemongrass, juniper, nutmeg, white fir, Idaho balsam fir.

Impaired memory – Use Young Living Single Oils: Peppermint, cinnamon, rosemary, basil, vetiver, rose, lemon, lemongrass, cardamom. Peppermint, incidentally, improves mental concentration and memory. Dr Dember conducted a study at the University of Cincinati in 1994 showing that inhaling peppermint increased mental accuracy by 28 percent. The fragrance of diffused oils, such as lemon, have also been reported to increase memory retention and recall.

Impaired concentration – Right Brain versus Left Brain. The left brain is logical, rational, and judgemental. The right brain is artistic and creative. Essential oils are believed to heighten right brain activity while increasing left brain integration. Dr Richard Restick, a leading neurologist in Washington, DC, stated that maintaining normal synaptic firing would forestall many types of neurological deterioration in the body. Essential oils high in sesquiterpenes, such as vetiver, cedarwood, patchouly, German chamomile, myrrh, melissa and sandalwood, are known to cross the blood-brain barrier. For general cerebral stimulants, use Young Living Single Oils: cedarwood, vetiver, sandalwood, ginger, nutmeg, myrrh, German chamomile, spikenard, eucalyptus globulus, frankincense, melissa, patchouly, fleabane, helichrysum. Helichrysum increases neurotransmitter activity. Nutmeg is a general cerebral stimulant and also has adrenal cortex-like activity.

Immune-system to support transformation – Use Thieves and Young Living Single Oil helichrysm.

Lymphatic system changes – Essential oils (therapeutic-grade) have long been known to aid in stimulating and detoxifying the lymphatic system. Use Young Living Single Oils: ledum, sandalwood, helichrysum, myrtle, grapefruit, lemongrass, cypress, tangerine, orange, rosemary.

Fatigue (tired or exhausted from minor exertion) – Use Young Living Single Oils: lemongrass, juniper, basil, lemon, peppermint, rosemary, nutmeg, black pepper, thyme, melissa, cypress.

Psychological recapitulation (the need to gain clarity on personal issues) – Use Young Living Blends: Highest Potential or Magnify Your Purpose.

Feeling the need to cleanse, detox and purge – Recommend Young Living Liver Cleanse and Rejuvenate Kit.

Stress and high anxiety levels – Use Young Living Single Oils: lavender, chamomile, blue tansy, marjoram, rose, sandalwood, frankincense, cedarwood.

Some of these symptoms are being felt by a great many people. Many are rushing off in panic to their doctor, chiropractor, herbalist, and so on, and are usually told that there is nothing wrong with them. And this is the truth. For all these symptoms are just temporary and simply indicate that deep and powerful physiological transformation is occurring as we make progress on the path to enlightenment.

Find out how to join and become part of the Young Living Oils family today..

JOINING YOUNG LIVING OILS
To join and become part of the Young Living Oils family you will need to give them the sponsorship details below.

SPONSORSHIP INFORMATION FOR JOINING:
NUMBER: 702686
NAME: PSA LIFE MASTERY LTD
JOINING BY TELEPHONE:
- Telephone Young Living Oils on 01480 455088
- Press 1 to continue in English
- Press 3 to place an order or to speak to customer services in the UK

- You will be asked for your sponsorship number **702686** and name **PSA LIFE MASTERY LTD**

You will be asked for your own details and your Young Living Oils order. You will be given a membership number to use for future orders

JOINING BY INTERNET:

- The website address is **www.youngliving.com**
- Go to the "Young Living Oils UK"
- Go to "Join Us"
- You will then be asked for your sponsorship details. Type in **702686** and the name **PSA LIFE MASTERY LTD** will appear.
- Enter in your details and the place your order. You will be given a membership number to use for future orders

http://www.psalifemastery.com/yloils.html

NOTES

PSA WORKSHOPS

Initiation to MS-REM super reiki awakens the divine in you, attuning your mind, body and spirit, opening the pathway of the soul to wholeness. MS-REM includes daily practices for you to deepen, widen and live your divine connection. By connecting you to powerful transforming spiritual energies and practices, you learn to walk your talk and live your spirituality.

For healers, seers, wisdom seekers and absolute beginners alike, these workshops offer a wonderful opportunity to go beyond theoretical knowledge to actually live and breathe spirituality.

http://www.psalifemastery.com/workshops/workshops.html

STUDIO PSALM PHILOSOPHY

'Our philosophy is to bring you the very best of the world's products, therapies and ideas.'

CD's

Titles include:

A Map to God Initiation

A Map to God White Gold Earth Alchemy

A Map to God – Integrating Transformation

Reiki

Platinum Wesak Attunement

Qabalah

The Seven Alchemical Levels

http://www.psalifemastery.com/philosophie.html

RETREATS

There are retreats to relax, be pampered, rejuvenate and heal.

Alternatively, there are retreats that expand on this rejuvenation theme to enhance spiritual transformation.

Psychological recapitulation practiced in group daily is, I believe, a profound key to accelerated enlightenment. Come and live the daily disciplines so necessary for your own enlightenment process – be part of a group, who joyfully embody these disciplines, for ten days or longer.

http://www.psalifemastery.com/retreats.html

http://www.psalifemastery.com/testimonials.html

EVENTS AT STUDIO PSALM AND IN LONDON

Project: Earth Alchemy Seminars

A series of life-changing, unique and visionary events, gatherings of great hearts, minds and spirits, which bridge the gap between science and spirituality.

Come and *network* with and *listen* to leading lights in the fields of science and medicine, spirituality, politics, global climate crisis, the performing arts and accelerated learning and genius.

Help us focus on *solutions* for global climate crisis and planetary shadow.

THE **TRANSFORMATION**

Understanding leads to insights, insights create awareness, awareness leads to Transformation – learn about the science of miracles and experience profound spiritual energies.

A unique and powerful one day workshop with award winning health writer and journalist Hazel Courteney and Dr Susie Anthony

http://www.psalifemastery.com/events.html

FILMS

Television and films are a major distraction and cause us to be programmed by superficial, false, social values. Be choosy with what you feed into your consciousness. If you must watch, some good films;

Always, Batman Begins, Bulworth, The Bulletproof Monk, Chocolat, Ciderhouse Rules, City of Angels, Coach Carter, Dances with Wolves, Dave, Dead Poet's Society, The Disk, Dragonfly, Education of Little Tree, Fisher King, Field of Dreams, Forest Gump, Galaxy Quest, Ghost Baraka, Goodwill Hunting, The Green Mile, Harry Potter, Horse Whisperer, The Kid, K-Pax, The Last Samurai, The Legend of Baggar Vance, Life is a House, Lord of the Rings, The Matrix, The Mists of Avalon, Minority Report, Manchurian Candidate, National Treasure, Never Ending Story, Out on a Limb, Pay It Forward, Patch Adams, Paycheck, Phenonemon Michael, Powder, Prince of Tides, Seabiscuit, Star Wars – all of them, Star Trek (serials and films), The Sixth Sense, Steel Magnolias, Signs, Shawshank Redemption, Tea with Mussolini, Terms of Endearment, Tuesdays with Morrie, Total Recall, What Dreams May Come

VOLUNTEERS

We need your help – consider a volunteer or part exchange package where you donate your time and skills to assist us at the Studio Psalm in return for tuition.

Contact: 01749 679900

psalmlifemastery@aol.com

CHANGE FOR KIDS
Integrity-Intelligence-Intentionality in Action

AIMS:

- to make a sustainable, long-term difference to the lives of children through the foundation and development of spiritual values and awareness of the 'bigger picture'.
- to help and educate children through their leisure time and holiday activities, in order to develop their physical, mental, emotional and spiritual capacities that they may grow to full maturity as individuals and unlock their best potential.
- raises awareness of environmental issues.
- promotes community and team spirit.
- teaches children to find their passion and follow their bliss.
- to instill authentic leadership skills.

THEMES TO BE ADDRESSED:

- Emotional Resilience
- Psychological Intelligence
- Spiritual Integrity
- Community and Sustainability
- Nature and the Environment
- Ancient Wisdoms, Myths, Legends and Prophecies
- Creativity in Communication and Conscious Languaging
- Quantum Physics and the Science of Miracles
- The Healing Power of Laughter
- Therapeutic Grade Essential Oils for Health
- Meditation and Relaxation
- Optimal Fitness & Health - Super Wave Resonance Exercise
- The Magic of Music and Movement
- Optimal Nutrition – How foods influence our moods

psalmlifemastery@aol.com